ALL MY MOTHERS
AND FATHERS

Also by Michael Blumenthal

Sympathetic Magic (poetry)

Days We Would Rather Know (poetry)

Laps (poetry)

Against Romance (poetry)

The Wages of Goodness (poetry)

Dusty Angel (poetry)

Weinstock Among the Dying (novel)

When History Enters the House: Essays from Central Europe

To Woo and to Wed: Poets on Love and Marriage (editor)

ALL MY MOTHERS

AND FATHERS

a memoir

Michael Blumenthal

HarperCollins*Publishers*

Grateful acknowledgment is made to Stephen Dunn for permission to quote from his poems "The Routine Things Around the House" and "Eggs."

HarperCollins books may be purchased for educational, business, or sales promotional use. For information, please write: Special Markets Department, HarperCollins Publishers Inc., 10 East 53rd Street, New York, NY 10022.

FIRST EDITION

Designed by Nancy Singer Olaguera

Printed on acid-free paper

Library of Congress Cataloging-in-Publication Data is available upon request.

ISBN 0–06–018629-1

02 03 04 05 06 RRD/❖ 10 9 8 7 6 5 4 3 2 1

FOR MY SON, NOAH,

WHOM FATE HAS DEALT A KINDER HAND

AND, IN SO DOING,

HELPED TO RECTIFY MY OWN

FOR AMOS AND JUDY

AND IN MEMORY OF MY TRUE MOTHER,

BETTY GERN BLUMENTHAL (1907–1959),

WHOSE GOODNESS AND LOVE SAVED ME

A first-generation American father possessed by the Jewish demons, a second-generation American son possessed by their exorcism: that was his whole story.

—Philip Roth, *The Anatomy Lesson*

Had my father lived, he would have lain on me at full length and would have crushed me.

—Jean-Paul Sartre, *The Words*

That's how you lose your own life, of course, devoting yourself to your parents. . . .

—Paul West, *My Mother's Music*

But what should a kind-hearted boy do who hasn't yet learned to defend himself against all his mothers and fathers?

—George Konrad, *The City Builder*

CONTENTS

Life happens to us; then we, in the act of remembering, happen to it. At times the wished-for life—with its understandable desires for a greater happiness, or a more easily achieved redemption—intrudes itself upon the actualities of the one lived. Nonetheless I have tried herein, as the poet Robert Lowell suggested, to "say what happened," to recount my own humble episodes of happiness and disappointment to the best of my ability to remember them, and, in Lowell's words, "pray for the grace of accuracy Vermeer gave."

Some of the names of individuals within the story, however, have been changed in order to avoid embarassment or discomfort to the persons involved. I am nonetheless grateful to all those who made an appearance, the living and the dead.

PROLOGUE

The tragic hovers in the corners of the house.

It shivers in the pillows and the sheets.

It winds its slender rope around

the half-completed and complete.

—"The Happy Nihilist," from *Against Romance* (1987)

When my grandmother's life came to a sudden halt four days after my father's birth in Frankfurt-am-Main, Germany, on September 10, 1904, my father, Julius Ernst Blumenthal, was hardly left alone in the world.

Before dying—perhaps from the fatigue of bringing this last child into the world—my grandmother had gone to the well seven other times. She had already given birth to six daughters and an older son to keep her surviving infant company in the cruel, heartless world into which she had sent him as her final act among the living.

My grandfather Max, a small-time kosher butcher in Frankfurt's Jewish ghetto, must not have had a light load to bear as the newly widowed father of eight. And, like anyone in his shoes would have been, he was in no position to make many demands on whatever woman might come along to help him lighten the burden of his rather substantial progeny. So—when a neighbor introduced him to Janette Lissauer, an eager Jewish widow from the neighboring town of Oberürsel—it was only a matter of months before my father's motherless infancy was endowed with a new stepmother.

Janette Lissauer, however, was clearly a woman whose interests were more dominated by the need to find a husband for herself—and a father for her two fatherless children—than by a wish to become a stepmother to a needy brood of eight. And it must have been my father, the youngest, most vulnerable, most needy of the lot, against whom his stepmother vented the lion's share of her rage at having found herself in so difficult—and, in her own mind, so *unchosen*—a predicament. "My schtepmutter, she never luved me, bis auf the end von her life," my father repeatedly told me as I was growing up, "ven she could finally beleev was ein wunderbarer sohn I was."

So it was surely not a random event that caused my father, at the ripe age of fourteen, to apprentice himself to the reputable German fur wholesaler Meyer und Vogel, Gmbh, in Nuremberg, thereby escaping the domain of his wicked, domineering stepmother and virtually following in his beleaguered father's footsteps (it being hardly a great leap from selling meat to selling furs).

If you look at the photographs of my father, the ones taken in the early 1930s after he was promoted to traveling salesman, he might well have passed for a German matinee idol: His jet-black hair, slicked down with pomade, shimmers in the light, and—in his gray, wide-lapeled suit and a shirt so white it makes the gray seem almost charcoal—he has that thin, tightly strung look frequently associated with romantic men, coupled with a seductive, sideways glance that always prevents his gaze—slightly androgynous, vulnerable, and charming—from meeting the camera head on.

These were the years when Julius Streicher and his henchmen were already parading down the streets of the Jewish ghetto in Frankfurt with whips and clubs, shattering the store windows of Jewish shops like my grandfather Max's kosher butchery, where he struggled to support his second wife and their then ten children. These were also the years—just a few before the Nazis actually passed the *"Rassenschande"* laws that made such liaisons illegal—when it was suspect, if not downright dangerous, for a young Jewish male to be seen in the company of an Aryan woman.

My father—passing through the Bavarian countryside in the spring of 1934, when he offered a lovely, blond-haired opera singer and innkeeper's daughter named Claire Haas a ride at a Baden-Baden bus stop—may, of course, have been too removed from all this to pay much attention. He may already have been a man too mired in his own fate to beware of falling in love with someone his life would never allow him to possess. Or he may merely have wanted to strike back at his father for marrying a woman *he* so hated. He may have wanted to wound the man who had wounded him.

Nonetheless, after a three-year-long romance conducted in hotel rooms, the backseat of my father's chauffeur-driven limousine, and the first-class compartments of trains—the Nazis hot on her trail and her lover seemingly incapable of defying either them or his father—Claire Haas boarded a plane for Santiago, Chile, to join the Stuttgart Opera's South American tour.

Many years later I was to find among my father's papers a copy of an unused Chilean work permit which he—clearly intent on following his lover—had applied for and received. But for some reason—perhaps, as he would explain it later, because of his loyalty to his deeply religious father or perhaps because of his loyalty to a deeper, more self-destructive force that lurked within—he lacked the will (or the courage) to claim what he most wanted: He allowed the one true object of his passions and desires, the one truly *chosen* woman of his life, to elude his grasp.

∼

1 | BEGINNINGS

It is a gift if one is born happy. Those who are born
unhappy are incurable.

—HENRY MILLER

IT HARDLY SEEMS LIKELY that I was born happy. For there are other
mothers and fathers in this story as well.

My biological mother, Nelly Atlas, a rabbi's daughter from a
small German town near Leipzig, met my father, Berthold Gern,
on a moshav in Palestine by the name of Moledet near Afula, just
west of the Sea of Galilee, several years after Berthold left Germany in 1934. Their first child, Daniel, died of infantile typhus
when he was ten days old. All the evidence points to the fact that
my mother Nelly—having then given birth to my brother and sister—wasn't all that wild about bringing a fourth child into the
world, particularly under the circumstances into which I was
born on March 8, 1949.

My parents had come to the States for what was to be a two-
week visit in the fall of 1947, just before the outbreak of the War
of Independence, to celebrate my grandmother Johanna Gern's
seventieth birthday at the home of my father's sister and

brother-in-law, Betty and Julius Blumenthal, with whom my grandmother lived in the Washington Heights section of Manhattan.

The Blumenthals, like most German Jews who managed to get out in time, had left Nazi Germany at virtually the last feasible moment, for a simple reason: to avoid Hitler's gas chambers and crematoria. After several years as a busboy at New York's Hotel Governor Clinton, Julius had managed to work his way back into the only profession he had known since entering the doors of Meyer und Vogel at age fourteen—the fur business. Within just a few years—thanks to an unending supply of charm and flattery (*"Gnädige Frau,"* he greeted every woman who entered his showroom, "in this coat, you will schtop the traffic.")—he had been able to build a fairly successful business as a retail jobber on West 29th Street, allowing him, his wife, and his blind mother-in-law to move into their sunny, five-room, sixty-eight-dollar-a-month apartment along Fort Washington Avenue, at 801 West 181st Street.

So it was with a great deal of anticipation (and a certain amount of envy) that my biological parents set out from Tel Aviv with their four-year-old daughter, Judy, and two-year-old son, Amos, one afternoon in October 1947 for what they thought would be a brief reunion with their comparatively worldly and successful New York relatives.

But, as fate would have it, just after Berthold and Nelly Gern's arrival in New York and the celebration of my grandmother's seventieth birthday at Café Geiger on East Eighty-sixth Street, the Israeli war against the British intensified. And Julius Blumenthal, whose life's motto was, *"Es ist nicht nötig dass man lebt, aber mir dass man seine Pflicht tut"* (It isn't necessary to live, but to do your duty), decided he simply couldn't allow his wife's family to return to such an insecure, dangerous existence.

After turning the obituary pages of the German-Jewish weekly *Aufbau* one morning just after the Gerns' arrival, he noticed in the FOR SALE column an offering of a five-acre, ten-coop chicken farm in the small, heavily Jewish community of Vineland, New Jersey, just three hours from New York. Leaving the house early the next morning for what he said was an appointment with a customer, he drove 120 miles south on the New Jersey Turnpike, plunked twelve thousand dollars in cash on the table of South Jersey Realty, and returned that night to proclaim his brother- and sister-in-law the proud new owners of a three-bedroom brick-and-shingle house, five acres of land, and a purchase-and-sale agreement for 7,500 two-week-old baby chicks, to be delivered a week from that Monday to their new home at 1066 East Sherman Avenue, Vineland, New Jersey.

"I don't know how we will ever make it up to you," Berthold Gern, on the verge of tears, told his brother-in-law.

"Ja," his wife, Nelly, concurred, "it is so generous. I don't know what we could ever give you in return."

"You would, I know, do the same for us," Julius Blumenthal assured his relatives. "After all, *Es ist nicht nötig dass man lebt, aber nur dass man seine Pflicht tut.*"

And so, with a quick flick of Julius Blumenthal's eager pen and an overnight trip to Montreal to apply for residence visas to the United States, my parents Nelly and Berthold, along with their children, Amos and Judy, packed themselves into Julius Blumenthal's burgundy-colored 1946 Chevy and headed south on the New Jersey Turnpike. There, approximately a year later, amid several thousand other farm-fresh eggs incubating their way toward life or some family's breakfast table, I made my first, tentative motions toward the light and air of this world.

❧

My adoptive father, Julius Ernst Blumenthal, had met my mother, Betty Gern, in the small German town of Georgensgmünd, just outside Nuremberg, in January 1936, when he stopped at the widow Johanna Gern's house at 16 Friedrichsgmündstrasse to pick up the key to the Jewish cemetery where his stepmother's son lay buried.

My father must, of course, have been depressed by Claire's departure, frightened by the ominous march of Julius Streicher and his SS troops through the streets, increasingly terrified about his own life and future. And his stepmother, the loveless, ever-withholding Janette Lissauer, must still have been deeply wounded as well by the death of her only son from her first marriage.

So that, on that morning when, ever dutifully, my father went to get the cemetery key, he must have been pondering his own death as well. He must—his true love gone, his real mother dead, the Nazis already hard on his heels—have felt a terrible emptiness . . . a fear, a longing for comfort.

I picture my mother—a shy, pretty young woman of nearly thirty—that day my father first came by the old stone house to lay some flowers on his stepbrother's grave. I imagine her standing in a back room, peeking out from behind a curtain, then entering the foyer, eyes lowered toward the floor, where her eager mother had summoned her to meet the dashing young Jewish furrier from Frankfurt.

There were, no doubt, not many men for a young, fatherless woman like my mother (whose only brother, Berthold, had already fled Germany for Palestine) in a small town like Georgensgmünd; not many opportunities for romance or escape. So that—seeing the handsome, dapper, charm-oozing figure of Julius Blumenthal at her door—a deep glimmer of hope must have passed through her. And, finding this innocently available girl and her widowed, ambitious mother—both of them eager to welcome a man like himself into their home and hearts—my father must have suddenly felt fate smile down on him. For here, finally, he could have *both* a loving mother and a shy, devoted wife.

And so, arriving to claim the cemetery key—the key to death—on his miserable stepmother's behalf, my father must have felt instead that he had found the key to a new life. And what did it matter that he felt little of the passion he had felt for Claire Haas for this not exceptionally pretty Jewish girl who hesitantly reached her hand toward him, hardly daring to look up? It wasn't, after all, passion he was after any longer, but safety—not really a wife he had been looking for all these years of kissing women's hands, but a mother . . . a mother at whose living breasts he had never fed, into whose living eyes he had never had a chance to gaze.

So, on February 2, 1938—hardly a year after the love of his life had departed for South America—in a small ceremony in the Black Forest town of Freiburg, presided over by Rabbi Fritz Sheuermann, Julius Blumenthal married Betty Gern, thereby acquiring both a wife and a new mother with whom to soothe his wounded, grieving heart.

I will never know, I suppose, at what point during—or after—my mother's pregnancy it was decided that I was to be adopted by my aunt and uncle. Perhaps as they drove south that very afternoon on the New Jersey Turnpike, thinking gratefully of their childless relatives' generosity and of the burden of having two young mouths to feed on the income to be generated by a small family chicken farm—the idea first hatched itself as a possibility in my parents' minds. Or maybe it was only a year later, when

Betty Blumenthal looked down one morning to find a small brownish lump on her left breast, and a radical mastectomy was performed on the forty-year-old woman, leaving her in a state of weakness and depression for which the most effective cure, according to her doctors, would be to "give her something new to live for."

What a convenient solution it must have been! On the one hand, a childless woman who had, in some sense, "nothing to live for"; on the other, her newly arrived immigrant brother and sister-in-law with two young children and a chicken farm they were uncertain would provide them with even a subsistence living. Whatever the reason, on March 15, 1949, just seven days after I uttered my first tentative cries, I was handed from the potentially nurturing breasts of Nelly Gern into the arms of Betty Blumenthal, and took my place among the dying of the world.

"The day vee picked you up in Vineland," my parents would say throughout my early years, "vee vas so happy." And so, throughout the first years of my burgeoning consciousness, the answer to that ever-present childhood mystery—"Where did I come from?"—seemed to be that babies were "picked up" somewhere, like a special delivery package, or a disease.

But meanwhile, here were these two families for whom mortality had entered from opposite directions—the one husband poor, relatively unskilled, the shards of a far-off war's bullet still implanted in his left arm, soon to be the father of a third child; the other charming, middle class, childless, faced with a dying wife and a blind, aging mother-in law. And the perfect solution must have presented itself: They would exchange death for life, barrenness for hope, the farm of thousands of unfertilized eggs for a single, fertilized egg.

And with that trade—carried out as cleanly as that of my

boyhood hero, Duke Snider, from the Dodgers to the Mets—I, too, exchanged "uniforms"; and Berthold and Nelly Gern, my natural parents, became my aunt and uncle, and Julius and Betty Blumenthal, an impotent Jewish furrier and his wife, became my father and mother.

~

2 | GOLDEN DAYS

I hold a candle to your face:

 In the light, the lines of you

are a latticework of loss—

three mothers, two wives,

an uncertain son

who thrashes about

in the brine of your eyes,

calling you *father, uncle* . . .

mother.

If all men want mothers,

what might we,

having none, want?

We could break

from that design—

take back the stolen rib

and the fig leaf, take back

the diaphanous heart,

take back the fluttering eyelids.

Father,

hermaphrodite,

mermaid and minotaur,

read this

in any language:

Lese dieses

in jeder Sprache.

Be water, Father,

be blood.

—FROM "FATHER," FROM *DAYS WE WOULD*

   RATHER KNOW (1984)

SO IT WAS THAT I WENT from being an infant hatched alongside the chicken coops of 1066 East Sherman Avenue in Vineland, New Jersey, to a room beside transmogrified pelts of mink, Alaska seal, Persian lamb, and chinchilla, in apartment 53 at 801 West 181st Street in Manhattan, a boy raised in a play whose characters, from the outset, were cast in confused and conflicting parts. It was, in fact, a play only one of whose central characters—my nearly blind grandmother Johanna (mother of both my biological father and my adoptive mother), with whom I shared a bedroom for the first twelve years of my life—played an unambiguous and unchanging role.

It was a play whose first ten years, I was only to discover later, were permeated by the unspoken secret of its origins, a play whose original script, I, its central character, was never allowed to read. And so—like any other child of any other "normal" family—I went about playing my assigned role as the dutiful only child of Julius and Betty Blumenthal, unaware that the woman at whose missing breast I had been placed was already only a single breast away from the grave, or that the father who, by all appearances, had "fathered" me was incapable of fathering anyone. Unaware that my household's only actual link to what was my blood lay in the person of the seventy-five-year-old woman, her white hair gathered in a bun, who reached out weekly from behind the Sabbath candles to bless me in the encroaching dark.

I am three years old, and my father takes me downtown to make a recording of Mario Lanza's "Golden Days" as a birthday present for my mother. It's a time when a dollar bill can still buy things: a pound of rice pudding at Horn & Hardart's, a whole pepperoni pizza, a silk tie, a two-minute recording of anything you can grind out, recorded in the quiet anonymity of a green-curtained booth somewhere near the garment district, where my father peddles furs.

Among my father's great loves are Mario Lanza and his *The Student Prince,* a love he maintains with the same fierce, undivided loyalty with which followers of Callas and Caruso, Tucker and Peerce, Domingo and Pavarotti, will later love their heroes. Along with the dulcet tones of Eddie Fisher singing "Oh, Mein Papa," it's the voice of Mario Lanza belting out, "I Walk with God," and, of course, "Golden Days," that fills our five-room apartment in Washington Heights.

I should, I suppose, be amazed to discover that, beyond the two words of the title, my father doesn't know a single syllable of "Golden Days," a song he must have heard, played, and sung several thousand times during the years of my childhood. Even now the scratched and warped 45, with the words "MICKY and Dady, GOLDEN DAYS, 5.1.52" scrawled on the label in red ink, reveals—along with the birdlike, contorted chirpings of a three-year-old boy—my father's commendably cantorial voice chanting the two words: "Golden days . . . da DA da da da da da DA . . . Golden days . . . da da da da da da da DA . . . Golden days . . . da DA da DA da da da DA . . . Golden days . . ."

It doesn't occur to me that there is any *meaning* to this lapse on my father's part—to not knowing the words to the song he loves most. I don't, for that matter, yet know that listening means much of anything, that listening says something about both the listener and the speaker. I don't yet know that listening—like gifts you buy someone, like the way you honor their choices in life, their griefs, their happinesses—reflects a kind of *attention.*

I don't yet know how difficult—how nearly impossible—it is for anyone to really listen if no one has ever listened to them.

∽

My mother and grandmother are kind, loving women, and I—lucky boy—am the apple of their collective eyes, my grandmother's pair of which, alas, has gone almost totally blind. She—the one person in all these tradings and exchanges whose biological relationship to me actually matches her role, and who is also my roommate—loves me, perhaps out of sheer proximity, most of all her three grandchildren, and showers me with whatever love and attention her ever-diminishing sight allows, which includes tickling my feet so much when she changes my socks that I burst into fits of delirious laughter.

For both my mother and grandmother, my academic achievements—which lead, to my prematurely advanced reading level, to my skipping second grade—are a source of great pride, and my grandmother, whose mind functions like a forerunner of the modern computer, is more than eager to help me with my math homework, with me calling out numbers and various functions ("times," "divided by," "minus") to her in German, and she coming up with the answer before I can blink an eye.

On one occasion, when, my third-grade teacher has the audacity to give me merely an *S* (satisfactory) rather than the ultimate *SO* (satisfactory/outstanding), my mother races, head down, up Fort Washington Avenue, bent on rectifying what must clearly be a mistake, and returns with a line of uninterrupted *SO*s that puts me right up there with the brilliant, encyclopedia-reading accountant's son who will be my nemesis throughout my elementary, junior high school, and high school years—and, later, my Harvard colleague—Warren Goldfarb.

We're a large bunch, the Blumenthals are, with all my father's collected sisters, brothers-in-law, nephews, and cousins, and the major family event seems to be our periodic excursions to a place called Mohansic Park, where we have humongous family picnics, during which my father takes Super 8 movies, I (the only truly young child present) am tossed into the air by Uncles Leo, Hugo, Julius, Fred, and George and our family friend, Helen, and we engage, collectively, in the Blumenthal national sport: ring-around-a-rosy. At times, a neutral observer might conclude, all we need is a bunch of girls in dirndls and Julie Andrews singing, "The hills are alive . . . ," and—*voila!*— there you'd have it: *The Sound of Music.*

What we have instead, though, is a bunch of once beautiful, now slightly overweight women with pocketbooks (my father's sisters); my somewhat less attractive but sweet-visaged and cheerful-seeming mother (also with a pocketbook); my thickly bespectacled, matriarchal *Omi,* my aging uncles; and my mania-cally upbeat father, filming, playing the harmonica, and singing *"Im Salzkammergut, da Ka'ma' gut lustig sein."*

Summers, when we venture out to the more remote Pine Hill Arms Hotel in the heart of the Catskills for our customary two-week vacation, our leisure activities get more spectacular to match the scenery: My mother and I ride the summer chairlift at the Belleayre Ski Center, my father (who can't swim) jumps Johnny Weissmuller–like into two feet of water, and my grand-mother lies in a lounge chair, trying to decipher the obituaries in the *Aufbau.*

Christmas—or, rather, Hanukkah—and Passover are spent in Vineland, where the whole biological mess is happily reunited and we seem like any other family of aunts and uncles, grand-mother and cousins. I sit on one end of the seesaw, with Judy on the other and Amos in the middle, and my mother and grand-mother stand on either side, helping us to maintain our tenuous equilibrium. My uncle feeds the chickens and collects eggs; my aunt places them on the basement grader and then into cartons; my grandmother asks someone to read her the Vineland Egg Auction prices listed on the front page of the local paper. It is all, in an immigrant sort of way, rather normal. We are having lots of fun.

My father fares no better behind the wheel than he does in the recording booth. Along the New Jersey Turnpike that leads from the pelts of Washington Heights to the eggs of southern New Jersey, our car can perpetually be found pulled over into the breakdown lane, with my father behind it talking to some Smokey the Bear–looking state trooper.

"Good day, Officer Tumilinsky," my father says, reaching into his breast pocket to remove a small plastic wallet stuffed with business cards as he struggles to read the officer's name-plate. "My name is Julius Blumenthal . . . a great pleasure."

While other boys I know have fathers who often get tickets for speeding or failing to come to a complete stop at Stop signs, it is only *my* father, it seems, who is perpetually stopped for driving too *slowly* in the passing lane, entering via the exit ramp, or failing to drive with his lights on after dark. The reason is that we are usually lost: Not only along the familiar route to Vineland, but in the thirty or so years he and my mother have been vacationing at the Pine Hill Arms, my father has never once been able to reach his destination without first wandering off toward some far-out-of-the-way New Paltz or Buffalo.

"I have chinchilla, silver fox, Peruvian mink, Alaska seal, and—this month only—some very special leopard coats . . . the best prices in New York," my father, handing the trooper a fifty-cent costume jewelry necklace he has bought from some panhandler in the fur district, is saying as I roll down the car window. "Come down to my showroom with your wife and—I guarantee you—we will find something that will schtop the traffic. . . . Believe me," he continues, "I will sacrifice something for you."

Time and again, to my utter incredulity, the trooper and his wife *do* show up at 231 West Twenty-ninth Street the following week, always leaving with no less than a mink boa or a remodeling of some dilapidated Persian lamb stole. "You see," my father says, kissing the woman's hand as he leads her to the elevator, "I told your husband I would sacrifice something for you. In this coat, Mrs. Tumilinsky, you will schtop the traffic."

It is, no doubt, the utter onslaught of his verbiage—the faltering English, the Old World gentlemanly charm—that does it. But, one way or another, I don't remember my father *ever* actually getting a ticket. And, the more traffic violations, illnesses, wrong numbers, and missed coin tosses at tollbooths he is able to accumulate, the more sartorial splendor, it seems, the wives of state troopers, surgeons, and tollbooth attendants are able to display.

"A pleasure to meet you, Officer Tumilinsky," I hear my father saying as he starts the car, simultaneously squeezing a few more business cards into the trooper's hand. "God loves you, and so do I."

Within minutes we're back on the road, cheerfully headed for my father's next mishap, singing, *"O Jugend, O Jugend, was warst Du so schön"* (O youth, O youth, how beautiful you were), or an old Bavarian beer-drinking song, *"Trink mir noch ein Tröpfchen"* ("Drink another drop for me"), along the way.

I have only one dream insofar as my parents are concerned: *English*. Like Jason longing for the Golden Fleece, like Tantalus thirsting for his beckoning grapes, I too, ache—not for balm or salvation, but for the sweet syllables of what, after all, is my native-born tongue, the language (as I see it) of life. I want to speak the language of Duke Snider and Ricky Nelson, of John

Kennedy and Elvis Presley, of Dick Clark and the American Bandstand . . . *not* the language of Göring and Goebbels and Himmler and Hitler, not even the language of Goethe and Schiller.

"Such a pleasure to see you, *gnädige Frau Froehlich*," my father greets my elementary school principal, a tall, statuesque woman by the name of Frohlich, in his few syllables of the national vernacular, "God loves you, and so do I."

Our house, in my opinion, is a kind of leper colony of the wrong tongue. *"Du, Du, liegst mir im Herzen,"* my father is invariably singing just as a friend of mine—or, worse yet, one of the girls in my class—calls. *"O Jugend, O Jugend, was warst Du so schön."*

I beg. I plead. I prostrate myself before them. "Please, please," I whine like a wounded dog, holding one hand over the receiver, "can't you speak English just this *once*?"

To their credit, they sometimes try. "Good day, young Mr. Wortman," my father says to my friend Richie as he enters our house, "and how is your dear mamama, and the rest of your family?"

But no sooner is a friend comfortably ensconced in my room, no sooner do I allow my relentless guard a moment's reprieve, than my grandmother's voice cries out from the kitchen, *"Mikey, kannst Du mir bitte ein Moment in der Küche helfen?"*

Everywhere I look shame, my loyal servant, awaits me. My creeping, blind, obituary-scouring grandmother, whom I love—what possible social credit can she bring to the life of a young boy? What small emoluments of allure and sensuality? My crazed father, cruising the neighborhood with his furs and kissing the hands of widows and widowers, what possible competition is he for the likes of Donna Reed's fly-fishing husband or Beaver's father, or the guitar-strumming family of Ozzie Nelson?

"Please, dear God, please," I go to bed murmuring under my breath while my father makes me recite the German litany *"Heile, heile Segen, Morgen gibt es Regen, Übermorgen Schnee, dann tut's Mikey nimmer weh,"* "please let me wake up normal and ordinary, in a world without umlauts and accents."

But there are also moments of reprieve—moments when I can seemingly penetrate the legitimate English-speaking world of my countrymen, as on those occasional Sunday afternoons when my parents take my grandmother and me to Lindy's on 51st Street for cheesecake. Lindy's is famous at the time, if not for flesh-and-blood celebrities, at least for their signed black-and-white portraits decorating its window, which suggest that, by merely sitting down at one of the tightly-clustered, deadly uncomfortable tables, you can rub shoulders with the likes of Frank Sinatra, Tony Bennett, Ed Sullivan, Lawrence Welk, or—if you are among the truly chosen—one of my parents' true American heroes, Milton Berle.

Hardly have we been ushered to our table, my parents and grandmother chattering away in their usual *Nürnberger Deutsch* while I try to distance myself from their humiliating foreignness by making sure no one I know is around, when the door opens and in walks—smoking a big fat cigar, his mink-clad wife on his arm—none other than Milton Berle himself.

I'm ecstatic. Here, in the very flesh, seated literally a few feet away from me, is both an embodiment of America and a potential escape from my parents' table. No sooner have Berle and his wife been served their slices of "Lindy's Famous New York Cheesecake," to the awestruck gazes of half the population of Teaneck, New Jersey, but I'm out of my seat and standing beside Uncle Miltie, trying hard not to inhale lest one of his wafting curlicues of thick cigar smoke enter and clog my asthmatic lungs.

"Hi, Uncle Miltie," I venture bravely, doing my very best Arnold Stang imitation. *"Cheep, cheep, cheep."*

There's a prolonged silence as Berle, clearly irritated by my premature invasion of his cheesecake break, exhales a blackish cloud of cigar smoke at my boyish face.

"Hello there, young fella," he finally offers after an interminable pause, reaching out to place a cold hand on my face. Then, grasping a chunk of my left cheek between his thumb and forefinger in the same way my uncle Leo does, he turns and twists the small nodule of flesh, causing me to wince in pain as he says—as if for the benefit of everyone else in the room—"Great to meet you, son," then pats me on the shoulder like a third-grade teacher sending a disorderly student back to his seat, and redirects his attention toward his cheesecake.

Deeply embarrassed at having failed to make a more enduring impression on one of my family's few American icons, I reseat myself at my parents' table.

"Solch ein Massel," my father says. "Milton Berle."

"Und," he adds before I can even respond, "such a beautiful coat his wife has on. . . . Cerulean mink. Something, let me tell you, that would schtop the traffic."

I realize, to my relief, that I can barely hear what my father is saying. I'm too busy trying to hide my face in my cheesecake. I'm too busy rubbing my burning cheek.

Then there is the matter of their age. "What a beautiful grandchild you have." People stop them on the street, pinching me on the cheek. "You must be so proud." "How come your parents are so old?" my friends ask. "Were you a mistake or something?"

I *had*, of course, been a mistake, and so, at times, my whole life—the wrong parents, the wrong language, perhaps even the wrong astronomical alignments filling the house—seems a mistake as well. *Why, oh, why, can't we just be like everyone else?*

Like it or not, however, I'm wedded to this constellation—wedded to walking my grandmother, on warm summer nights, up the hill to Bennett Park, where, while other kids play stickball and a game called ringolevio, I read to her aloud from the boldface, exuberant letters of the German-language obituaries.

"*Inge Heinemann, née Bendauer,*" I intone, like Goethe. "*Geboren 7.2.04, Karlsruhe, gestorben 9.13.58, Bayside, Queens.*" But what I long for is the local *patois,* the language of Stevenson and Kennedy, Frankie Vallee and Dion, Robert Young and Walt Disney. To be young and free and *really* American, I think—*that* must be the heavenly condition!

"The world is a terrible place," a poet once wrote, "with room for tennis." And it's something very much like tennis I want—tennis, whiskey sours, the *New York Times,* and a home where no one is singing, "*Im Salzkammergut, da ka'ma' gut lustig sein!*" America, I think, is the place of life and light. Germany was the place of death. And it's life I want, preferably in English.

The names on the buzzers in our lobby have little in common with the Welches, Johnsons, O'Briens, Whites, and Athertons of nearby *goyische* Hudson View Gardens. Ours, rather, are like a who's who of Holocaust survivors and Jewish Communist theorists: Marx, Engel, Fleischmann, Fleischhaker, Hertz, Monat, Strauss, Pollack, Lilienfeld, Katzenstein, Bergmann, Blumenthal.

In addition we have in our building a kind of immigrant precursor to today's HMO: Dr. Monroe Frieder, our dentist, lives on the first floor in apartment 5; Dr. Victor Feith, my father's internist, on the second floor in number 29; Seymour Kirsh—a gastrointestinal specialist (much needed by my grandmother)—is in apartment 38; Dr. Fred Lehmann—the ear, nose, and throat man—resides in apartment 47. For pediatrics, my own Man Friday, Dr. Stephen Musliner, must actually be summoned from next door in 815; and for oncology, a specialty we'll soon need, Dr. Fred Weissmann will have to cart his little black bag to our house all the way from lower Fort Washington Avenue, two blocks away.

There is one glaring departure from the otherwise *goyischrein* register of tattered, Scotch-taped names beside our apartment buzzers. It's the superintendent, Mr. Suess, a tall, dour, laconic man whose well-known heart condition we do everything possible to exacerbate by playing what we call "imaginary baseball" in the courtyard between our building and the more "integrated" 815.

Having been sternly rebuked by Suess on several occasions for breaking Mrs. Laubheimer's second-story window with one of the pink rubber Spaldings we use for punchballs, we now attempt to lure the ailing and mean-spirited superintendent from his ground-floor apartment—from which he emerges, brandishing the long, spearlike rod he uses to change lightbulbs in high places—by going through all the motions (and sound effects) of a full-fledged game, while hitting and tossing what are, in fact, only pocketfuls of air.

"You damned boys!" Suess emerges from the service entrance screaming. "If you don't get the hell out of here, I'm going to have the whole bunch of you thrown out of the building, I swear to God!" Assured by my parents that an anti-Semite lurks behind every corner—not to mention every sharp-edged wooden pole—I take it for granted that "the whole bunch of you" means us Jews, just as I later take it for granted that my parents are right when they insist that my cousin Amos's rejection by Phi Epsilon Pi, an exclusively Jewish fraternity at Rutgers, is evidence of rampant anti-Semitism.

Like the quintessential *goy* who, by now, lurks both in my mind and in the nationally broadcast households of the Cleavers and Nelsons, Suess does one other thing I have dreamed, throughout my childhood, that my own father might do: He goes *fishing*. Every Sunday morning, often as early as 5:00 A.M., he leaves the building for some charter boat out on the Hudson, inevitably returning later that day, like an urban Captain Ahab, a huge bounty of fish dangling from his wrist. Much as we all hate Suess, these mysterious marine exploits of his—as contrasted with the various cardiac emergencies, diabetes, angina pectorises and other illnesses of our own fathers—endow him with the near-legendary quality I, for one, dream—no, *pray*—that my father will one day embody as well.

And one morning, indeed, the day comes. To my utter shock and amazement, my father enters my room one Saturday night to inform me that "I von't be home ven you vake up tomorrow morning . . . I am going fishing mit Suess."

What prompts him I will never know. But, all day, like an expectant father cruising the maternity ward, I wait on pins and needles, imagining my father, Julius Blumenthal, the Mario Lanza of the chinchilla cape, engaged, Cousteau-like, in mortal, hand-to-hand combat with the demons of the high seas. "My father," I boast to my astonished friends Raymond Fleischhaker, Frankie Engel, Steven Fleischmann, and Ronnie Berger over a game of punchball, "is out fishing with Suess."

Agog with anticipation, I wait and wait until, finally, beaming from ear to ear and carrying five of the largest fish I had ever seen, my father, accompanied by our ever-saturnine superintendent, emerges from Suess's dilapidated station wagon. *"So, da,"* he, suddenly halo bedecked, announces. *"Ich habe sie gefangen"* (I caught them).

For what seems months (though it is only a matter of days),

I am ecstatic. *My* father—*my* maladroit, hand-kissing, God-blessing father—is a fisherman! *Good-bye, Arnold Stang!* I shout happily. *Hello, Clark Gable!* Possessed and exuberant, for the first time in my life my fantasies of my father extend beyond the halls of Congregation Beth Hillel and Bloch & Falk's Kosher Delicatessen to the deep Antarctic waters, the Great Barrier Reef off the coast of Australia, the gorilla-dense jungles of Rwanda and Uganda.

But my fantasies, ebullient and weighted with the tangible as they now are, are short-lived. For, sometime about a week later, while rummaging around on my father's desk in search of a pen, I find the bill: $114.65, payable to Wolf's Fish Market on Amsterdam Avenue.

I say nothing, though I suspect—from his rather depressed reaction to the sudden diminution of my filial enthusiasm—that my father must know. In any event, I console myself, he had tried. And there wouldn't, thank God, be further opportunities. Because the very next week, while reaching up with his infamous spear to change a blown bulb near the top of the elevator shaft, Suess suffers a heart attack and dies.

Though hardly a fishing boat, there is one place where my father seems utterly happy and entirely himself: in the third row of Congregation Beth Hillel of Washington Heights, between St. Nicholas and Audubon Avenues. Unlocking the small wooden compartment just below his name-plated third-row seat, kissing his prayer shawl along its Hebrew-inscribed edge, and finally opening his German-Hebrew prayer book, my father enters a kind of private heaven of ritual and song, a place where his own stifled cantorial ambitions and reflexively observant Judaism can find, momentarily, a common voice.

Singing along to *Ein Kelohenu* and *Adon Olom* with our cantor, Fred Kornfeld, and the synagogue's all-male choir (among whose members, it occurred to me long after, my father really should have been), my father enters into a kind of rhapsodic Eden, a place of engagement and satisfaction not even his much-beloved furs can offer. If the fur business is his mistress, it seems to me, then Judaism and, with it, this synagogue, are his muse, as—with a musical sense far more intuitive than learned—his voice rises above those of the rest of the amassed faithful and, with quivering lips and rapturous eyes, he praises the Lord and mutters the names of the dead into the air.

I, of course, am rather unmoved by all this, urged on only by my father's slightly (ever *so* slightly) contagious enthusiasm (and repelled by his bad breath) as he bends toward me to indicate the proper place in the prayer book, yet always somewhat embarrassed by the seemingly excessive religiosity of his Old World fervor. That there is something decidedly "uncool" about this, something decidedly un-American, I have no doubt, and, on those rare High Holiday occasions when classmates of mine like Toby Dolinsky or Ruthie Pollack or June Fine from more assimilated families are among the congregation, I do all I can to huddle down inconspicuously in my seat so as to dissociate myself from my father's resonant bellowings.

Yet, it occurs to me later as I struggle to retain moments of affection and respect for him, it is here—as well as at the window of Karl Ehmer's decidedly nonkosher delicatessen on East Eighty-sixth Street, where, when he thinks no one is looking, he inhales slices of ham—that my father is utterly in his element, an Old World Jew among other Old World Jews, a refugee from Hitler among other refugees from Hitler, a man who, at least temporarily, has found his voice among other men seeking to regain theirs in the vast cacophony that is America.

∿

There is yet another member of my "family" who, though not really related to anyone, is as present as dawn and dusk in our lives. Why she is always there—eating with us, vacationing with us, spending every birthday and holiday, hovering over every sickbed, with us—I will probably never really know. Yet I have hardly any memory of the first ten years of my life that Helen isn't part of.

Helen lives, in a manner of speaking, with her husband, Dr. Victor Feith—a man in whose company I never see her—in apartment 29. From below her window I can easily, and frequently, whistle, or call her name from the narrow side entranceway to our building. A kind of second mother to me, a figurative (or literal—which, I'll never know) live-in mistress to my father, she's the muse of our family, whose creamy chocolate pudding topped with a dollop of whipped cream and fresh-baked waffles with maple syrup console me through infinite attacks of asthma, earaches, hives, and allergies. What's more, she's a poet, a virtual Edna St. Vincent Millay to my father's Rod McKuen, her simple rhyming poems in German providing a kind of "benediction" for every occasion:

> *Und so die Tage kommen und gehen*
> *Als wir uns'ren Mikey wachsen sehen,*
> *Und weiss er doch mit jedem Strich:*
> *Ach, Mikeylein, wir lieben Dich!*

> (And so the days come and go
> As we watch our Mikey grow,
> And may he know at each new height:
> We love dear Mikey with all our might!)

So naturally and seamlessly is Helen a part of our lives—so natural does it seem to me to have a married woman with a living daughter and two living grandchildren, whose husband still lives with her in the very same apartment, accompany us on every vacation, sit at our table at virtually every meal, be a kind of nurse of first resort for every medical emergency—that it isn't until many years later that I began to truly question the logic of her perpetual presence.

Nor does it seem strange or unusual to me—already inhabiting, albeit unconsciously, a world in which my aunt is my mother and my mother my aunt—that a photograph of me should sit, sandwiched like that of a small prince, between those of Helen's actual grandson and granddaughter atop her piano, or that, for reasons I cannot fathom, her own daughter and husband seem to utterly *detest* this seemingly kind and maternal woman. Since, by now, literally everything—my own origin, my mother's mysterious illness—is shrouded in mystery, why shouldn't Helen's presence be as well?

In Helen's personal life, too, some great mystery lurks. Perhaps, I speculate, it has to do with her dead daughter, Traude—dead of some mysterious "illness" in Germany at age seven—whose portrait hangs just beside Helen's triumvirate of "grandchildren" to the right of the piano. Maybe Helen killed her own daughter? Or perhaps some terrible act of negligence—some awful betrayal, some unforgivable act of infidelity—has so alienated her husband and daughter that she must take refuge beneath my blind grandmother's weekly *Shabbos* blessing, and my father's equally blessed challah and kiddush cup, as a way of finding, again, her place in the world?

Occasionally Helen's presence in our midst—although usually beneficial—seems quite literally a refuge. One memorable Friday evening, she appears at our Sabbath table holding a handkerchief to her swollen, bleeding upper lip, the undeniable extrusion of a large welt also emanating outward from her right eye. Clearly not the result of a mere love tap from the venerable and distant Dr. Feith. Not yet realizing, of course, how easily the love and admiration of one's friends and the utter disaffection of one's own family can be directed at the same person, I can't imagine what satanic and otherworldly inspiration might have moved Dr. Feith to uncoil some part of his anatomy into the face of his loving, and lovable, wife.

Along with her constant availability and poetic gifts, Helen has numerous other virtues that make her presence amid the already wide penumbra of my parentage and *ersatz*-parentage most welcome. Above all, she speaks English—*real* English—almost like a native. Along with that, she reads *real* books—biographies of Churchill and FDR, the diaries of Anaïs Nin, scholarly studies of Mozart and Bach—in English! Unlike my dull, perpetually ill, umlaut-riddled immigrant parents—Helen is smart, talented, educated, competent. She not only keeps my portrait on top of her piano but actually *plays* the thing—Mozart, Chopin, Bach—not "Golden Days." Counterpointing my father's German-speaking Polonius and my mother's depressed and withdrawn Emily Dickinson, Helen seems a woman of dignity and culture—even, I suspect, of passion.

It is she, rather than my mother, who teaches me to walk, to draw, who helps me learn to read. It is she who writes poems for me, makes me chocolate pudding and fresh-baked waffles; it is she who has mounted my photo in that dignified and austere place amid the melodies of the great German composers. Surrounded by three such women—a blind old woman, a mastectomized mother, and an intact, articulate third woman—whom else would a young boy choose?

"I love Helen more than I love you!" I once yell at my mother in a fit of rage. And something in me, with a child's candor, is no doubt speaking the truth.

Whether I love Helen more or not, it's nonethless my *mother's* skirt I cling to—cling to, in fact, so tenaciously that, whenever she tries to leave the classroom after walking me up the hill to P.S. 187, the principal, Mrs. Frohlich, has to be summoned from her office to separate us, me with tears streaming down my face.

My best friends Raymond and Ronnie's mothers, Milka Fleischhaker and Molly Berger, walk them up Fort Washington Avenue to school as well. Yet Raymond and Ronnie seem able to take leave of their mothers without the heartrending scene I, almost daily, enact. But—the best efforts of a succession of teachers that includes Mrs. Bohrer, Mrs. Grundeen, Mr. Orange, Mrs. Rosenberg, and others notwithstanding—I seem unable to say good-bye to my mother without the divine intervention of the principal, who usually succeeds by literally forcing my hands away from her skirt and pushing my mother out of the room.

The cast of characters I am left with, once Mrs. Frohlich succeeds in severing me from my mother's skirt, are, for the most part, a relatively benign—and mostly Jewish—group of kids.

There's Chris Ijima, decidedly *not* Jewish, whose father teaches music at Music & Art, and who—in addition to being the class's best athlete and all around smartest and most popular kid—seems to play every instrument an orchestra can accommodate, including that to-me-exotic-and-multilayered creature, the French horn.

Along with Chris, there's perhaps the most dissonance-producing creature in our entire class—a prematurely tall, stiff, liturgically postured girl in wire-rimmed glasses by the name of Suzanne Cosack, who wears a large gold cross suspended from a

chain around her neck, and who, in the midst of all us circumcised bar-mitzvah boys-to-be, seems destined for the hallowed
halls of Mother Cabrini High School next door . . . and then
straight for the Cloisters.

Clearly, in our prepubescent eyes, Suzanne is already more
than halfway to a nunnery—or at least to a front seat among the
flock of my father's unlikeliest of all TV heroes, the Right Rev-
erend Bishop Fulton J. Sheen. Suzanne's high-Catholic and
rather mysterious presence among us also engenders a kind of
prurient gossip: The head of Mother Cabrini herself, we are led
to believe, immersed in a formaldehyde bath in a glass tank
resembling a fish tank, is on display in the very lobby of her
namesake institution for all the world—or, at least, those coura-
geous enough to enter the revolving doors—to see.

None of us, however, already harboring the guilt-and-fear-
inducing conviction that it was the Jews who killed Christ, have
the nerve to do so, so Suzanne simply continues about her quiet,
studious ways, a lone catechist among the *daveners* and shiva sit-
ters, battling the encyclopedia-memorizing accountant's son,
Warren Goldfarb, for the role of smartest kid in the class—
followed, after a significant ellipsis, by Chris Ijima and, an
incredibly distant fourth, me.

Then there's the ironically named (given his father's occupa-
tion), and fittingly omnivorous Sidney Salmon, who lives in the
large pinkish high-rise on Fort Washington Avenue and whose
father, he never hesitates to remind us, is *rich*—just as he, the
older "son" and heir-to-be of S. Salmon & Sons, Wholesale
Meats, will someday be rich, hovering above us in his hefty and
moneyed magnificence. Sidney, unlike Chris, is a kind of obese-
in-training, and *dumb*, but when he gets that massive young
frame of his behind a baseball, the thing really takes off—usually
up over the schoolyard fence and right across Fort Washington

Avenue, where one of the dorks, like me, inevitably runs to retrieve it.

Worst of all, however, is Johnny Jacoby, a prematurely large and freckle-faced bloke who, as it happens, always winds up sitting just to the left of me in class, and who makes use of that strategic location—and my own hardly intimidating physical presence—to turn my left arm into a punching bag. I like Johnny well enough, and I think he likes me, but what I *don't* like is the constant pain in my arm, along with the fact that I'm scared shitless to hit him back.

Compared with Mark Abramowitz—who sits in the first row and engages in a practice that will make him a lifelong legend to the rest of us—however, I am both wildly popular and a physical specimen akin to Sonny Liston.

Mark, who must weigh all of thirty-five pounds, even by sixth grade, has the habit (one could hardly call it a habit—it's more like an obsession) of picking his nose *en plein air*, and then mounting the small balls of coagulated snot onto the first knuckle of his left hand, from where, with an energetic flick of his right index finger and a "Hi-yo, Silver! Aw-a-ay!" he sends small bullets of aggregated mucus shooting around the room, when he thinks the rest of us aren't looking.

Someone, of course, always *is* looking, and it doesn't take long for little Mark to become the object of an ostracism so severe that even Mr. Orange, our fifth-grade teacher and a man seemingly without human sympathy, begins to take pity on the poor creature, rather than on me, whose battered left arm has rapidly begun to swell as a result of Johnny Jacoby's ministrations.

The classmate I, *goy* lover that I am, am most interested in amid all this—even more than Chris Ijima, who is, after all, Japanese—is Frankie Morris. What a name! I keep whispering it to myself: *Frankie Morris*. Frankie is not only more athletic and, in that deeply Clark Kent American way, *handsomer* than I am, but, in his reserve and cocky, self-satisfied demeanor, already so "other" from the rest of us hyperactive Jews that I quickly decide it is him, and him alone, I most covet as a friend. Frankie also lives in what is widely known to be a "non-Jewish" apartment building on Fort Washington, and has a mother, Mrs. Morris, who (I can hardly swallow each time I see her) is actually *young* and *pretty* . . . and, what's more, speaks impeccable English, and a father—this part really blows me away—who actually *looks* like Superman, and is a *cop* to boot!

Frankie, however, my assiduous courtship notwithstanding, wants no part of me or of my kind, and one day—as I follow him, all idol worshippy, home from school—he simply turns to me and says so. "You're not my friend," he says, calling a spade a spade, and so it is: *I'm not his friend.* But then again I'm no Mark Abramowitz either. And my left arm is really starting to hurt.

But what is it, I wonder now, that so traumatizes a young boy parting from his mother before a rather ordinary school day? Maybe, it occurs to me, I know something no one else yet knows:

Maybe what I know is that I will soon have to part from her forever.

~

3 | THE EIGHT DAYS

... I remember the long looking-glass; with the drawers
on either side; and the washstand; and the great bed on
which my mother lay. I remember very clearly how even
as I was taken to the bedside I noticed that one nurse
was sobbing, and a desire to laugh came over me, and I
said to myself as I have often done at moments of crisis
since, "I feel nothing whatever." Then I stooped and
kissed my mother's face. It was still warm. She [had]
only died a moment before. Then we went upstairs into
the day nursery.

—Virginia Woolf, *A Sketch of the Past*

THEY ARE STILL IN THEIR original metal canisters, the old 8 mm
films my father shot in the years between 1949 and 1959, still
marked with their original, now brown, labels: MICKY LEARNS TO
WALK, 1950. GOLDEN DAYS, 1952. FAMILY PICNIC, MOHANSEE PARK,

1954. VINELAND: AMOS, JUDIT, OMA & MAMA, 1956. FARM LIFE, 1956. OUR LAST FILM FROM OUR DEAR MAMA, 1959.

When I go to watch them, however, the figures are almost always cut off, dismembered by the cameraman's poor aim, by his frenetically moving the camera from place to place, scene to scene. It is, in fact, almost impossible to splice together a narrative from all this: Things seem dissociated, random. People appear for a second, then are never seen again. If there's any thread of consistency, in fact, it's the repetition itself: yet another brief segment of my grandmother and mother walking arm in arm in Fort Tryon Park; yet more footage of me with an earache, yet another hello and *Auf Wiedersehen* at my aunt and uncle's chicken farm in Vineland.

The only person, in fact, who seems captured in any essential way is the cameraman himself—my father—in those rare scenes in which someone more tranquil and focused is holding the camera. What is constant about him—what seems, at least, to constitute some kind of "Portrait of My Father as a Middle-Aged Man"—is that he is perpetually in motion, agitated, running, lifting, singing, playing the harmonica, waving his white handkerchief. He seems—to my own more tranquil, middle-aged eyes—like a human maelstrom: cajoling, kissing, hugging, entertaining anyone and everyone he can get his hands on, incapable of letting any action (or, more precisely, any *in*action) take place without dominating it. Not even the respite of melancholy seems able to contain him as he moves—with an energy so relentless and manic it exhausts even the viewer—through friends and family alike, stooping occasionally to lift me into the air before setting me down and moving on to the next person in line.

In fact, it occurs to me now, if there's any unevenness at all to the attention he distributes energetically to all around him, it's the somewhat diminished level of it he directs toward the melancholy but kindly looking woman carrying a black pocket-book who is almost always off to the side of the action. She seems, in a way, like the date he might have arrived at the party with, only to have someone else in mind when it came to dancing. Sometimes she looks away, and I could swear—or am I imagining it?—that I see a slightly exasperated, though patient, look come over her face, a faint expression of tedium and ennui. And she is, indeed, the least flamboyant of the women—all the others being my father's extroverted, rather beautiful sisters.

But, then again, why should she be all that beautiful—or that cheerful? She doesn't, after all, have that much longer to live. She's my father's wife, my soon-to-be-dying mother.

I never pronounce the word *cancer*—or the word *dying,* for that matter—during the last year of my mother's life. But, that fall of my tenth year, after we return to Washington Heights from our usual two weeks in Pine Hill, my mother enters the hospital for some "tests."

What exactly they are, nobody says. But, the next morning, I ask my father what she has gone in for, and then watch the cup suddenly tremble in my grandmother's hand as she bursts into tears, and I observe my father's foot gently kicking her under the table.

"Why are you so depressed?" I ask my mother repeatedly over the next several months as she bends over the Biedermeier dresser in my parents' bedroom to brush her hair. "What's the matter?"

"I'm not depressed," she replies, with an obviously forced cheerfulness. "Nothing's the matter."

And so, to all my questions, there are no answers, as doctors appear and disappear, my mother vanishes into various hospitals and comes back, and my grandmother's cup continues to tremble in her hands, spilling bits of coffee-drenched challah all over the table. I have only words—occasional, strange-sounding English words like *pleurisy*—for hints: hospitals with odd, sometimes otherworldly, names like Doctors', Harkness Pavilion, St. Luke's, Mt. Sinai—along with a child's uncanny ability to sniff out the truth, no matter how many lies are created to disguise it.

My father, somehow, seems almost entirely absent during these months—a kind of mythic figure who comes and goes, shlepping furs and various delicatessen items from Horn & Hardart's, kissing his customers' hands and schtopping the traffic. It is, in fact, only the presence of my grandmother, Johanna, and the ubiquitous Helen, along with the progressively more solicitous attentions of the other mothers in the building, that serves to fill in a landscape suddenly rendered barren by the increasingly withdrawn, depressed figure of my mother.

Where *is* my father during these months? I wonder. Somehow relentlessly present, yet, as an emotional figure, almost entirely erased from my memory, so there is not a single conversation of any kind I remember having with him between that morning my mother first goes into the hospital and the night of her death some twelve months later.

Perhaps, I imagine now, he is already launching a kind of "preemptive strike" to make sure he won't be, again, the abandoned child reaching up toward the breast of his living mother to find only a void. Perhaps he is merely teaching me, in the enacted reality of his fears and disappointments, the Golden Rule I am just at this time beginning to learn at school: Do unto others as others do unto you; disappear before someone else disappears—before someone who desperately needs you can learn to hold on.

My mother, withering away from cancer and in the company of my nearly blind grandmother, adopts a rather unconventional hobby for a bunch of German-Jewish Holocaust refugees: watching professional wrestling.

At least twice weekly, occasionally accompanied by my father, we sit huddled before the living room black-and-white TV, watching the Graham Brothers, a fleet-footed Argentine dropkicker by the name of Antonino Rocca, and—my mother's absolute favorite—a humongous, four-hundred-pound-plus hulk by the name of Haystacks Calhoun have it out with various opponents, most of whom Calhoun reduces to a semicomatose pulp with his most infamous of moves: throwing them to the canvas, standing at their side, and simply falling on them.

My mother and grandmother, for some reason, find Haystacks's rather unballetic demeanor not only admirable but downright lovable, and we are thrilled, not merely to watch our hero in action, but to listen to him recount his weekly eating habits—consisting of some forty-odd T-bone steaks, several dozen eggs and slices of French toast, and all sorts of other protein- and carbohydrate-loaded delectables—to various ABC announcers during the intermission.

We love Haystacks with the kind of fierce and unflagging loyalty I had heretofore reserved for the likes of Duke Snider and Sandy Koufax, and maybe, it occurs to me later, one of the reasons my mother, growing thinner by the day, is so wild about the Haystack is that she, too, feels as if the weight of the world is about to fall on her—as it is.

| SUNDAY

She is sitting on the large bed with my father. It is late September. The bedspread is a dark burgundy; the sun hovers like a lozenge over Fort Washington Avenue. I've just walked down the hill from my aunt Erna's house and am sitting alone in the living room reading. Suddenly I hear a sound like a stifled bird's cry coming from the bedroom. I go on my tiptoes and open the door.

I watch her sitting there, on the bed with my father. He is holding her hand. In the other hand my father is holding a white pail. It is the same pail my grandmother uses to urinate in. But now it is my mother, her head held like a spigot over the white porcelain, who is using the pail. A strange light is shining in her eyes. She holds her face above the pail, vomiting into it.

I don't want to look, yet I feel a strange fascination with what I am seeing. The vomit is deep green, like pea soup. I can't help myself, and just keep standing there, watching my mother's throat heave like a clogged garden hose over the pail. Suddenly my father looks up and sees me. He asks me to go get my mother some mints. I walk out into the living room, where the mints are where they have always been—on a small, silver tray beside the kiddush cups in one of the Biedermeier cabinets my parents brought from Germany. They are white, just like the pail.

I take the tray and go back into the bedroom. My mother has stopped vomiting now, but the vomit is still there in the pail. She smiles and takes some mints from my hand. "Thank you, darling," she says. "Thank you, darling." She speaks English.

I turn to walk out of the room. She is still sitting there, on the bed, holding my father's hand. "Thank you, darling," she says again. "Thank you." It is the last time I ever see her sitting up.

| MONDAY

The men come early in the morning—two of them, dressed in white and black. They wheel the large bed silently into the corner of the room. It stands there like a huge, white dinosaur, silent as sleep. It stands in the same place where I slept as a child, dreaming of falling. But now it is my mother who is falling, and she falls into the fresh sheets, white as the pail was white, clean as snow.

Suddenly the house begins filling with people, strangers in dark suits carrying small black bags, relatives I haven't seen in a very long time. I walk into the room, a comma between the clauses of the long sentence of intruders who have been in and out of the apartment all morning. I want to turn the large crank at the foot of the bed and make my mother's head go up again. There is something fun about turning it, like yanking water from a very deep well, helping it to rise.

But my mother won't rise. It seems as if all the rising has gone out of her, and she just lies there, an old boxer too tired to get up after being knocked down for the last time. Still, I turn the crank and crank her head up until she nearly looks into my eyes.

Leaves are falling from the trees outside on Fort Washington Avenue. It is Monday, September 21, 1959, in the year of our Lord.

| TUESDAY

I wake, sick to my own flesh with the thought of her. I get out of my bed. I feel like a fever carrying a body, and walk back into her room. She just lies there, perfectly still, a large spider's web of tubes running from all sides of her like cables into some celestial battery.

I stand at the door and stare, as if I were scouring the heavens in search of a galaxy. I wait and wait. But nothing rises. Nothing except for a small armada of bubbles rising into the glass bottle hooked up beside her. They rise into the dense liquid like the last breath of a drowning swimmer, like words trying to say: *I am still here, son. I am still here.*

| WEDNESDAY

For weeks after she dies, I ask everyone who was near her those last days when it was that they last heard the sound of her voice. I must already know that the voice is the heart's harp, and I want to know what chord, in the end, issued from hers.

I, too, have taken to bed—with the flu. All day we exhale, the two of us, our illnesses into the feverish air. Now it is nighttime. All day I stay in bed, mimicking her. But now I rise, opening the door to the bedroom, and stand there watching. I feel as if I am standing on a threshold to somewhere I have never been. I feel as if I were *her* mother, as if I myself were a woman. She just lies there on the high bed, cranked nearly down, eyes half open.

I go in and stand beside her. I can hear her breath rising, like a wounded animal's, from beneath the blanket. I can see her right arm extending into its circuitry of sugar. I place my small hand on her arm. Her eyelids flutter. I whisper, as softly as I can, as if not wanting to wake her: "Good night, Mom."

There is a long silence. It seems as if my words are passing to somewhere very far off. She opens her eyes, as if she has suddenly been called back from somewhere she is eager to get to. I feel two fingers curl, ever so lightly, around my own.

At first she says nothing. Then, as if by a heroic effort, her lips begin to move. It seems as if hours pass before a word finally comes. "Good night, darling," I hear her say, "Good night, darling"—words that will echo for years through my silenced life.

| THURSDAY

All morning I beg them to let me into the room. "Later," they keep saying. "Later, later." All morning I listen to the sound of the bedroom door opening and closing, opening and closing. I can hear them all descending on her—the neighbors; her brother Berthold; my father's sisters; a flotilla of doctors with their little black bags, the rabbi with his assorted *brocha*s. Our house is a nest of death and, like bees arriving to gather pollen, they've all come to gather around her.

After I beg all morning to enter, someone—I can't remember who—comes and leads me to the bedroom door. I look at the hallway clock. It is two in the afternoon. Opening the door, I see the burgundy bedspread again. I feel afraid, at first, to turn my head toward the large ghost of the bed where she lies.

Finally, though, I do turn my head. And what I see terrifies me: Her eyes, glazed as if they are coated with shellac, are wide open, staring up at me. Years later, in my hunger for the mock coherence of metaphor, I watch two Chinamen pull a northern pike from the St. Lawrence River, and in the death struggle of that huge fish I see again those eyes as I see them now. But now I have nothing to compare them with. Looking as if into a deep, bottomless well, I look, for the first time, death in its very face and call it Mother.

But she doesn't answer. Like a trapped fly dissolving into a spider's web, she lies there, the mute syllables of another country issuing from her. "Mother!" I call out again. "Mother!" "Mother!"

| FRIDAY

I wake to a commotion of rabbis and the scent of dying. Death itself has slinked through the halls like a serpent during the night, choking the breath from her. Now, returned to her original innocence, she is merely a body again, and I can't overcome the desire to kiss her. I want to go into the room where her body lies. I want to hold her one last time, to place my mouth against her mouth and breathe the life back into it.

I start toward the room. Hands restrain me. Voices say: "Not yet. Not yet." What can I do? I wait, listening to the sound of doors opening and closing, wheels rolling down the hallway, the whispered voices of strangers. I know what they must be doing, but can't believe it. "Wait," they tell me. "Just wait. We'll let you in."

No one knows what they are doing. No one knows how long a man mourns, mutely, for a child's missed mourning. Suddenly the small concertina of wheels and doorbells stops. The whole house grows terribly silent. Someone comes into my room to get me. It's my friend Raymond's father, Kurt, our accountant. I am crying. "You can go in now," he tells me. "You can go in now."

Slowly, I turn the knob to the bedroom door. I turn my eyes from the burgundy bedspread to where I hope I will find her. The hospital bed is still there. The sheets are still perfectly white, as though not even death has been able to dirty them. But she is gone. They have taken her away while they held me prisoner in the back room. Now she isn't even a body any longer.

| SATURDAY

All day I watch the World Series on TV. Small processions of grief echo like commercials through the house. The low stools are being recalled from their closets like pinch hitters. For months, I have emptied my sadness into her. But now that they have taken her body, I no longer want to know the grief of bodies. I want, merely, to think of strikeouts and passed balls, the living heroics of the great catch.

That night, the ball game over, my father calls me into the room where she died. I stand before the Biedermeier dresser, my eyes to the floor, as he bends to open the bottom drawer. There— neatly folded as if waiting, still, for her body—is her pink nightgown. I watch it rise like a loaf of bread in my father's trembling hands, moving toward me.

Slowly my father lifts the nightgown to his own lips. He whispers a blessing in Hebrew. Then, instead of the body I so wanted to kiss, my father holds the empty nightgown against my face and whispers in German: *"Gib' uns're Mama einen letzten kuss"* (Give our mother one last kiss). Terrified, I close my eyes and feign the puckering sound of a kiss as I feel the cold silk pressing against my lips.

| SUNDAY

It's a beautiful day. I am at my friend Raymond's, where they have sent me to play. I can hear the church bells ringing along Fort Washington Avenue. I look out the window and see a long serpent of black cars lined up along the curb, a procession of shoulders wrapped in fur entering them. I can't keep myself from watching as they drive off. I try to look into the windows of each of the cars. I don't want to miss, again, her body.

Then, suddenly, I find myself sitting on the floor with Raymond, laughing wildly. I laugh and laugh until my whole stomach hurts, but I can't stop. *Your mother has just died,* I say to myself. *How can you be laughing this way?*

I've forgotten everything else about that day, though I have tried for years to remember. I have forgotten when they came home, what they said, whether or not the rabbi took me into my room again to say it was all for me. But I remember, always, that long, wild, bellyaching laugh and the long serpent of black cars, and wonder for years if, had I wept then, I might have been spared the long, silent weeping since.

I wonder if, had I wept then, I might have wept for real.

∾

4 | MALHEURS

It is almost night

when the joys of this life

finally find you again:

Looking for tulips beneath the ice.

—"Melancholy," from *Days We Would*

Rather Know (1984)

THE MORNING MY MOTHER dies, after I open the bedroom door and see the empty white hospital bed, I go to the kitchen and sit down at the table.

There's a commotion in the house, people coming and going, and—though I don't at the time phrase it as an actual question—I ponder it anyway: *Now* what do I do? What is a boy supposed to do after his mother's dead body has been carried out of the house?

So I do what my family always does in times of overwhelming grief or anger: *I eat.* Baby food custard, the kind I've always loved. I don't remember the brand, but it is creamily consistent (the consoling marriage of cream and eggs), like the Horn & Hardart's rice pudding my father brings home from the fur district.

I don't exactly remember who is sitting there at the table with me while I eat, but I'm quite certain it's Helen, my uncle Berthold, and my grandmother. I stir the custard for a long, long time before eating. I hear a hiss of air escaping from the lid when I open the jar and watch the circular motion of the spoon as I stir. The custard tastes so very good that—in moments of grief, even forty years later—I still eat custard pudding.

"She was so young." I, already an archivist of utterances, say to my uncle a bit later, while trying to determine my mother's last words. "She was only forty-two."

"No," my uncle corrects me, "she was *fifty*-two. She lied to you about her age. She thought you would love her more if she was younger."

Two thoughts cross my mind at once: The first is that—with one magical swoop of my uncle's tongue—my mother has been given ten extra years of life. The harsh injustice of a woman being plucked so young from this life has been somehow mitigated, made less painful. The voice, I realize, can give gifts.

And then, close on its heels, comes the second thought: How terribly insecure she must have been about my love, this woman whose own body couldn't nourish me, who was too ashamed of her scarred and dying body ever to even allow me a peek. She must have known that what would be revealed would be traumatizing to a nine-year-old boy.

"I love Helen more than I love you!" I remember the words I had spoken in a moment of anger. I think to myself now that she must have believed me—must have believed that I loved that other woman, that woman of the intact body, that woman who had been able to bear children, that woman who was not so visibly among the dying, more than I loved her. And maybe, it occurs to me, I did.

So I sit at the kitchen table and eat my custard pudding and think of what they have done with her body—of where I might still find it, how I might still kiss it good-bye, how I might touch it for the last time—that body I have little memory of ever having touched, aside from clinging to her skirt.

Then, after eating my custard and walking by the bedroom again to make sure they hadn't—in a moment of remorse, a moment of mercy—put her body back, what do I do? What does a ten-year-old boy *do* after his mother's dead body has been carried out of the house? Go out and play baseball? Watch the World Series? Stick a piece of bubble gum on a string and fish for change beneath the subway gratings?

No, he doesn't do any of those things. What he does is he goes looking for sympathy, for someone who will tell him the truth, someone who will let him grieve.

I realize now what I must always have realized, must always have known the way only a child knows the unspeakable and the unspoken: That our house was not a place of truth, not a place of sincerity. I must have known very early on that my family members—especially my father (that kisser of women's hands, that flatterer of women's bodies)—didn't really mean what they said or say what they meant . . . that the place of the fur was a place of untruth. And I must have decided very young that what I most wanted to be was a man who *said* and *meant* at the same time.

So what do I do after eating my custard pudding, after checking once more for my mother's body, after determining as best I can that the last words to have issued from her lips were the "Good night, darling" she had whispered to me from her deathbed that Wednesday night? What I do is walk up the stairs to the sixth floor of our building, to apartment 61, where my friend Ronnie Berger lives, and ring the doorbell.

Months before—when no one had said a word to me about what was really wrong with my mother, when no one had told me she was dying—Ronnie's mother, Molly, had asked me how she was. And because I *knew*—because a child, in the deepest recesses of his heart and soul, *always* knows—I fell, sobbing, into her arms. And so Molly Berger's home, her arms, her body, became for me a place of truth, that place of sincerity I had always longed for.

There is something else that must be terribly attractive to me about the Bergers' apartment, that must imbue me with the sense that their house, if not my own, is a place of truth. It's Mr. Berger, a man completely without charm. In fact, as I will later say, mockingly, of some of my academic colleagues, he is terribly "serious." A journalist for a classical radio station in New York, where he hosts a weekly German-language talk-and-music show, he is a man who works with words. Words, I sense, that mean something, words that embody a kind of sincerity. Words that can give life.

David Berger's study is filled with what seem to me terribly sophisticated tape recorders and audio equipment. There is a sense of solitude I associate with his work, a sense—which both frightens and attracts me—that it takes place in the world of men, without the kissing of hands, without the seduction of women. I know—subliminally but clearly—that here is a man who makes love to his wife, who doesn't need to charm strangers or flatter women or be the best-loved man in the fur district. I think: This man is quiet. He works alone. He doesn't waste words. He loves his wife. *This* is what a man is. And these thoughts intrigue and frighten me.

And I sense something about Molly Berger as well: that here

is a woman who is both motherly and intact. Here is a woman who can stand the truth. And so, at that moment when I am simply overcome by the truth—the truth, first, of my mother's long illness and, now, of her dying—it's to Molly Berger's door that I go. From the histrionic, confused, charm-ridden, death-ridden, overeating confines of my own house, I go upstairs.

Molly Berger answers the doorbell and stands gazing at me for several seconds across the threshold. There is a look of compassion mingled with respectful distance on her face. She must, I realize as I stand staring at her, already know what has happened.

"Is Ronnie home?" I ask, in a more or less customary tone of voice.

"Sure, come in. He's in his room."

I start down the hallway toward my friend's room, past David Berger's study, where I notice him in his usual posture of adjusting various knobs on the recessed wall unit of stereo equipment and tape recorders.

"Hi, Mr. Berger," I whisper.

"Hi, Michael," David Berger replies. He seems only a tad more attentive to my presence than usual, lost in his habitual state of reverie before his tape recorders and microphones. In the background a baritone voice is singing in German.

"Would you like some milk and cookies?" Molly Berger's voice calls after me from the kitchen.

"No, thank you," I reply, continuing toward my friend's room. I suddenly realize that I don't know, really, why I have climbed the stairs to Ronnie Berger's apartment. I don't really want to cry. Maybe it's that I just want to be pitied.

"Hi, there," I say shyly.

Ronnie Berger looks up from the floor, where he is gluing together a model submarine as I enter. "Hi, there. Wanna work on this with me?"

I'm not really sure *what* it is I want. But Ronnie's proposal seems as reasonable as any. And so, on that late September morning of my tenth year, while my mother's dead body is still being transported down Fort Washington Avenue from our apartment to the busy halls of the Riverside Memorial Chapel on Amsterdam Avenue and Seventy-sixth Street, I sit gluing tiny fragments of World War II submarine fuselage together on the floor of Ronnie Berger's sixth-floor apartment.

That night after her death, as my mother's pink nightgown is rising toward my lips in my father's hands, what am I thinking?

Closing my eyes to the faces of hundreds of living women in the years since, I have often asked myself that question as my face turned away from their faces, my eyes from their eyes.

I remember the bottom drawer of the large Biedermeier dresser as it opened. I remember my father, dressed in blue flannel pajamas, reaching down into the drawer, scooping the nightgown up in his palms like an old Bedouin woman carrying straw through the fields. I remember him bringing it, first, to his own lips, where he plants a soft, seemingly feminine kiss against the silk, and then lowering it once again.

I remember a sudden sense of dread coming over me. The image of the empty bed from which my dead mother's body had been taken that morning again flashes through my mind. I remember feeling as though I have no avenue of escape, as though I am in that room with a man who is not really a man, a lover of women who is not really a lover of women. I remember the dread, and I remember the revulsion, and I remember the terrifying sight of that pink nightgown moving toward my lips in my father's hands.

And I remember a terrible, bottomless feeling of being trapped—by a man who loves his own symbolism more than he loves his son, a man who can't bring his whole eyes and lips and heart into contact with a living woman, a man who can only kiss the dead cloth that once dressed his wife's disfigured body, a man too deprived of grief in his own childhood to allow me, his son (though I am, without yet knowing it, *not* his son), to grieve.

But I don't want to kiss the empty nightgown of a dead woman's body. I want to kiss a living woman, a dying woman—yes, even the dead woman who has been secretly removed from the apartment that very morning. What I surely *don't* want to kiss is the dead woman's dead nightgown. I don't want my living eyes to gaze into the face of such a double death.

But I've already been deprived of the kiss I want to bestow. And, now, as the pink nightgown rises in my father's hands, I am overcome by revulsion and anger and loathing and shame. And my eyes won't open, and my lips won't form their kiss, and—as I feel the cold silk press against my face—something in my ten-year-old heart vows to avenge itself against the grief-stricken, unconscious man standing beside me. I must be secretly thinking to myself that, someday, he will pay for my humiliation and shame and loss, and for my aborted grief.

The day after my mother's death, our rabbi, a deeply religious, salt-and-pepper-bearded man by the name of Dr. Hugo Stransky, comes to talk to me.

"It is not a good idea for you to go to the funeral," Stransky informs me. "Your mother wouldn't want you to be there if she were still alive."

The idea that my mother wouldn't want me there to say good-bye to her as she is lowered into the ground—like the idea that she wouldn't have wanted me to say good-bye before she was taken out of the room the morning before—comes as a shock.

"But I *want* to go!" I wail. "She was my mother."

"Yes," the rabbi answers. "I know. . . . But you will do her memory more good by staying here."

"But then I will never see her again," I insist.

"Yes, that's true," Dr. Stransky replies. "You will never see her again."

But never, I must already realize, is a terribly long time. Never is too long to live in a world where the funny and the serious, the living and the dying, are constantly divided. Never is too long a time not to be able to look a dead woman in the face and say good-bye. Never is too long not to be able to look a woman in the eye.

For the second time in my still-young existence (my father's sister Clemmie had died of a heart attack on a flight between Cleveland and Miami in 1957), the shiva stools are removed from their closets and spread out, half-moon fashion, around the living room. I don't know it yet, but—my father being the youngest of ten, and all his sisters having married significantly older men—these stools are about to become our apartment's semipermanent furnishings: Like grown-ups playing on dollhouse furniture, my family sits around and mourns. But I, who wasn't allowed to be at my mother's funeral, am not allowed to be present for this part of the ritual either: I'm told to stay in my room.

A few weeks later I find myself about to enter the long hallway of our apartment, between the room where my father keeps his furs and the bedroom I share with my blind grandmother. Suddenly—as I emerge from the bathroom and my father from his roomful of transmogrified skins—it occurs to me to ask him something that has been on my mind now for a very long time.

"Papa," I say, "when you always talk about 'picking me up' in Vineland, what do mean?" I had recently, somehow—no doubt prompted by my mother's death—begun to question exactly how and where in Vineland I had been "picked up." Was it at a supermarket? At the synagogue of which my uncle Berthold was president? At Vineland High School, where my cousins Amos and Judy went?

I need to know. *Picked up?* What could the words possibly mean?

"Well," my father begins slowly, in German. "When you were born in Vineland, Berthold and Nelly already had two children, your cousins Amos and Judy. They had just arrived from Israel, and I bought them the chicken farm, so they had to work very, very hard, and didn't have much time or money to take care of another baby.

"Your mama," he continues, somehow omitting himself, "always wanted very much to have a baby of her own, and she was just recovering from being sick. So I said to her, 'Betzele, let us take this sweet little boy.' And so we went to Vineland when you were just eight days old and picked you up. You were our million, and you brought so much happiness into our Betzele's life."

What did all this mean? I remember thinking. Was my dead mother no longer my mother? My living father no longer my father? Was my "aunt" Nelly—that woman I had always, more or less, disliked, and who, I felt, had never much liked me—now, somehow, magically, my *mother*? My "uncle" Berthold my father? My "cousins" Amos and Judy my brother and sister? Should I now love my dead mother less? My living aunt more? Why didn't my mother just go ahead and *have* "a baby of her own"?

"You were our million," my father repeats, interrupting my reveries. "And you gave your dear mama, may she rest in *sholem*, something to live for."

About a week after my mother's death, I run into my friend and neighbor Frankie Engel's mother, Toni, and his younger brother, Jerry, at the elevator.

"Where's your mother?" Jerry, all of about six, asks me innocently, while his mother turns beet red.

"She's on vacation," Mrs. Engel responds before I have a chance to.

"Yes," I agree cooperatively. "She's on vacation."

"Will she be back *soon*?" Jerry is a curious little tyke, and his question—as I have neither had a chance to say good-bye to my mother, nor have I seen either her dead body or her funeral—echoes a fantasy that's been much on my own mind since her death: She'll be coming back.

"Yes." Mrs. Engel once again preempts my own uncertain response. "She'll be back very soon."

She'll be back very soon. The words echo in my own mind and heart, not as a forced explanation to a child, but as a very real fantasy: *She'll be back very soon.* And now, for what will be months—no, years—my childish, disbelieving, ever hopeful mind begins imagining possible scenarios: I will arrive one morning at the breakfast table and—*whammo!*—she'll be there. I will go into what is now my father's solitary bedroom to say good night and—miracle of miracles!—she'll be in bed again with him. I will turn the corner of Fort Washington Avenue on my way home from sixth grade, and—wonder of wonders!—there she will be, as if she had never been taken away.

But the most vivid fantasy of all—the one that combines my secular fantasies with my profoundest religious hopes—is the one that (as time goes by and none of my other fantasies of her resurrection materialize) will take place, à la Moses and the Burning Bush, at my bar mitzvah: The curtain of the Ark will be parted for Rabbi Stransky and Cantor Kornfeld (and me!) to remove the Torah scrolls and—*baruch hashem*—there she will be.

But my bar mitzvah, alas, is still years—and numerous unexpected events—in the future. Like Frost I have miles to go before I sleep . . . and much to endure before my dear departed mother, blessedly, will be returned to me again.

My father—with a bad heart, a grieving ten-year-old son, and a blind mother-in-law in tow—is suddenly among the ranks of the newly widowed. And I, apparently already an aspiring poet of sorts and ever the devoted son, welcome his first birthday as a widower with the following verse:

> If every father on this earth
> Were half as good as you,
> The God and all his Angels
> Would have nothing left to do.
>
> If every father did so much
> To help his children by,
> Then every single boy and girl
> Would never have to cry.
>
> And now dear father comes the day
> On which you too must rest.
> And every time I think of you,
> I'm thinking of the best.
>
> Now that you are home today,
> I'm also very glad.
> And one more thing I'd like to say
> Is "Happy Birthday Dad."
>
> *Your loving son,*
> *Micky*

My father's unconscious, however, along with his ever-helpful sisters, seems to have other things in mind than "helping [me] by." From the moment my mother's cancer-ridden, twice-mastectomized body is lowered into the ground, his six surviving sisters, the Sirens of our story, dreading that they might have to lend a hand in caring for their ten-year-old nephew (who isn't, after all, *really* their nephew) and his blind grandmother, begin a frenzied search for a wife for their widowed brother.

Suddenly a flotilla of plastic models, children's books, polo shirts, and Erector sets arrives in the mail from someone who goes by the mysterious name of *"die Witwe Kahn"* (the widow Kahn), and to whom—when she finally makes an appearance in my life some weeks later—I take an instant, visceral dislike.

To say that Alice Kahn *née Bernheimer frühere Guggenheim* is not the kind of woman who can easily endear herself to a ten-year-old boy who has just lost his mother is to be blessed with a gift for understatement. Hunchbacked, a deep frown perpetually pasted to her face, accompanied by a yapping, overweight twelve-year-old English fox terrier inappropriately named Ami, she has recently been widowed by her second husband, Fritz (who, like her first, died of a heart attack—on Thanksgiving Day). Fritz had been a German-Jewish industrial glove tycoon of a sort, who had gone from selling a shoebox full of cheap mechanic's gloves to running a miniempire from his dimly lit basement in Jackson Heights.

"I think both her husbands died voluntarily," I say to my friends of my potential stepmother, "just to avoid the prospect of staying married to her."

Alice Kahn, indeed, is every grieving boy's archetype of the wicked stepmother. Thanatic, fearful, parsimonious beyond the gravest necessity, she is so transparently incapable of anything even bordering on genuine human affection that her very presence—the very *possibility* that she might be brought on as the replacement for my gentle, loving, ever-dying mother—sends me into paroxysms of fear and depression so violent that, but for the knowledge that I can't abandon my father and blind grandmother, I might consider fleeing to the chicken-dust- and flea-ridden confines of Vineland where, at the very least (I now know) my true flesh and blood dwell, and won't (or so I hope) abandon me.

"Wen hättest Du am liebsten dass ich heirate?" my father asks me. "Whom would you like most for me to marry? Helen"—he begins, wisely, with the name of my recently widowed first choice—"Gisela," his long-suffering, never-married seamstress, whom I have always liked—"*oder* Frau Kahn," the twice-widowed, willfully childless purchaser of children's toys whose interest in me, I immediately intuit, extends no further than as a door into my widowed father's vulnerable heart—to be used for that purpose and immediately slammed shut.

"Helen oder Gisela," I reply, referring to the two women already reliably ensconced in my affections. The third alternative, I feel, is too unspeakable to name.

I don't remember what, if anything, my father says in response. But one thing I *do* know for certain: On October 5, 1960, just over a year after my mother—the dying woman to whom I was adopted by a man whose own mother had died in childbirth—is lowered into the ground, that same man—who in his life had been graced with a stepmother who had never wanted or loved him—presents me with the third mother of my not-yet-eleven-year-old life.

Her name is Alice Kahn.

Though I don't realize it at the time, with the death of my mother and the ascent of my stepmother, my childhood—and, with it, any and all happiness I would know for years—has effectively come to an end. Without so much as a peep from the woman who is my natural mother—indeed, with her silent acquiescence from the chicken-dust-infested walls of Vineland—the slow dismemberment of my childhood world begins.

My grandmother—followed shortly, and more gradually, by Helen—is, naturally, the first to go, as my stepmother—with the demonic power characteristic of the psychologically damaged—relentlessly "lobbies" my fathers' sisters behind the scenes to help bring about her eviction. One evening, as the growing chill between the oddly cohabiting twosome of my father's mother-in-law from his first marriage and his second wife is coming to a head, my "uncle" Berthold—staying at our apartment as he does every Monday night while delivering his eggs—arrives for his habitual 8:00 P.M. glass of beer. On this occasion, however, there's a fresh, rather hefty bruise just below his left eye.

"What happened?" We all gather around him, expecting to hear yet another inner-city horror story from our increasingly "mixed" and dangerous streets. The horrific events on this occasion, however, are slightly more intimate: My uncle, it seems, had found himself occupying the elevator just moments earlier in the exclusive company of my father's seamstress sister Tina, who lives just three floors below us in apartment 25. As one of the leading emissaries of my stepmother's campaign to evict my grandmother, Tina, apparently, felt this to be her golden opportunity: Slapping my uncle in the face with a solid right, she ordered him, in very few words, to "get your goddamned mother out of my brother's house," an act that—due to a combination of my and my father's love for my grandmother and my aunt Nelly's hatred of her—had, until then, been resisted.

My aunt Tina's right cross, however, which lands squarely on my uncle Berthold's cheek, is apparently enough to get the job done. Some two weeks later, her accumulated belongings gathered into four antique suitcases, my eighty-four-year-old blind grandmother—the only woman who now stands between me and my stepmother's vengeful and penurious cruelty—is packed into my uncle's Chevy station wagon and taken to live with my aunt and uncle in Vineland.

My grandmother—the one person aside from Helen whose love I'm sure of, the only person I truly trust—is now out of the house, sitting alone in my aunt and uncle's darkened Vineland living room among the chicken dust. Whenever I can accumulate the shekels from my work at Strauss Cleaners and from shoveling out cars, I take the A-train down to the Port Authority Bus Terminal after school on Friday and board the late afternoon bus that follows the New Jersey Turnpike through the thriving metropolises of Camden, Bordentown, and Millville to visit her.

My cousin Amos is already off to college at Rutgers, and Judy's working as a secretary in Philadelphia, so what awaits me is the prospect of spending the weekend navigating between my dispirited aunt, who *hates* having her mother-in-law living with her, and my grandmother, who spends most of our "private" time together weeping. On Monday morning, after three such delightful days, I get up at 5:00 A.M. with my uncle and drive to New York, where I attend my classes at the prestigious Bronx High School of Science and he delivers his eggs.

What the hell, I must wonder, as I sit in my aunt and uncle's living room, is *wrong* with all these women? Why so much hatred? Such lovelessness? Why such a death-embracing lack of joy? Why can't any of them—aside, that is, from my blind and helpless grandmother, and good-hearted Helen, whom my stupid father refused to marry—be like Mrs. Berger or my friend

Leslie's mother, Mrs. Millett? Or, for that matter, like my dead mother? Why is this poor old woman weeping? Why won't this younger woman, her daughter-in-law, give her any love? Or me?

There are no obvious answers to these questions, I realize. But what I'm not yet aware of, blessedly, is one of life's most unbendable rules: The wrong people, no doubt, will be made to pay for these sins in the end.

Shortly after my father's marriage to my stepmother, he, Helen, and I, like three people on some sort of clandestine "date," are seated at the RKO Coliseum on 181st Street and Broadway, watching what would become one of my father's all-time favorite movies, a kitschy 1961 remake of Marcel Pagnol's eponymous 1932 classic, *Fanny*. The horrific American version—a work of art to rival another of my father's favorites, *The Sound of Music*—stars one of his true musical heroes: the sentimental French crooner Maurice Chevalier.

Chevalier plays the role of the elderly Monsieur Panisse, a—get this!—*impotent* gentleman who falls in love with, and marries, a much younger woman, Fanny. Fanny (played by Leslie Caron), however, is already pregnant by her younger lover, Marius (played by Horst Buchholz), who has left her for sailing adventures elsewhere. A certain biographical resonance with my father's own story has, no doubt, utterly evaded his fantastically repressed consciousness—as it will mine, for the next forty or so years—until I begin writing this book.

My father and Helen have, apparently, seen the movie before—multiple times, I venture a guess—so that this showing, my father explains, is for *my* benefit. I'll love it, he assures me. And I *am*, in fact, rather enjoying myself, when what I don't yet realize is the fatal moment arrives:

About half an hour from the beginning, a scene takes place in which M. Panisse and two other men, one of them played by Charles Boyer, decide to play a prank on strollers along the Marseilles shoreline promenade by placing an old top hat in the middle of the street—an obvious challenge to any passerby—with a large stone hidden beneath it. First, a local shipyard worker comes walking toward them, rising to the challenge and proceeding to painfully—and, of course, comically—stub his toes, an event that sends my father into such paroxysms of laughter that one of the ushers must be summoned to try and quiet him down, as his embarrassed son slinks beneath his seat.

The usher, in fact, succeeds in briefly silencing my father just as, on-screen, a local priest comes walking down the same street. As Panisse and his cohorts cover their faces in horror, his holiness, too, kicks the booby-trapped hat, catapulting my father into renewed waves of bellyaching laughter so loud and so heartfelt that tears begin to stream down his cheeks.

Once again the usher—with a "If you can't control yourself, sir, we will have to ask you to leave the theater"—descends toward our row, by which time most of the viewers seated near us have either broken out in peals of laughter themselves, moved to other seats, or gone to complain to the management. My father—prompted, perhaps, by both myself and Helen feverishly trying to quiet him—calms down for a minute or two, but the recollection of the priest's right foot meeting the stone apparently proves too much for him: Seconds later, with an amplitude and force even louder than his original outburst, he is again doubled over in his seat. Just a minute or two later—with Helen holding him by the arm, and me trying to hide my face, lest anyone I know is in the audience—we are unceremoniously led by the usher up the aisle and back out onto Broadway.

Years later I will wonder: Was my father's outburst during

Fanny something like my own outburst of laughter on the day of my mother's funeral? Could it be that his laughter was merely crying in another form?

My stepmother, it becomes clear to me virtually from the day she moves into our apartment from Fritz Kahn's house in Jackson Heights (a move she agrees to only under great duress, I having convinced my father that, having just lost my mother, I don't need to lose my friends as well by moving away), is inordinately devoted to prayer. Almost every day, she sits in a corner of our apartment, her little black German-Hebrew prayer book conspicuously opened to the page marked *"Morgensgebet einer unglücklichen Ehefrau"* (Morning Prayer of an Unhappy Wife).

It has never occurred to me that the Jewish religion—or the attentions of the Deity in general—might be so responsive to the special needs of its constituents. But, daily—indeed, several times a day—there she is, invoking the particulars of her situation to the god of Abraham, Isaac, and Jacob, and then proceeding, as soon as the door closes behind my father and her yapping fox terrier, to torture me to the point of tears with innuendos and accusations that it is I, the mournful little troublemaker, on whose behalf she has been forced out of her two-bedroom mini-castle just a stone's throw from La Guardia Airport.

As soon as I begin sobbing, she's down on her knees, both arms wrapped imploringly around my upper calves as she—tears running in big dollops down her abundantly freckled cheeks—*begs* me not to say anything to my father about what she has done, lest he send her packing. And, indeed, I *don't* say anything—having already sensed that my father's role in my life is fundamentally one of a betrayer, and not wanting to edge my way any closer to the orphanage doors by further exciting his already diseased heart.

But, by the time my father and little Ami return home from the fur district, my stepmother has independently worked her way into a tizzy over the subject, and within minutes—foaming at the mouth like a rabid dog, his face red as a beet—my father is hurling invectives into the air in German and trembling with a rage at once so out of control and terrifying that I feel I have no other recourse but to place myself, tear-strewn and begging for all I am worth, between my by-now-nearly-hysterical parents, pulling desperately at my father's pants leg in the hope that I might restrain him long enough to avoid having yet another one of my parents' bodies dragged, this time openly, through our apartment door.

By the time the uproar ends—my stepmother cowering, prayer book in hand, in a corner, my father wiping the saliva from his lower lip with a cologne-soaked handkerchief—the damage is done. And it's usually only a matter of days before I— at the ripe, sophisticated age of twelve—will be off with my father to the office of Dr. Leon Werther, cardiologist, where I watch, terrified, a vast web of little metal nodules being pasted on my father's chest and connected to an electrocardiograph.

Paralyzed somewhere between awe and desolation, I see the small, electrified needle hump and stagger as it charts the series of peaks, troughs, and straightaways that signify the perpetually worsening condition of my father's four-chambered organ. Some twenty minutes later, having been told that my father's condition is "not quite a heart attack, but a substantial worsening of the cardiographic picture," we're back home, where my father is put, immediately, to bed, hovered over by his sobbing, prayer-book-toting wife, the volume no doubt opened to "Prayer of an Incipient Widow."

I am, in fact, so certain that each ensuing night is going to be my father's last that I wake every morning, run to my parents' bedroom door, and—even before making sure the sun has risen—listen for the faintly consoling sound of my father's breathing.

There is also the matter of my forthcoming bar mitzvah, an event—given that it is, however indirectly, an affirmation of my existence—my stepmother approaches with the same humorless chagrin with which she greets all other evidence of my living presence. Reframed, however (as, for her, every human occasion inevitably is), as an "investment opportunity," the festivities take on a much more luminous significance, offering her one of those much sought-after occasions where religious redemption and profit might cohabit under a single roof.

My stepmother's many friends (*die lustigen Witwen*—"the merry widows"—as my father calls them, after his favorite operetta) and other family friends and relatives have, naturally, made inquiries—usually addressed to my stepmother—as to what I might want by way of gifts on my ascent into Jewish manhood. She, in turn, the great arbiter of children's pleasures, responds to these inquiries without consulting their intended recipient.

It should, therefore, come as no surprise to me when—instead of the usual checks, books and sports paraphernalia befitting such an occasion—my pre-bar mitzvah gift table is piled high with electric blenders, kitchen utensils, embossed stationery, perfumes of dubious gender-appropriateness, and other items that make it appear, at the very least, that my parents are either at the forefront of a kind of prefeminist Jewish avant-garde or about to have a daughter bat-mitzvahed.

My stepmother, ever on the lookout for number one, has, of course, requested gifts for me that only *she* could conceivably use. So, after the event is over and the accounting made, I find myself the proud recipient of a handful of checks and multiple copies of Max Dimont's *What Is a Jew?* while she makes off with a portable script typewriter, an armada of blenders and juicers, a new toaster, a dresser top full of perfumes, a new iron, and several years' worth of stationery on which to imprint her voluminous correspondence with AT&T, Ohio Edison, Phillips Petroleum, and the German-Jewish diaspora of merry widows.

"*Solch ein goldiger Junge,*" the widows each say in turn on the receiving line, pinching my cheeks like Milton Berle. "Such a sweet boy. Mazel tov."

But something far worse takes place on the day of my bar mitzvah than the loss of a few hypermasculine gifts. When the time comes for the opening of the Ark and the removal of the Torah scrolls—that moment toward which my ever-hopeful, ever-disbelieving heart had been straining now for almost three years—when the congregation president Dr. Simon pulls the curtain and I, my heart pounding not so much with fear as with the expectation of God's longed-for miracle, gaze longingly toward it, it is *not* my mother's longed-for face that appears there above her habitual long skirt: It is merely the various maroon-and-gold wrapped Torah scrolls, those five Books of Moses, in none of which my mother's name appears—and none of which have even the slightest thing to say to a boy whose vision of the Resurrection has just been shattered forever.

My stepmother's penuriousness—a miserliness of such an all-consumingly thorough nature it makes Silas Marner seem like a philanthropist—becomes, once all possible rivals for my father's affection have been eliminated, our household's dominant motif, leaving its flotsam and jetsam everywhere I turn. The bathroom sink, when I wash, is regularly filled with a kind of post-Holocaust navy—the floating carcasses of used but not fully postmarked postage stamps, which my stepmother, the first great American immigrant recycler, endeavors to resurrect into a second life on similarly redeployed envelopes.

Wherever I retreat *La Belle Dame Sans Merci* follows me, demanding that I drink up the three drops of orange juice I have left in the glass or lick the side drippings from an empty glass of milk, asking me to turn out the lights, or to check the long-distance phone bill to see if any of the calls are mine.

Sent across the street with a quarter to buy a twenty-two-cent head of lettuce, I am so assiduously reminded of my three-cent debt (which, I must confess, I frequently combine with two cents of my own to buy a pack of baseball cards) that I, fatigued by the whole process, often respond with a full nickel, allowing my stepmother, in her beloved investment tradition, to garner a 20 percent return on her initial expenditure.

Though almost entirely oblivious to the larger world around her, she is, however, not averse to my reading to her from the daily *New York Times*.

"Phillips Petroleum?" she calls out from the kitchen.

"Fifty-eight and three-quarters," I reply.

"Bethlehem Steel?" comes next, in double trochees.

"Thirty-nine and five-eighths."

"*Oy veh. Das ist furchtbar.* Ohio Edison?"

"Twenty-seven and a half."

And so it goes, with me seeming to have graduated from reading the obituaries in the *Aufbau* to my grandmother only to arrive at this.

Most of all, however, I dread those rare occasions when we find ourselves in restaurants, where my stepmother, a devoted practitioner of the wear-'em-down theory of psychology, so insists that I eat all the (free) month-old pickles on the table and gulp down all the "milk" (usually, in fact, a chemically reconstituted, no doubt carcinogenic substance called "Coffee Light") in the small silver pitcher that I find it the lesser of two evils merely to acquiesce rather than continue to be subjected to her harangues about waste and high prices.

My parents' finances, with my stepmother's ascent to power, are also organized around a very simple principle: Whatever has been hers (her and her second husband's, Fritz Kahn's, house included) remains hers; whatever has been my father's and mother's (and, therefore, presumptively, one day, mine) becomes, immediately, the joint property of Julius and Alice Blumenthal. Their joint living expenses are to come, with rare exceptions, from *his* income; her ample dividends and new investments, however, remain in *her* name. Why would any sane man, with a child, who had just remarried a "rich widow" agree to such an apportionment of riches? Many years later I will finally find out.

My father, to his credit at the time, tries to resist the overwhelming aggressive powers of his second wife, but to no avail. Like a psychological steamroller annihilating everything in its path, her persistent repetitiveness, not unlike my father's "God loves you" and "schtops the traffic," wear down every attempt at resistance. Ultimately, it seems, it is always easier—at the very least, quieter—to give in than to fight.

In a very real sense, I am beginning to realize, my father and I—each trying, in his own way, to defend himself—are now in the same boat.

Along with their more sadistic and masochistic preoccupations, my father and stepmother are also clearly masters of what Freud called "bungled actions"—comical, always entertaining, slips and mishaps that, on occasion, lead to embarrassing situations.

"You vill never believe vat happened mit us, dear son," my father informs me as my parents reenter our apartment one Sunday near the end of my high school career.

"*Jawohl*," my stepmother seconds. "To make such a terrible mistake. . . . I vas red in the whole face."

"What happened?"

"Ve vas sitting in the Hirsch Funeral Home," my father begins, "und I vas saying to Alice vhat a surprise it is that no one von the family looked to be around."

"Und your father vas introducing himself to everyone and saying to them all vhat a vonderful voman Mrs. Katzenstein vas, and may she rest in *sholem* like he is alvays doing," my stepmother interrupts.

I always describe the Hirsch Funeral Home, a place given to conducting funerals with the one-after-another rapidity of certain local Jewish catering establishments, as "the bar mitzvah factory of the other end." On any particular Sunday some dozen funerals—mostly of German-Jewish refugees with names like Dingfelder, Strauss, Baumgartner, Berger, Schwartzschild, and Fromm—take place simultaneously in its interchangeable chapels of elegy and adieu. "My parents' version," I explain to my girlfriend at the time (who is forever astonished that, whenever I call, they seem to be just back from a funeral), "of Monday night football—a way of keeping themselves busy in old age."

"*Jawohl*," my father continues. "Und then, all of a sudden, the *Rabbiner* was standing up and giving the sermon und schpeaking about the family, und he started talking about 'the deceased Gretel Lisberger.' Und ve suddenly realized that ve vas in the wrong funeral."

"Such a *shlimazel!*" My stepmother invokes the Yiddish word for "misfortune." "The Katzensteins were such good customers."

~

Then there was that cold, unforgettable night when, after a series of frantic late-night phone calls, my parents and I rush down to the General Post Office at Thirty-third Street and Eighth Avenue in Manhattan to retrieve the sympathy letter my father has just written to Hugo Baumgartner.

Having heard that very morning that Hugo's wife, my parents' fifty-six-year-old friend Lotte, who had been fighting a losing battle with breast cancer, was close to death, my father immediately sat down and uttered forth that venerable staple of his literary repertoire, the condolence letter.

"My dear Hugo," the letter began:

> I cannot tell you how shocked and saddened my wife und I are by hearing this terrible news of the dead of your dear and beloved wife and our great friend Lotte.
>
> We know, of course, what you und your family haf suffered in the months of your dear wife's sickness, und she has been every day in our prayers and thoughts. Just this past Shabbos, I said a special prayer for her and for your family in the Synagogue, in the hope that dear God Almighty should hear our prayers and bring to her and to you in your suffering relief.
>
> As you know, it is just more than one year since I lost my dear beloved Betzele, also to this terrible cancer, so I know from the buttom of my heart what terrible suffering you have lived, and pray for you that she may rest in Sholem. It is only good that she was blessed from God in her life mit two such wonderful children as your two boys, who will grow up I know in loving memory of their dear beloved mama Lottchen.

Und I know—as was the case mit my beloved Betzele who passed away more than a year ago 9.25.59—that you see in your heart what a good und loving husband you have been to her, may God bless and keep her, and what two wonderful boys she has brought into the world mit which to keep her memory.

My wife and son join with me to say Kaddish in memory of your dear wife und our beloved friend Lotte whom we will remember only mit the best und loving memories, may she rest in Sholem, and for whom we will say this Shabbos a special Hallelujah that her suffering is finally over and for the good memories and special friends she has left on this world.

Our thoughts and prayers are mit you in your sorrow. God loves you, and so do we.

With all our blessings,
Julius Blumenthal & family

I will never forget the expression on my father's face when, later that long-ago evening, a neighbor casually mentioned that she had just been to visit Lotte Baumgartner, who was feeling much better. Nor will I ever forget the frenzied search-and-rescue mission that followed, as the three of us piled into the car and headed down to the General Post Office.

I'd never seen so many bags of mail in a single place. The thought of having to retrieve the small white envelope addressed, in my father's nearly hieroglyphic scrawl, to "Mr. Hugo Baumgartner & family" seemed, even to an eleven-year-old boy, an insurmountable task. But retrieve it we did, after hours of sifting through thousands of letters destined for zip code 10033.

Later I can't help but wonder what it would have been like

for a still-living woman to read a letter of condolence for her not-yet-transpired death. I wonder why my father seemed so eager to pronounce a woman dead while an unfinished life still blazed within her.

When I'm not reading to my stepmother from the stock market quotations or going to school, I spend every spare hour trying to figure out how to earn some of the precious legal tender she so arduously preoccupies herself with.

Unfortunately I can channel my entrepreneurial zeal no further than the downstairs storefront of Julius Strauss Dry Cleaners on 181st Street, for whom, every afternoon between the hours of four and six, I deliver garments to various apartment buildings around Fort Washington Avenue and Cabrini Boulevard in a frenzied effort to raise enough money to pay for college.

Among those buildings, rising majestically over the grassy banks of the Hudson, stand the matched set of five red-brick high-rises that are Castle Village, well known as inhospitable to (and largely unaffordable by) the neighborhood's merchant-class German Jews. Awed by the very sight of the elegantly clad doormen, and by names like Welch, Fox, and Crane taped to the buzzers (not to mention the generous tips usually forthcoming from behind their doors), I scud eagerly down 181st Street, often stopping to treat myself to a malted and a pack of baseball cards on the way in anticipation of my bounty.

Perhaps most amazing of all are the *women* who often answer the door to claim their freshly cleaned garments, many of whom are unlike any member of their gender I have ever laid eyes on. Tall, blond, wearing long pastel nightgowns and jewelry—yes, jewelry!—in midafternoon, they waft long trails of perfume out into the hall ahead of them, their white-toothed, Ozzie-and-Harriet smiles and perfect English leaving me with a longing to be American and *normal*—yes, normal!—so profound that I remount the hill toward Fort Washington Avenue literally praying to die and be reincarnated in some not-far-off East Hampton as a Barkley or a Gardner.

By now, of course, the ideal of the golden shiksa is firmly entrenched in my consciousness, only aided and abetted by the tall, luscious, clean-smelling, middle-aged women—just think of it, *mothers* all!—who, like a host of Rapunzels, come to the doors of even more exclusive Hudson View Gardens to deposit their coins and newly minted dollar bills in my eager hands.

It is these very coins and dollars that seem to me, a young boy still in search of his lost mother, to be the only avenue into my stepmother's cold and ever-calculating heart. And, by the time my senior year approaches I have—between a succession of summer jobs, delivering dry cleaning for Julius Strauss, and shoveling out the snowed-in cars of the world—stowed away enough money to *almost* pay for the first year of college at the state university for which I am destined.

So it's with great delight, not to mention relief that I arrive home one afternoon to find a letter from the local chapter of B'nai Brith, informing me that, on the basis of my outstanding scholastic record, I have been awarded a four-hundred-dollar scholarship (the full annual state university tuition in those days!) for my first year of college. The check, I am told, will be in the mail shortly, and I'm to be congratulated on my fine academic performance and the great promise I hold out, for both myself and the Jewish community, for the future.

Being blessed with a stepmother who sends me out with a quarter for a twenty-two-cent head of lettuce and then asks for the change, the thought of four hundred *free* dollars suddenly descending on me—dollars that will liberate me from having to say any further thank-yous to the father who (I am relentlessly told) "has sacrificed everything for you"—sends me into effusions of gratitude, and I find myself whispering a blessing to the elusive and inscrutable gods as I wait for the precious shekels to descend and free me from the dark tabernacle of Dow Jones and electrocardiographs.

But months go by with—to my surprise and growing suspicion—no mail addressed to me beyond the usual renewal notices from Reader's Digest Condensed Books and Stamps of the World. Finally, with but a few weeks remaining before the due date of my tuition bill, I arrive home one afternoon to find my father alone in the house.

"Dad," I say, "you didn't happen to see that check that was supposed to come from B'nai Brith for my scholarship?"

"Oh, that," my father answers rather glibly. "*Jawohl.* It came, and I sent it back."

"You *what*?" For one who should, by now, be accustomed to betrayals, I've retained a remarkable innocence.

"*Ja.*" I can feel a hint of pride in my father's voice as he speaks. "I sent it back to the B'nai Brith."

"Why on earth would you *do* that? I *earned* that money with my grades in school. What right did *you* have to send it back?"

"No son von Julius Blumenthal is going to take charity." My father, by now, is oozing a kind of fierce, uninhibited animus. "And anyway," he continues, kissing me a bit too tenderly on the lips for my own comfort, "with a father like me, who would sacrifice anything for you, why in the world do you need the B'nai Brith?"

How can I dispose of her, the wicked witch of Dow Jones and *davening*? I dream, I pray, I flirt with thoughts of matricide and dismemberment; I petition the fickle gods nightly for relief from my and my father's ordeal.

There is, in fact, no cruelty I don't imagine inflicting upon my deranged, death-dealing stepmother. Trembling with rage, my fists clenched into tightly humped nuggets beneath the sheets, I fantasize about tying her to a chair, then kicking her so powerfully and repeatedly in the face that her features themselves will be splattered all over the plastic- and sheet-swathed furnishings she so religiously guards from the defilement of human hands.

I could send away for a gun through the mails, I think, then pump some dozens of bullets into various parts of her and watch her bleed to death while I smoke a cigarette and—like my favorite fictional detective, Mike Shayne—suavely imbibe a *Schnapps*. Or I could, in a variation on Oedipus, gouge her eyes out and doom her to a life where not even the small scobs of dust, not even the five droplets of orange juice remaining in my glass and for which she lives, will be able to summon her attention from the netherworld where her panicked, humpbacked consciousness no doubt dwells.

My father, as I see it, is, along with myself, merely a victim: He has never loved her. He didn't want to marry her. He has merely been forced, by his overzealous and manipulative sisters, the Sirens, into a marriage with a penny-pinching, despondent widow who has robbed him, and us, of all our joie de vivre, who has transformed the presiding melody of our household from "Oh, what a beautiful morning" to that famous Schumann *Lied*: "*Ich grolle nicht, und wenn das Herz auch bricht*" (I don't complain, although my heart is breaking).

And, I question the gods, hasn't he already suffered enough, my poor father? A mother dead before he could even get his mouth to her nipple; a wicked stepmother who detested him; Julius Streicher and the SS patrolling the streets of his city; his true love in some far-off Chile; exiled to a new country at the age of thirty-three; a wife dead of cancer before he was fifty-five? I want to save him—to return him once more to his life of cruises and singing, of harmonicas and Mario Lanza . . . to his "Golden Days."

There's yet another fantasy I have—a safer one, less satisfying but less messy. I'll first poison the bitch, something quick but hopefully painful. Then I'll dig a hole in her beloved six-by-eight-foot backyard—which, if one takes the intensity of her rhapsodizing about it seriously, might as well be the Garden of Versailles—and bury her there, heaping shovelfuls of dirt over her pouting, freckled face as the last gasps of asphyxiation cover her malevolent features.

I imagine how the trial would go if I were found out: I would, of course, argue in my own defense. I would simply explain who I and my father were, what she had done to us, how she had made of our once relatively happy home a dungeon of doused lights and the orisons of an unhappy housewife. No jury, as I imagined, could possibly convict me, an innocent child whose life had been joined to that of a wicked witch as unjustly and haphazardly as Hansel and Gretel had been led to the gingerbread house by following the beautiful white bird.

I dream, I fantasize, I hope and hate, but I do not—*cannot*—act. Like a young Hamlet, strung out between vengeance and indecision, I pace and fret, weep and rail, dream and hope. Couldn't some benign natural force, some dramatic intervention from above, remove her from our lives? The good, after all—my mother, my father's mother—die so young and easily. Why, now, can't the evil perish as well? Why, powerless once at keeping the tragic out of my life, do I now feel powerless once more to remove the demonic from it?

And so, a child filled with a man's hatred, I rage and fantasize, wait and deliberate. And—like all rage not acted upon, like every killing instinct that cannot find its rightful object—my rage goes where I want, above all, to place my stepmother's wretched and tormented body: *underground.*

∽

5 | MUSES

She knows the darkness

is only a passage

between light and light,

that the wisteria

climbing the house

are real, and lust

only tenderness gone wild

in the wrong field.

She is the one who is

always fertile in times

of barrenness, the one

with the silver hair

carrying a candle

through the long tunnel.

She is Halcyon,

calming the waters

after all my deaths;

she is Eurydice,

refusing to fade

when I look behind me.

She is the one

who wakes

with her arms around me

when I wake alone.

— "THE WOMAN INSIDE," FROM *DAYS WE*

WOULD RATHER KNOW (1984)

THE FIRST UNDRESSED BODY of a woman I get to see is my blind grandmother Johanna's. I see it, naked in the moonlight of the bedroom I share with her. I watch its vast folds of flesh, sagging like an old turtle's when she rises from the high, creaky bed in the corner of the room to urinate into the rusted bedpan. With the inner, still inarticulate gaze of a three-year-old boy, I look out toward the ghostly, naked, drooping figure that stands before me and think: So this is a woman.

She can't, of course, know I am looking—this blind, dazed, groping, confused creature who rises from the bed to the tinkly crescendo of hairpins falling from her night table, who lifts her stained nightgown and stretches her other hand out into the vague unspecificity of the room to find a place to relieve herself of the burdens of her own body. She can't know how each night I watch her open the small green bottle of white pills she takes for her chronic constipation and watch her unfasten the pins from the bun at the back of her head so that a gray waterfall of hair plummets down her back and she becomes, to my still-questioning eyes, a kind of old girl of near death, a corpse disguised as a wind-up doll that can defecate and pee.

Nor can I know, as she stands in the middle of the room five flights above the streets of Washington Heights, that I am staring at the naked body of death—a body I will write about as a grown man many years later—through the moonlight of early childhood:

> Eyes of a child:
> watching the ghost of you
> fold like thick dough
> from the creaking hand of the bed,
>
> Thighs sagging
> like crepe paper in the night,
> your hair tired tinsel
> on a tree held beyond its occasion.
>
> You would go to pee—
> the bedpan held between your shaking limbs,
> a tired old plumber,
> a wind-up doll
> on its last rotation.
>
> The urine
> played
> like rain
> against the sides,
>   woke me . . .

The first woman
I
saw naked,
the first woman I
        loved,

Holding your eyes
in your fingertips,
touching
to see me,
insisting
that the mind's eye lay in the heart,
that the world's one dimension was darkness,
that touch was the light,
sense the window.

And now still
your lesson:

Only those who will touch can see me,
Only those who can't see will listen . . .

Only the blind reach out to find me.

"Johanna"

Then there is my mother's body—which I never actually see (or, if I do, I somehow erase from my memory) but which is known to me primarily as something appended to the small pillow of cloth I sometimes see lying inside her brassiere on my parents' bed. A white omelette of false flesh, it suggests to me a place where no questions can be asked, and from which no answers will be forthcoming.

But I know that my grandmother's body, my mother's never-seen-but-known-to-be-disfigured body—the bodies of these two moribund creatures—are the images of woman I carry with me throughout my childhood.

So that, whenever the breathing, life-hungry body of a younger, healthier woman later becomes familiar to me, the scarred and defaced bodies of those first-loved women rear their ugly heads once more, and I cry out, in anguish and in fright: *"No!"*

There is also a third woman's body in the house—a nearly perfect one in fact, except for its knobby head of brass and its lower torso of mesh and steel grating.

Whenever the endless parade of stoles, coats, and boas is periodically undraped from her shoulders, I find myself staring long and hard at the firm, neatly stitched breasts of my father's mannequin, whom I name Lucretia. Whenever I can, I sneak into the fur room to embrace this cold, unyielding, partial yet somehow seemingly perfect creature. I stand on my tiptoes to kiss the long, brass neck, which, in my ravenous imaginings, responds like a ripe avocado to the ministrations of my lips and tongue. I think: Yes, maybe somewhere there's a woman's body like this—a tight, firm, unstained, undefecating thing with a face, with a living face and eyes.

Whenever I hear the click of the front door behind my departing parents, I make a beeline for the fur-room door and sway Lucretia's body from the brass wheels connected to the steel mesh of her lower torso. From this position I lower her onto her back against the rug in front of my father's full-length showroom mirror, then throw myself in a fit of passion on her cloth-and-metal body.

On one such afternoon, not long after my mother's death, when I am no more than eleven, I suddenly feel a strangely unfamiliar tingling sensation at the center of my body. It feels as if I'm going to pee, yet somehow different, more pleasurable. So I don't quite know what to do as a strange, seamy, viscous discharge suddenly oozes from my erect penis onto Lucretia's stitched cloth belly. Afraid that I'm about to urinate onto the most sensuous member of my father's small harem, I run for the bathroom, leaving a trail of small, thick droplets in my tracks.

Over the next several years, my romantic interludes with my father's passive, metallic yet somehow beautiful mannequin—with or (I hope) without my parents' knowledge—continues. Continues, that is, until the day I am scheduled to leave for college. That morning, with a combined sense of nostalgia and lingering desire, I stick my head through the fur-room door, hoping to catch a final glimpse of my beloved. But there, in the exact spot where the object of my tenderest ministrations once stood, now sits only my stepmother's snarling fox terrier, Ami.

They had obviously removed her during the night, no doubt in the same surreptitious manner in which they had taken my mother's body away years before. Perhaps, I console myself, they suspected that, in the excitement of leaving home, I wouldn't notice. Or maybe my father, once again, wanted to spare me the pain of a final good-bye.

My stepmother has a problem: Much as she would love to rid herself and my father of my adorable adolescent presence, to do so means giving up the one thing in life she is even stingier with than love—money.

I'm fourteen, a year short of even the illegal summer employment she will eventually dredge up for me, and I want to get away from her *almost* as much as she would like to help me do so. But, at my age there's only one usual summer solution, the one with an ominous ring for refugees from Nazi Germany, regardless of its cost: *camp*.

My friend Leslie Millett's mother, a widow at least endowed with the attribute of loving her son, has uncovered a rather attractive-sounding place named Farm Camp Lowy in Oxford, New York, not far from the Borscht Belt that will be home to my future summer jobs. The word *farm,* at least, has a familial ring to it. Leslie's going for the full eight-week session, at a whopping $1,300, an amount that, translated into potential shares of Ohio Edison or Phillips Petroleum, will, I know, send dear Alice toward apoplexy. So I hedge my bets and begin begging for a four-week stay at a bargain-rate $650, a small price to pay, I figure, for ridding yourself of that most heinous of living creatures: the stepson who makes dirt and needs love.

Reluctantly, and only after a massive lobbying campaign by Leslie, Mrs. Millett, Ronnie Berger's mother (she, too, wants to save me from the Wicked Witch of the East), and Mr. and Mrs. Farm Camp Lowy themselves, my parents agree to the month of July, when they will be off planting their tushes on the famously dubbed "Adenauer bench" (named in honor of the postwar German chancellor whose government's reparations payments helped maintain those who usually occupied it) in downtown Fleischmanns, New York, population 312.

The camp turns out, indeed, to be a farm, on which I manage to secure for myself the volunteer "job" of stable boy, a rather manly and pastoral activity that requires moving horse manure around from one pile to another in wheelbarrows, along with saddling, bridling and brushing the horses and getting bossed around by the head horsewoman, Jane Somebody, who fits every New York Jewish boy's fantasies of Annie Oakley.

I like Jane, I like the camp, but what I decidedly *don't* like is the daily feeling of guilt the $650 price tag has aroused in me, along with the fact that I manage to strike out four times during our first interbunk softball game and am therewith consigned for the rest of my stay to the loathsome category of "nonathlete." There is also the blowing of some sort of bugle every morning at 6:30 A.M., a ritual apparently known as reveille, from the French, and I find it hard to develop an affection for either the bugles or the hour, at which time I would prefer to be in bed whacking off.

In the middle of all this arrives the traditional Parents' Day, during which the collected parents of Syosset, Far Rockaway, Hewlett Harbor, Flushing, and Sheepshead Bay are supposed temporarily to abandon their summer interludes of golf and mah-jongg and spend a day watching their usually rather urban and sub-urban little loved ones frolic among the sheep, cows, and horses.

For my stepmother, however, happily ensconced in her *Liegestuhl* on the lawn in Fleischmanns studying the Dow Jones averages, the idea of not only having to *pay* to get rid of me but of then having to pull together the gasoline money and energy to actually *visit* me reeks of the kind of masochism she is hardly prone to. And so, as the gates to Farm Camp Lowy open to wel-come in the well-fed hordes of bourgeois breeders—*not* my dar-ling parents but two of my father's dear sisters—ravishingly bleached blond Hertha and buxom, dark brown Tina the seam-stress—well rested from their vacation in nearby Loch Sheldrake, pull in by taxi to console their abandoned little nephew Mikey.

Shortly after I turn fifteen, an age at which little else occupies the minds of adolescent boys than thoughts of hot, initiatory nights with the opposite sex, my father decides to take me on a midwinter cruise to Bermuda aboard one of the widow- and widower-packed vessels of the Greek Line.

"It is life's greatest dream," he insists, despite all my protestations that I would rather stay home and go to spin-the-bottle parties with Judy Honigsberg and Lois Meinstein. "A cruise. . . . You will never forget it."

My father has always loved cruises. "My dream," he repeats endlessly. "The greatest *simcha* in life." When he marries my stepmother—despite her lifelong history of seasickness—he talks her into taking a two-week cruise to Jamaica and the Virgin Islands for their honeymoon. Armed to the gills with a lifetime supply of Dramamine, sleeping pills, and sedatives, they embark from a West Side pier—or, rather, they board the ship. For it requires little more than a step onto the deck of the sixteen-hundred-bed cruiser for my stepmother's constricted spirit to manifest itself by sending her body into paroxysms of reverse peristalsis so severe that half the ship's crew is soon running all over the deck, terry towels draped over their forearms and buckets of all sizes and shapes ready to be proffered from their trembling hands.

But it is too late to turn back, my father having already forked out some ten thousand dollars in 1960s currency for their little adventure. And so—for two solid weeks—my stepmother pukes and gurgles a compost of eggplant, spanakopita, and stuffed grape leaves seaward, cursing the gods that have brought her into the cruise-loving arms of Julius Blumenthal, Fine Furs.

"F. Harry Stow," my father mutters in broken Greek to the small flotilla of stewards and deckmasters who nervously await the next eruption from his wife's beleaguered stomach. "God loves you, and so do I."

But now, some three years later, it's I, with a stomach to rival Captain Ahab's, who am my father's cabin mate, and, instead of

rolling over onto the imagined, palpitating body of Judy Honigs-
berg or Linda del Casino, I devote all my physical energy to *not*
rolling off the three-foot-wide upper bunk of our bargain-rate
compartment onto the heart-diseased, diabetic shape of my
father.

"F. Harry Stow,"* my father greets every creature with an
even marginally Greek face. "This is my dear son Michael, taking
a cruise with his daddy. . . . God loves you, and so do I."

As I'd expected, there isn't, with the exception of the crew,
another being under the age of sixty-five on board. And as we sit
down to dinner that first night, I am met, to my utter non-
amazement, by a group of rag-necked widows and spinsters with
names like Lisbeth, Emma, Molly, and Friedel, arrayed like a
string of secondhand pearls around our necklace-shaped table.

"What a handsome young man!" each greets me in turn,
stroking the slick crest of my pomade-reinforced pompadour,
"and what a lucky father, to have such a handsome son."

"F. Harry Stow," my father replies to each one. "I told him he
will never forget this cruise, so long as he lives."

After four days of at least six meals a day and no exercise
beyond a game of shuffleboard with a retired jeweler named
Alfred Mendel from Poughkeepsie, New York, we arrive in
Bermuda, by which time my disdain for my father—or, rather,
my guilt at being the unappreciative son who isn't having a better time—has reached such epic proportions that I am actively
contemplating patricide. By the time we finally step ashore, my
only remaining fantasy is to be with a young, dashing, athletic
father who will rent a Harley-Davidson and whisk me off to the
bars and discotheques, where we will find a couple of well-
stacked blonds and male-bond into the night together.

*His version of the Greek *efaristo,* or "thank you."

But my father, tossing his "F. Harry Stows" and "God loves yous" left and right like a man tossing crumbs to pigeons, instead buys us two tickets on a tourist bus to Paradise Island, where he proceeds to rent a deck chair, wrap himself in a thick padding of blankets, and fall asleep on the beach (he can't swim), while I summon what little masculine bravery I possess and stroke my way toward the horizon.

Slightly aquaphobic from youth—when I wrestled with periodic bouts of asthma amid aborted swimming lessons at New York's Hotel Paris on West End Avenue and Ninety-seventh Street—I suddenly turn to find myself farther from shore than I had realized, and, seized by a soul-gripping panic, I begin thrashing wildly in an effort to navigate my way once more into the shallows.

"Dad!" I scream at the sleeping figure back on shore. "Dad! Save me! I'm drowning!" I must, for a moment, imagine that my father, like the legendary Clark Kent of that great metropolitan newspaper, will suddenly throw off his glasses and emerge, a kind of refugee Johnny Weismuller, rushing into the water to rescue me, his Jane. But my father can't hear my desperate cries even if he's awake—and certainly can't do anything to help. Increasingly certain that I am about to meet my Maker, here, some two thousand miles from kissing parties, Chubby Checker, and my long-held hopes of losing my virginity, I begin bobbing beneath the surface, taking small gulps of sea brine into my already congested lungs, while my father snores on into his dreams of lost youth and angina pectoris.

Just as I think I am rising for the last time into the light and air of this world, gasping for breath and feeling at least half grateful that I will be spared the return trip in the company of Emma, Lisbeth, Friedel and Molly, I feel a soft but nonetheless solid sensation at the tips of my toes. Having already begun reciting the mourner's Kaddish on behalf of my own demise, I suddenly recognize a familiar texture—sand! Allowing my wildly thrashing feet to fall by their own weight, I find myself standing, in what is no more than three feet of water.

Realizing that the gods are not yet prepared to claim me, here on Paradise Island amid the loneliness-inducing company of my father, I walk slowly, rather shamefacedly, toward shore. My father has just emerged from his nap when I reach his deck chair. "Well, son," he asks, sitting up and staring out to sea, "did you have a good swim?"

"Great, Dad," I reply, stone faced. "The water's terrific."

And so goes the one great adventure—aside, that is, from beating Alfred Mendel again at shuffleboard on the way home—of my Bermuda vacation with my father. When we get back to New York three days later—I having gained at least fifteen pounds and no longer able to fit into any of my clothes—we open the apartment door to find my stepmother—a rental nurse from Jewish Family Services at her side—in bed, tears streaming down her cheeks.

"*Lieselein!*" my father cries, running to her side. "*Was ist denn los?*"

"I hope you both had a good time," my stepmother lifts her head from the pillow to stare at us, her face contorted in pain and anger. "I haf been lying here all week in *terrible* pain . . . You should never haf left me alone."

"What happened?" I inquire from the doorway.

"It seems she's broken a vertebra," the nurse explained.

"How'd she do *that?*" I am still naive enough to think of my parents' lives from a causal perspective. "Did she fall?" "No," says the nurse. "It's very strange—it seems she broke it without actually doing *anything*."

"Such a *schlimazel*," my stepmother chimes in.

"A miracle," says my father. I swear I can see tears running down his cheeks.

My father, who has already subscribed to Reader's Digest Condensed Books and National Geographic Nature Stamps on my intellectual behalf, is always on the lookout for other ways to improve his mournful son's inner life—beyond, that is, buying me multiple copies of Max Dimont's *Jews, God, and History.*

One day, lugging his furs home from the fur district in the elevator, he sees our neighbor, Mrs. Engel, carrying a book he thinks might interest me: Harold Robbins's *The Carpetbaggers.* The next day—inscribed with the habitual "For my dear son Mikey, something *very* interesting for you. Love, Dady"— the book is right there on my desk. Once I flip open the cover, I'm hardly disappointed.

When I *really* start to get interested is somewhere in the middle of the novel, during the section entitled "The Story of Rina Marlowe." Rina Marlowe, it turns out, is a thirteen-year-old, rather sexually precocious girl, prone to taking off her bathing suit and other garments in front of the lascivious eyes (and, it will turn out, *hands*, and other body parts) of her adopted brother, Laddie.

"A dull ache began to throb in her breasts," begins a certain passage that immediately sends my right hand down toward my groin, "and she looked down at herself. Her nipples were clearly limned against the black jersey of her bathing suit. She looked up again at the boys. They were staring at her quite openly now."

Laddie, a luckier—no pun intended—lad than I am, also happens to have a bedroom at the head of the staircase just opposite his sister, who has a tendency—just as the very printed page is tormenting me—to torment him by leaving her door partially open, so that this is the kind of thing *he* gets to *see*—and I get to read:

> Rina had just crossed the room and was standing in front of the mirror, her back to the door, clad only in a brassière and a pair of bloomers. While he watched, she reached behind her and unfastened the brassière, then, half turning, stepped out of the bloomers. Holding them in her hand, she crossed the room and came back in a moment, carrying a bathing suit. She paused again in front of the mirror and stepped into the suit. Slowly she pulled it up over her breasts and straightened the shoulder straps.

This scene, which is too much for me—it sends me, in fact, to immediately soiling not merely my underwear but also my stepmother's immaculate, *echt deutsche* sheets—proves, a few pages later, too much for Laddie as well:

> . . . He caught at her legs and pinned them against the bed with his knees. He laughed wildly. "Now, my darling little sister, there'll be no more games."
>
> "No more games," she gasped, staring up into his eyes. His face came down and his mouth covered hers. She felt herself begin to relax.
>
> Then the fierce, sharp pain penetrated her body. She screamed. His hand came down heavily over her mouth, as again and again the pain ripped through her.

I can hardly believe my incredible good luck—nor the sudden radical improvement in my father's literary tastes. Why this— *this*—is better than his going fishing with Suess. *This* is what fatherhood *should* be about! And, on top of it all, what a lesson: If a man with a mere typewriter can do this to me, what, I can only imagine, can a real *woman* do? *This* must be what my English teacher, Mr. Canell, means when he keeps talking about "the power of literature."

Just as *The Carpetbaggers*—in which Rina and Laddie, now, seem to be fucking and humping away on nearly every page—threatens to utterly deplete my once seemingly endless adolescent supply of seed, the party's over: The afternoon after having dog-eared page 271 during yet another sleepless night, I return from school to find the book, to my utter rage and disbelief, *gone*: Mrs. Engel, my muse just the week before, has apparently seen me carrying the book around on the street and has informed my father in no uncertain terms that, his good intentions notwithstanding, this is "not *at all* a book for children."

And so now—just like my mother's body—my beloved book, too, is gone, without a word of explanation. On this occasion, however, my father is eager to make amends: The next day when I get home from school, there on my desk—inscribed with a note "from your loving Dady"—is a brand-new, hardback copy of Max Dimont's *Jews, God, and History.*

Beyond the vicissitudes of junior high school spin-the-bottle, the first flesh-and-blood woman I actually kiss is Margot Eisenberg of the East New York section of Brooklyn.

It's 1964. I meet Margot at a skating rink near my aunt Rosel's and uncle George's former home in Lakewood, New Jersey, where my parents are spending their usual one-week winter vacation at a hotel populated mostly by diabetics, arthritis sufferers, and fellow heart patients. Over my stepmother's violent objections and relentless sulking, my father has taken me—bored, by now, nearly to distraction after two days on this Magic Mountain of stress and high cholesterol—to Lakewood's one source of amusement for the under-sixty-five set: the indoor ice rink.

There—assiduously supervised by her mother, an old customer of my father's, and wearing a short pink skating skirt and tight halter top that make her prematurely inflated breasts look like small hot-air balloons—is Margot Eisenberg, cruising along on the ice at breakneck speed as I muster every ounce of my fourteen-year-old will to keep my severely bent ankles from breaking while I try to support myself in quasi-upright position along the railing.

"*Gnädige Frau Eisenberg*," my father says, dragging his tongue-tied son over to the other side of the rink and bending to kiss Mrs. Eisenberg's hand, "what a *simcha* to see you again. You remember me? Julius Blumenthal—you bought a beautiful Blackgama mink from me a few years ago, which schtopped the traffic. This is my dear son, Mikey. . . . And what a beautiful young daughter you have. God loves her, and so do I."

Mrs. Eisenberg does, of course, remember (how could she possibly forget?), and, to my father's delight, it turns out that she and her daughter are staying at the very same hotel where I am ensconced with my parents. By that evening, my father has already arranged with the maitre d' to have the Eisenbergs moved to our table, where, for the next three days, I sit, virtually speechless, gazing at the beckoning full moons of Margot's breasts.

Miraculously enough—and with what seems little effort on my part—Margot and I wind up kissing behind the escalator our last night at the hotel, and—her telephone number scrawled on a sheet of paper in my dungaree pocket—I return to Washington Heights confident that (hardly a year after the bar mitzvah that declares me, unambiguously, a man) I, Michael Blumenthal, am firmly in possession of that sacred rite of passage into puberty: a girlfriend.

Once home, I devote myself to my new enterprise with a religious fervor. I quickly find myself—over the strenuous objections of my father and the unexpressed but obvious delight of my stepmother, who no doubt hopes the worst might befall me—descending from the downtown A train at the New Lots Avenue station every Saturday night and—the one white boy in a crowd of what at the time were often still known as "niggers," "spics," and "Chinks"—taking a bus through the most dangerous section of Brooklyn until I find myself staring at buzzer 14F at 228 New Lots Avenue, from whose little metallic rectangle the name "Eisenberg" beckons like a sexual holy grail.

At the time the Beatles' hit single, "I Want to Hold Your Hand," has every adolescent in the Western world cruising the streets humming its tune. But it isn't at all Margot Eisenberg's *hand* I want to hold but those scrumptious, beckoning, initiatory breasts—those nearly hallucinogenic-looking generous tits. Weekend after weekend, her mother having gone to bed, I back Margot against their dining room wall and shove the quivering serpent of my tongue more than halfway down her throat while reaching, like a drowning passenger in search of a life raft, for the steel-rimmed barricade of her D-cup bra.

But, beyond the occasional split second of what we refer to in those days as a "dry feel," the best efforts of my wildly jabbing left and right get me little more than a clutch of polyester and a sternly reprimanding "Not yet." Fatigued and frustrated, wanting at the very least to see close-up the twin objects of my fervor, I finally suggest to Margot that we go for a swim one Sunday afternoon at the Highbridge Recreation Center, located near my parents' apartment in Washington Heights.

The idea is that—stimulated by the refreshing rush of water in and around the various orifices and protuberances of her body, aroused by the sight of me in scrawny little bathing trunks bolstered by a jock strap—Margot will be unable to resist later submitting to the clutch and sweep of my efforts in my parents' hopefully empty apartment.

Everything goes just as planned until we get to the pool, where Margot emerges from the girls' locker room wearing a two-piece lavender bathing suit whose top enticingly surrounds a pair of boobs significantly larger than even my rapacious imaginings have been able to conjure. No doubt realizing that I am by now in a state of mesmerized erotic titillation sufficient to render me virtually possessed, Margot decides to milk my erotic subjugation for all it's worth. Walking coyly to the diving board, she proceeds to stand on it for what must be a full minute, bouncing lightly into the air on her tiptoes so that her breasts juggle playfully into the oblique light while I wait, moon mouthed, at the shallow end of the pool.

Finally, having apparently had enough of reducing me to a throbbing pulp of tumescence, Margot takes three purposeful steps toward the end of the board, bounds lightly into the air, and—executing what seems to my aquaphobic gaze like a swan dive worthy of Aphrodite herself—disappears below the neatly sliced surface.

On the cusp of my first real-life orgasm, I wait breathlessly for the shimmering reemergence of Margot Eisenberg's body into the beatified light. But—to my utter amazement, and the raucous delight of everyone gathered around the pool—what emerges from the depths and rockets skyward onto the surface is not the ample, coveted flesh of my incipient conquest, but two off-white, eerily familiar-looking pillows of foam rubber, which proceed to bob and dance on the surface of the pool like small circular dories.

Momentarily shocked—indeed, stupefied—by what I am seeing, I am virtually the last person around the pool to catch on to what has just happened. With an amazement bordering on horror, a sense of betrayal both painful and familiar, I suddenly realize that what I see—floating as serenely as two sunbathers toward the sides of the pool, and somewhat reminiscent of my dead mother's own—are the unmasked, lifeless cloth breasts of Margot Eisenberg.

There is only one thing my stepmother is always glad to do for me: help me find jobs.

She's so good at it, in fact, that—undeterred by the child-labor laws—she manages, in the summer of my fifteenth year, to find for me the much-coveted, seven-days-a-week, fourteen-hours-a-day position of waiter, busboy, bellhop, pool boy, handyman, and children's counselor at a booming, thirty-bed resort hotel in Hunter, New York, known as Lustig's Lodge.

The job pays sixty dollars a week, straight cash, and—under the malevolent, gulaglike gazes of my stepmother's friends Irma and Alfred Lustig—I and the hotel's only other employee, a twenty-five-year-old, voluptuously endowed German by the name of Ursula Kalwa (also hired illegally, without working papers, and whose job description, as best I can tell, is cook/chambermaid/dishwasher/girl Friday) work our little fingers to the bone, finding our few moments of respite, as might be expected, in the pleasure of each other's company.

It begins, of course, innocently enough—with (for a fourteen-year-old, at least) deep nightly conversations about the meaning of life, the limited possibilities of altruism, and—of course—the Nazis, about whom Ursula's most memorable comment is how enraged her parents are at the reparation payments being made to the Jews. She's a small-town girl, from a little dot on the map named Dangensdorf, located somewhere between Hamburg and

Hannover, and has the kind of large, muscular legs and (after a glass of wine or two) slightly tipsy swagger that must have made her attractive bait for American servicemen stationed at the army base not far from her house. She's not too shy to show me a rather suggestive photograph of herself with one of them that she keeps tucked in her wallet.

Almost nightly, a forged draft card and an unimpedable hard-on in my pocket, we make our way "downtown" past the darkened cemetery to Hunter's only bar, the Dog's Tooth Inn, where I, with all the suavity and panache I can muster, order the one drink I know the name of—an old-fashioned—and wait, ever patiently, for Ursula to make her move, to please-oh-please help me make with her *Eine Kleine Nachtmusik*. In the interim, egged on by my earlier close call with Margot Eisenberg and my rising scatological fervor, I raid her room at midday, while she's off making beds, and—like a hound on a fox's trail—inhale in large, buoyant, intoxicated sniffs the mingled odors of crotch and anus that waft with their transporting, aphrodisiac power from her soiled underwear.

Weeks go by, with little more than this in the way of "action," until one night—obviously moved to a state approaching heat by my latest insights into the ethical imperatives of the ill and dying—Ursula thrusts her large, fully salivating tongue into my mouth on the bench behind the hotel swimming pool and—*kaboom!*—before I know it, there it is, in my very hand—*not* a piece of fabric, *not* some little adolescent's padded bra, but 100 percent certified beef—a real breast!

I'm ecstatic. Despite all my stepmother's efforts to avenge herself on the Nazis by incarcerating me in the work-camp-like confines of Lustig's Lodge, I've done it: I've held, there in my very palms, the thing even my panicked, fur-ridden father couldn't seem to land . . . the real, authentic, life-giving, *deutsch-geborene* item: tit.

I'm so happy, in fact, I feel like weeping, and, for the next month—always somehow waiting for what I expect will be the "next step" that never comes—I wildly and exuberantly massage the robust, initiating breasts of Ursula Kalwa. Everywhere—from the kitchen to the boiler room to the still-unmade bed of long-time hotel guest and famed psychoanalyst Theodor Reik—Ursula and I smooch and grunt and pet until I'm certain that I've reached, if not the pinnacle, than certainly one of the summits, of sexual gratification.

Unfortunately for us, however, one of our tumescent interludes happens to take place in the hotel kitchen on an afternoon when we are mistakenly convinced that our tyrannical bosses have already retired to their quarters. Hardly four hours after Irma discovers us—my arms clasped lovingly around Ursula's breasts from beneath her armpits—my father and stepmother march into Lustig's Lodge, order me to pack up my belongings and—with my stepmother muttering something in German about all the money I might have made if only I weren't so oversexed—truck me off, virginity intact, to spend the rest of the summer in Pine Hill reading stock market quotations out loud from the *New York Times*.

My father, no doubt shocked and distressed by my attempted re-creation of his aborted love for Claire Haas, goes into a flurry of activity, calling various German embassies and consulates around the country in an effort to have Ursula deported for sodomizing his son, but without success.

I do, however, get to see her one more time—almost a year later at the Port Authority Bus Terminal in New York City, the day she again arrives from Germany and is about to board a bus for a summer job at the Concord Hotel in Kiamesha Lake. She had written to me several times during the year, but, when I briefly see her that day at the gate, the previous summer's heat has been all but replaced by my infatuation with Judy Honigs-berg, and I feel only a tepid flow of the exhilarating juices that had socked through my fifteen-year-old body the summer before.

"Oohhh, baby." I feel a hand reaching up between my legs and grabbing me by the balls. "Why don't you come up to my place after lunch? Old Manny will grease you up and make you feel *sooo* good."

I'm working at yet another lodge this time—Round Hill Lodge in Washingtonville, New York, to be exact—and the voice (and the hand) is that of Manny, the *very* gay Filipino chef, who's taken more than a casual liking to what he must see as the nubile, sixteen-year-old fair-skinned boy in tight black pants that is me.

"Why don't you sit right in here, baby," he says to me almost daily, moving his hands in parallel position from the air above his waist toward his cock, "and turn around three times?"

Manny's about sixty-five, and lives upstairs with the assistant chef, a muscular Greek by the name of Peter. Thanks to the hotel's owner, a dyed-red-haired sixty-year-old by the name of René Goldmann, who came out of the bedroom zipping up his fly in midafternoon to interview me at his Waverly Place apartment earlier that spring, there's an atmosphere of preliberation libidinal gaiety at the hotel. Its clientele—aside from René's flurry of weekend guests from the West Village—nonetheless consists mostly of middle-aged German Jews from Forest Hills and Riverdale whose major activity, aside from eating, is playing bridge and, on occasion, rather shaky tennis. This time, it's not even my stepmother who's gotten me the job, but my cousin Amos, who made what at the time seemed like a bundle the previous summer as the hotel bellhop, and has now gone off to work at the Harvard of the Borscht Belt, Grossinger's.

Among the guests seated at my station are a rather attractive middle-aged couple, the Masterses, whose fifteen-year-old daughter's reputation as a blossoming sex kitten with a body that could schtop the traffic has well preceded her actual arrival—she's still off at some expensive summer camp—for Labor Day weekend. Mr. Masters, a used car salesman from Forest Hills, struts around the hotel grounds like some sort of German-Jewish combination of Norman Mailer and Enrico Caruso, wearing blue bikini bathing trunks from which his balls protrude into the Orange County air like miniature grapefruits. Mrs. Masters, meanwhile, a statuesque bleached blond who must once upon a time have been a knockout, wears a leopard-patterned bathing suit with a huge wave of black netting down the middle, in which her once-no-doubt-firm breasts, now defeated by gravity, wedge their way toward her navel.

Amid all these perambulations of balls and breasts—though Manny's got the hots for me and I'll eventually have them for the Masters's nubile young daughter, Ivy—it's neither Manny nor Ivy who inhabits my libidinal imagination, but my waiter: René's young hunk of a nephew, Robbie Bodenheimer. I'm, of course, already well on my way to a career as a healthy, normal, masturbation-racked heterosexual, but there's *something* about Robbie—about the uninhibited way he manages, almost every night, to wind up straddling one of the other busboys or waiters in only his tight, white BVDs—that captures my sexual imagination or, to put it more bluntly, just plain makes me horny as hell. I, too, would like to join in the riding and humping and wrestling, but I'm afraid that if I do I'll simply embarrass myself right onto Robbie's beautiful, still hairless chest.

So—when highly touted Ivy Masters finally arrives—I content myself with nightly visits to her small room just beside the boys' staff quarters, where I soak my hungry fingers in her vaginal juices and force my face down between her legs to a rather determined chorus of—I, to this day, still don't understand why—"Please don't eat me." (She must, I gather, find the act—one of life's great pleasures—somehow unappetizing.)

Robbie, meanwhile, seems able to make use of every possible opportunity to mount someone—even, on one occasion, a twelve-year-old female guest in a bathing suit, whom he has conned into a game of "bet you can't keep me down for a count of ten" that fills me with such lust and envy I am forced to run back into the hotel men's room to send a wad of my seed spurting into the toilet. For the rest of my life, it seems, I will continue to regret the missed opportunities of that summer—to wonder, indeed, how *he* managed not to embarrass himself all over those boys and girls he was so contentedly straddling. But my die, it seems, has already been cast—much to Manny's chagrin—with womankind, so I continue to moisten my chapped hands at the well of Ivy Masters's lubricating vagina, and to stuff my pockets with the dollar bills of the Masterses, the Fahrers, the Guttmanns, the Katzes, and the Loebs, God bless them all.

∿

6 | EGGS

As for the chicken and the egg

I say the egg was first. The egg is perfect.

It always was.

The chicken, like most children, an afterthought.

—STEPHEN DUNN, "EGGS," FROM *NOT DANCING* (1984)

ALL MY LIFE I HAVE felt a deep attachment to eggs.

As far back as I can remember—in the deepest frost of winter, in the stifling humidity of summer, in times of grief, and in times of contentment—eggs have always been there.

I remember the black grader in the damp, mildewed basement of my aunt and uncle's chicken farm; the constant hum of its small motor; the dull, insulated thump of eggs onto the slightly inclined rubber runway as they rolled to the bottom and were loaded into cardboard containers and cartons.

I remember the babies and pullets and mediums and jumbos, the browns and the whites, the tiny pinprick of focused light that surged, laserlike, from the candler to illuminate those mysterious interiors of white and yolk, and that elusive four-leaf clover among eggs, the double yolk. I remember that even rarer find—the calcium-deprived egg that emerged without even a shell to hold it in place. Sometimes, in fact, I felt that I *was* that egg—without a hard shell, a convincing poise, to hold myself in place—soft, vulnerable, yearning for cover.

I remember the warm feel of eggs just out of the hen's body, the sweetly familiar smell of chicken shit. I remember the Egg Auction, and the egg prices right there on the front page of the *Vineland Times Journal*. I remember the smeared, yellowy coils of chicken shit on my uncle's worn boots. I remember the twice-yearly arrival of hundreds of madly squawking yellow chicks; the proud, libidinal strut of the roosters; the huge bags of chicken feed stacked in the barn, onto which my cousin and I would bound in a mountain of dust; the blond, balloony ticks we would pick out of the scruffy hair of the farm dogs, Mickey and Fips, and splatter in tiny starbursts of blood against the porch.

During our visits to Vineland I also remember loading my uncle's station wagon with carton after carton of eggs on Sunday night to prepare for the three-hour drive to New York to sell his eggs door-to-door the next morning. There was something fitting, I later realized, about my uncle—calling out: *Life! Life!*—delivering eggs in the same, refugee-laden apartment buildings of Washington Heights through which my father carries his skins of mink and Alaska seal, his lifeless boas of chinchilla and mouton.

Yet something in these earliest of memories of my aunt and uncle must have said to me: *This is man and woman, this is life and death, this is the labor of the body.* I must already have known that *this* was the place of my true blood, that this man carrying eggs, and *not* the man carrying those furs, was my true father. I must have known all along that it was with the living egg, and not with the dead mink, that I would need to reclaim my life.

As the years pass I increasingly begin to wonder: Who *are* they—these people who bore me, my flesh and blood? This "aunt" and "uncle," who—I know from those early whispered secrecies, those taut innuendos of mystery—are something more, although for my first ten years I don't know exactly what? The adolescent girl whose tightly drawn underwear wrapped like a transparent shroud around her buttocks introduces me for the first time to the allures of an intact female body; the three-years-older cousin with whom I frolic between the chicken coops, wrestle on top of the musty feed sacks, whom I follow around the various baseball diamonds and football fields of Vineland, trying to learn how to be a man?

Who are they—this family whose fake-brick-and-shingle house my parents, my grandmother, and I visit at least three times annually for "vacations," from the windows of whose brightly wallpapered attic I see the outline of the black bullet still lodged in my uncle's triceps from the Israeli War of Independence in the morning light as he carries his yellow-and-white metal baskets of eggs from the chicken coops?

I look, now, at the home movies my father made during that period, their images moving frantically from face to face in an ill-sequenced narrative so scattered and dissociated as to seem postmodern, and what I see might, clearly, be the events of any "normal" extended family: My parents, my grandmother, and I, in all our comparatively "urbane" splendor, getting out of my father's maroon 1948 Chevy; my aunt and uncle—lumbering, "farmy," dressed in overalls and Vineland Egg Auction sun visors, throwing open the screen door to greet us; my two cousins, running from the yard or chicken coops, grabbing their little cousin—or should I say their brother?—by the hand, eagerly awaiting the packages of food and gifts their comparatively rich uncle has brought from the big city. It all seems—and, as I remember it, *felt*—rather cozy and familiar. For who could possibly know what strange subtext lurked beneath these surfaces? What wild convolutions of biology and destiny?

As I look at photos of them over the years, these four grown-ups and two children—the aunt who is my mother, the mother who is my aunt, the uncle who is my father, the father who is my uncle, the cousins who are my brother and sister—I can't help but notice how much more attractive "we" are. My father cuts a downright dashing figure—handsome, energetic, animated, well built. My mother is well dressed, reserved, feminine, unmistakably European.

My aunt and uncle, on the other hand, still look like a couple of Israeli kibbutzniks: Beak-nosed and peasanty, their bodies are a testimony not to grace but endurance, not to style but hardship. To say that they—particularly my aunt—are not beautiful, exactly, would be to substitute generosity for mere tact. So why not say it? They, particularly my aunt—this woman who bore me—are downright unattractive and could easily be typecast as migrant workers on a Rumanian dairy farm. Perhaps more significantly, they have a certain look not very attractive to a young child—the look of those who have had a difficult life.

Yet—given the obvious tension that must have existed in the midst of all this conviviality—little, in fact, seems strange. Summer nights, surrounded by a circle of brightly glowing coils designed to keep mosquitoes away, the eight of us—along with Mickey and Fips and a rotating menagerie of stray cats, kittens, and fireflies—sit in the front yard without a word about dyings or exchanges, and it might (yes, indeed, it *might)* be like any other extended family of immigrants in America—cousins, uncles, grandmothers, hooked noses, another tongue.

Is it only my imagination, I wonder now, or do I always have a sense that there is, somehow, more to it? That my aunt, in particular, always wants something very disturbing from me—wants me to *fail?* It begins, I think, with my success in school—my terrific report cards, my excellent exam scores, my skipping several grades—all of which slowly begin to distinguish me even from my almost equally successful cousin Amos. Or is it the fact that I—now the "son" of a better off, more successful father—have nicer clothes, better opportunities, the company of more urbane, ambitious friends? Does she, I wonder, sometimes have the feeling that they might have given away "the good one"? Could it be that this woman—this woman whose body, whose act of love, bore me, and who should, by all rights, be the one person on this earth unambivalently on my side—doesn't, in fact, *want* me to be happy?

The fact is I never like her, this aunt who is really my mother, this woman who, for whatever mysterious reasons, had given me life and then given me away. Occasionally trapped with her in the cold, clammy basement beside the egg grader, I feel somehow jeopardized, unwelcome—unloved. And, as for my cousins, what—from all those accumulated years of visits and embracings—is my most vivid memory of them? It's this: My cousin Amos, having climbed a tree in the front yard I am afraid to climb, is looking down at me, goading me on. Suddenly I see his face wrench forward—not unlike the way I will see my mother's face wrench forward over the white pail several years later—and a huge wad of spittle arches through the air and lands in my face. I remember wiping it from my eye. I remember how wet it felt, how slimy, mucuslike, cold. I remember it, as if it had been a voice saying: *This is not your place, your life, your family. This is not your flesh and blood.*

I belong entirely to no one. I am not *really*—as my stepmother, in one way or another, perpetually reminds me—my father's. I am, to be sure, not really (not even legally, as she has made a point of refusing to adopt me) my stepmother's. I am not *really* my aunt's and uncle's, who have given me away and whose name I no longer carry. I am not really anyone's. I am piecemeal, dismembered, scattered, my paternity divided, my maternity—or what I know of it—deceased, my brother and sister my cousins. I am the "only child" of a woman who repeatedly points out to me that she never wanted children. I am a boy with two homes and the keys to neither.

In Vineland, too, there is a diaspora of Holocaust survivors, in this case mostly chicken farmers with names like Edelmuth, Tänzer, Mayer, Hönig, Wolf, Gern. And there is also a small synagogue—Congregation Ha'al Shareev—of which my uncle Berthold is one of the founders and, throughout most of my childhood, president.

Slightly less repetitious, and decidedly more poetic, than his broken record of a brother-in-law—a bit, in fact, like a southern New Jersey equivalent of Moshe Dayan, a bullet in his arm instead of an eye patch—he presides over the congregation's various meetings, fund-raisers, and funerals with a kind of countrified *yekke* (German-Jewish) eloquence. All this leads me, at times, to fantasize about bringing both my father and my uncle together upon a single podium—Berthold as rabbi, Julius as cantor: David Ben Gurion meets Richard Tucker. Amos and myself, if worst comes to worst, can be choirboys.

Amid the duly congregated there's also a retired chicken

farmer by the name of Hugo Marx, whom my cousin Amos calls by the rather unflattering name *"Buh-ahh."* Marx, though I hate to admit it, merits this appellation. *"Hallo,* boys," he greets us, his breath reeking of onions, in the first-row pew we share with him. "And how"—he suddenly exhales deeply into the synagogal air—*"buh-ahh,* are you doing?"

Aside from synagogue and egg candling, there are other entertainments available in Vineland as well, usually in the company of Amos's friends Mike Wolf, Eddie Brown, Harold Munter, and Norbert Woolf. Eddie, the *goy* who lives just across the street on the other side of Sherman Avenue, in addition to being the best athlete, also does some very *goyische* things: For one, he raises, not chickens, but pigeons, and I—the putative son of chicken farmers and furriers—find it hard to believe one would bother raising anything one can't either wear or eat. Not only that, but, along and within the contours of the Browns' converted barn, there is, quite literally, pigeon shit everywhere.

Norbert Woolf, a massive hunk of a boy who usually wears overalls that even *smell* of chickens, can—by the mere heft of his weight—hit a baseball so far, and so hard, that I am often uncertain whether it has landed in what is still Vineland, or in neighboring Millville. Because he's so big, and I'm so (relatively) small, I try to keep a respectful distance from his tendency to use me, à la Johnny Jacoby, as a punching bag.

There's another blessing about a town like Vineland too: Unlike in Henry Kissinger- and Delmore Schwartz–occupied Washington Heights, it's not hard to be famous in a small place—or even, like my cousin Amos, third in his high school class. Not hard, even, to get one's name right *there*, on the front page of the *Vineland Times Journal*, just below the Egg Auction prices.

MYSTERY SHOTS SHATTER WINDOW, such a headline reads one

morning, just a day after a single BB pellet is fired into the attic window of my aunt and uncle's house, where Amos and I are playing Monopoly. Even the *Vineland Times Journal*'s reporter, it seems, has a certain unconscious wish to unite me with my biological ancestry: "Mystery shots shattered an upstairs window of the home of Mr. and Mrs. Berthold Gern at 1066 E. Sherman Avenue last night," he writes, "where the Gerns' two sons were playing."

It's from Amos and Judy as well that I learn the first rudimentary lessons of dating and courtship. Amos, who's got a crush on the smartest girl in his class, Elizabeth Kaufmann, keeps scrawled on a white legal pad elements of the "spontaneous" conversation he will initiate when he calls Liz for a date.

"Hello, Liz, this is Amos Gern. . . . Am I disturbing you?" the shooting script begins.

"I was wondering if you might like to go to a movie with me Saturday night—that is, of course, if you don't have other plans."

And so on, etc., etc., etc.

During my early childhood years, when I don't yet know that these two are my brother and sister, nor do I know if *they* know (or—at least in the case of Judy, who is six years older—remember), they are always kind to me, and Amos never hesitates to include me in activities with his older friends or to teach me how to ride a bike. Years later, in fact, he really makes an effort to help me escape the draft during the Vietnam War, and to have me serve as best man at his wedding—both, I now realize, brotherly, rather than cousinly, things to do.

Judy, on the other hand, is hardly making waves with her academic talents. What's more, she's in a high school sorority populated largely by fast movers, and has different things to teach me, as I discover one day while scouring the contents of her purse.

"Have you ever been kissed below the neck?" goes question one of the Delta Alpha Chi Sorority pledge survey.

"Have you ever been kissed below the waist?" the questionnaire continues, bringing my youthful, prepubescent blood to a near boil.

"Have you ever been kissed below the waist while kissing someone else below the waist?" By now it's getting to be too much for a boy who shares a bedroom with his eighty-year-old grandmother. Amos and Judy, it occurs to me, are having more *fun* than I am, and I suspect it's not merely because they are older.

Maybe, it now occurs to me in hindsight, it's because they know where they belong.

There's an African folktale I've always loved:

> A hunter takes his young son on a deer hunt in the forest. While they're walking in the woods, the father shoots a forest rat and gives it to his son.
>
> "Hold on to this," he says to his son, "in case we need it later."
>
> But the son throws the rat away. Later that night, having failed to kill any other game, they come to the spot where they were going to camp for the night. The father makes a fire and turns to his son. "Give me the rat," he says.
>
> "I don't have it," the son answers. "I threw it away." Furious, the father hits him with an ax handle, leaving him unconscious in the woods.
>
> The next morning, the son wakes and goes back to his father's house. He takes his belongings and puts them into a sack and starts walking through the woods away

from his father's house. Finally he arrives at a kingdom whose king has recently lost his only son. When he wanders into the king's tent, the king says to him, "From now on, you will be my son." At first the elders of the village don't believe the boy is the king's son. But after a while, when he goes out and slays a horse and seduces some maidens with the other boys, he's accepted by the court and is honored and decorated.

But, years later, the boy's real father, the hunter, wanders into the king's village during a festival. He sees his son riding a horse, immediately recognizes him, and says, "Get down from that horse! You are my son, and must return to your house with me."

The king rushes out of his tent and—on seeing that the boy's real father has come to claim him—has his servants saddle up some horses. The boy and his two fathers then leave the village and ride out into the bush. Suddenly the king produces a sword from his sheath, gives it to the boy, and says, "Now—me or your father—which one will you kill?"

And maybe that, too, is my question: Which one would I kill? I remember those Monday nights in Washington Heights when—like the father in the African folktale—my uncle came to our house and slept in my room between long days of delivering cartons of eggs door-to-door. I remember sitting at the kitchen table with both my fathers—the father of the fur and the father of the egg—as my uncle sat drinking beer from a tall glass.

As my uncle and I got ready for bed, he always took two quarters from his pocket and pushed them toward me. And, every Monday night, I pretended to refuse the two shiny George Washingtons moving at me from my actual father's hand. And each time my uncle pushed them back. Until, finally, I gave in to what I wanted to begin with, and this strange ritual of insistence and refusal came to an end.

Thinking about it now, I wonder what the meaning of that often-repeated event was. I wonder what was behind the persistence of my refusal, that repeated play whose ending was known at the outset, that conversation in which "No" means "Yes" and "Don't" meant "Do," in which "I don't want" meant "I want," and "No, thank you" meant "Yes, please."

"The death of a man's father," Freud writes somewhere, "is the most significant event, the most decisive loss, of a man's life." Yet here I am, with the most significant event of my life not yet having happened—*not once but twice,*—with both my uncle and my father still alive and kicking, solid as bookends.

"If there is no longer a Father, why tell stories?" Roland Barthes asks in *The Pleasures of the Text*. But what if there are *two* fathers? What if you're a man who not only hasn't been blessed, like Sartre, with his one father's early death, but who's stuck with the crazed chorus of *two* living fathers, the first refusing to claim you, the second refusing to die?

Maybe, I realize, thinking back on those Monday nights of beer and quarters, all I have uttered since has been an effort to imbue that sequence with an actual sincerity, to take the sword from the hand of my adopted father and drive it homeward toward the true coinage of my actual paternity.

Maybe all the stories I've been telling are aimed at reaching out once more toward the beckoning hand of the egg and away from the hand of the fur. Maybe those stories are an attempt to change, as the poet Cavafy wrote, the "great No" of my childhood to a "great Yes"—to take the hand of my actual father once more and allow its living coinage to fall out and sing?

∾

7 | THE GRADUATE

All's misalliance. . . .

—ROBERT LOWELL, "EPILOGUE"

IT'S TIME TO SHOP for colleges, and—though I have very good grades and excellent SAT scores from what is widely acknowledged to be the best public high school in the country—I behave like someone accompanying friends to a restaurant he really can't afford: It's primarily the right side of the menu—the prices—I peruse. In addition my so-called high school guidance counselor, Mr. Alkali, is far more interested in guiding the serves and backhands of the tennis players he coaches than in the academic futures of his tutees.

"Looks good to me," he says, when I present him with my choices: two state universities and, for some strange reason, my "dream" institution: the University of Rochester. Rochester, indeed, *does* summon me for an interview, but when I examine the plane fares from New York—a whopping thirty-five dollars each way—I decide that this will be more than my stepmother can take, and refuse. Months later I'm off, without the help of either my parents or the B'nai Brith, to the state university's "elite" liberal arts campus, Harpur College—bargain-rate tuition four hundred dollars a semester, for which I have a New York State Regents Scholarship.

Soon—thanks, no doubt, to her *Morgengebet einer unglück-lichen Ebefrau*—my stepmother will succeed in luring my father, relieved of his crying and desperate son, out of my ancestral confines of 801 West 181st Street and into her *sanctum sanctorum* near the west end of La Guardia Airport. But first, of course, they must get me and my best friend and roommate-to-be, Siegfried Mortkowitz, to Binghamton, New York—Thruway tolls, gasoline taxes, *Mrs.* Mortkowitz, and all.

The Mortkowitzes, Polish Holocaust survivors who own a dry cleaning store in the Bronx, are too poor even to have a car, so—with my father, stepmother, and I squished in the front seat, and Siggy and his mother, along with all his worldly belongings, crammed into the back—the five of us jam into my father's silver gray 1961 Chrysler New Yorker and head up the West Side Highway toward the hoped-for mutual liberation of the New York Thruway and Route 17 West.

Siggy and I have a good time en route—as my father cruises toward his customary maximum speed of fifty miles per hour—playing various games like Twenty Questions and charades. My stepmother, meanwhile, her eyes firmly on the toll booths and the gas gauge, is in a relatively contemplative state, no doubt already planning to appropriate my remaining possessions, while Mrs. Mortkowitz, who, from the sound of it, can barely breathe, is hunkered somewhere beneath a mass of down comforters and feather pillows in the far-right passenger seat.

Even here, heading up Route 17 toward Monticello, my father has not lost his salesman's solicitousness and charm. Every five minutes, to my stepmother's alarm, his head makes a full 180-degree turn from the driver's seat to inquire of the hardly visible Mrs. Mortkowitz, "You are comfortable, Mrs. *Mos*kowitz?" to which, inevitably, comes the muffled and equally accented answer, "Yes, fine, Mr. Bloomingdale."

And so it goes, all two-hundred-odd miles northwest of the city, the Bloomingdales and the Moskowitzes and their collected progeny heading for the hoped-for Valhalla of Binghamton, New York. When, after what must have been at least a seven-hour drive for what should have required, of the ordinary human being, no more than four, we finally pull into the mud-and-construction-filled campus of Harpur College, my father puts the finishing touches on this German-Polish mission to upstate New York by asking the security guard for instructions on how to get to "*Bimming* (instead of "Bingham") Hall," an address he will proceed to use for the next year while directing my mail to venues as diverse as Birmingham, Alabama, and Brimington, Maine.

But by this time neither Siggy nor I could care less: We believe we are about to be free.

It's with Ivy Masters, in my college apartment in Endwell, New York, that—after what feels like years of doing what she calls "the minifuck," a nearly surgical procedure during which I insert my penis some five-eighths of an inch into her vagina and withdraw before ejaculating—I finally get to do "the act." It's a poor substitute, in my hierarchy of pleasures, for oral sex, but what the hell?

No one, it seems to me, is more thrilled by the fact that we are finally having sex than is *Mrs.* Masters, who not only immediately places her orality-shy daughter on the pill but—virtually every weekend Ivy comes up from Forest Hills to visit—sends along a not-very-kosher but extremely phallic-looking salami, "just in case," as Ivy conveys the message, "you get tired."

I *don't*, in fact, get tired—Why should I? I'm, after all, just starting out in this game—and the salami is usually rather delicious. (If I can't, I console myself, peaceably eat Ivy, I may as well devour her mother's salami.) And, after years of longing for Robbie Bodenheimer, minifucking, and having to content myself with wetting my fingers in Ivy's vaginal emissions, this actually "doing it" feels awfully good.

I've moved, not only *into* sex and *away* to college, but—even without my stepmother's help—*up* along the Borscht Belt hierarchy of summer jobs: Now I've followed in Amos's dollar-drenched footsteps once again, and am a busboy at the *crème de la crème*—Grossinger's of Kiamesha Lake, makers of Jenny Grossinger's famous Jewish rye, occasional home to the likes of Jack Benny and Mort Sahl—even to a heavyweight boxing championship contender, a 230-pound Argentinian by the name of Oscar Bonavena.

"Me heavyweight champion," Bonavena chants every morning at eight, as he invades the Grossinger's kitchen from his training camp in the Ski Lodge to down a half dozen huge steaks and two quarts of orange juice for breakfast. "Me heavyweight champion."

Bonavena is not quite the only *goy* doing his training amidst Grossinger's *glatt* kosher corridors. There's also Daphne Magnuson, a sumptuous blond from Westport, Connecticut, whose grandparents—people with an incredible name: *the Walzes*—actually raise horses on Block Island. Daphne, rumor has it, much like Robbie Bodenheimer before her, likes to wrestle in all sorts of pre- and postejaculatory positions, and, what's more, is the only member of the dining room staff not among the Chosen People, which means, of course, that she's the one who, if I had my druthers, would be chosen by me.

But I'm a bit shy and have a bad case of the uglies that summer, and can't imagine what this Gidget lookalike could possibly see in the likes of me, a conceivable composite of Golda Meir and Bob Dylan. So that, while Daphne's apparently humping away at night with two-thirds of my Ashkenazi brothers, I content myself for most of the summer with her bringing my favorite delicacy—a glass of apricot nectar—to my station at least twice daily and making comments that suggest to me that, although it's Nelly Gern's face I see gazing back at me from the mirror, it's *me* she wants after all.

Finally, on the last night of the summer, just after Labor Day, and before Bonavena finally leaves the hotel en route to a ten-round unanimous decision for Joe Frazier in Madison Square Garden, I manage to pluck Daphne, almost literally, off the motorcycle of some local *goy* from Liberty and land her, with a *Hi-yo, Silver! Awa-a-a-y!,* in my bed, where, to my unbridled joy, we wrestle and fuck each other into a summer's-end oblivion.

Chocolates. Chocolates. Chocolates. Chocolates. Away at college, away at work, away almost anywhere, the boxes periodically arrive—packed with Estée bitter chocolate, imported marzipan, Cognac-filled chocolate cherries, and chocolate-covered waffles.

"*Für meinen lieben Sohn,* my million," the enclosed card invariably says, in my father's traditional bilingual scrawl, "with love from your DADY."

Chocolates, cruises, secret bank accounts, secret mailboxes ("Write to your papa in secret—Why should there be secrets between a son and his good DADY?"). No mistress (not even, I suspect, Claire) has ever been so assiduously and relentlessly courted as I—a hormonally intact, dispositionally heterosexual, postadolescent male—am now courted by, of all people, my own father.

Years later—when I first discover the psychologically astute insight that the best thing a man can do for his children is to love his wife, and when I first experience problems trying to sustain intimate relationships with women—it begins to occur to me that, at least in part, the source of my difficulties is that the love of my father's life has never been either of his wives, or, for that matter, any of the other women whose hands he now kisses.

It's been me, his only, adopted son.

Since all forms of love bestowed on me must be bestowed illicitly, it is not only chocolate but that other form of sweetness— money—I am forced to receive in secret. Like my uncle Berthold's twin quarters proffered my way, and at first refused, every Monday night in Washington Heights, my father, too, pushes money toward me—in my stepmother's basement (when she's upstairs), in his car when I accompany him downtown, and in the form of secret bank accounts, the passbooks to which he periodically presents me with, either in person or by mail.

Poor him: He can't even love his own (adopted) son in the open. And his poor son: I, of course, *want* the money—just as I so badly want his love—but the very circumstances under which it is offered makes it seem dirty, forbidden, illegitimate, tainted. And so, just as I did with my uncle, I push the money away with one hand, and reach out, longingly, to receive it with the other, something like a mistress being made love to in a cheap motel.

Years later, on at least one occasion, the outcome of this pecuniary mating dance is not only unfortunate but costly. One day in New York, as I am about to depart on a month-long trip to Indonesia, my father shoves five hundred-dollar bills into what he believes to be the inside pocket of my raincoat. It's merely the lining, however, and as we innocently walk, a bit later, to the habitual doctor's appointment to which I am accompanying him, my father's illicit payoff, unnoticed by either of us, apparently goes blowing down Madison Avenue, destined either for a sewer or, perhaps more mercifully, the grateful hands of some homeless person who truly needs it.

The psychological lesson in all this, however—unlike those five hundred-dollar bills—will not be lost on me: In some sense, I realize, I am learning that money, too, is a form of love (or, as Wallace Stevens put it, "a kind of poetry"), and I will come, like it or not, to feel that whether, and how, it is given, or withheld, determines to some extent whether or not I am loved. And yet nothing, even then, prepares me for the lessons regarding money I am to learn later.

It's not Wallace Stevens but an Irish poet—a relatively unknown, perpetually drunk, flamboyantly gay (it is, after all, only 1968) cohort of California poet Jack Spicer, by the name of James Liddy—who gets me started on what (and there is no way between heaven and earth for me to grasp, or anticipate this yet) will ultimately be part of my career. And it's not even Liddy's work that proves to be my muse: It's his crush on my new best friend, Larry.

Liddy is the Visiting Poet—a title that, at the time, seems as exotic to me as Astronaut-in-Residence—at Harpur College, the first living specimen of poet I have ever encountered, and Larry, who's lost his literary virginity well before me, is taking "James's," as he calls him, course in Contemporary Irish Poets. Liddy's roving eye—which, it seems, frequently lands on the kind of hardly postpubescent Jewish boys from New York City in which Harpur specializes—has alighted, to his unending flattery, on Larry, complete with hand-delivered poems placed under his door at midnight, desperate phone calls, and epistles ("To Larry, who has entered the sensual secret . . .") sent and received at all hours, sometimes special delivery . . . and sometimes when I'm there.

I, too, have a "crush" on Larry, but of a different kind. A book, for the first time in my life, has truly spoken to me—D. H. Lawrence's *Women in Love*—and it is not the relationship of either or both of the couples that truly interests me, but that of Gerald and Birkin, that "other kind of love," on whose longing the novel ends. It is also the time of the Vietnam War, and, with it, of late-night, intimate discussions among male students concerning what to do, and I—my half-failed seductions notwithstanding—am feeling a need for this "other" kind of love as well: What I feel a need for is a friendship with a man whose intensity will, I hope, both mitigate the aching need for girls that fills my nights and days *and* the longing for a father, a brother—anyone—with whom I might truly form a platonic attachment.

Larry—along with our mutual friends Bobby and David—is one of these men, a potential Gerald to my Birkin, and I'm not too pleased, either by James's late-night phone calls, nor by the romantic verses he places under Larry's door. I'm—how else to say it?—jealous, and it's jealousy, not poetry, that proves to be my muse: Tentatively, painfully, ineptly, I begin scribbling in the dark.

Graduation, 1969: It's Isaac Asimov on the podium, speaking of the possibilities of life on other planets, but *I'm* very much on the ground, staring up at my stepmother's bitter and bored expression beside my father in the grandstand.

My parents—with all the enthusiasm of Yasser Arafat and Syrian president Hafez al-Assad attending Yom Kippur services—have come up for my college graduation (I'm a respectable, if not sensational, 147th in a class of 568), as has my girlfriend, Daphne (the very same one I landed that last night at

Grossinger's), from what is now her undergraduate school at Oneonta State. Seated beside each other in the stands, Daphne and my father are, to say the least, an odd juxtaposition, a bit like having Elie Wiesel on a blind date with Claudia Schiffer.

After Asimov's speech and the remainder of the ceremony—during which the Phi Beta Kappas are called separately—my father politely rouses my stepmother from her reveries of Phillips Petroleum and Standard Oil, and they make their way, with osteoporotic tentativeness, down the stands and onto the gymnasium floor, where the assembled parents, relatives, and spouses-to-be are congratulating the graduates.

"Was ist denn los?"—"What happened?"—my father, ever the man with an encouraging word, asks as he finally reaches me. "You were always such a good student. Why didn't they call *your* name?"

That night, at a local steak-and-seafood restaurant called the Red Lion Inn, where I also work as a waiter, things only go from bad to worse, as—in the decidedly mixed and incongruous company of Daphne, myself, and my stepmother—my father, the great charmer, mutely sits there, the expression of a just-escaped Holocaust survivor indelibly glued to his face.

"Your father, he is very, very upset." My stepmother turns to me when Daphne and my father head off to the loo.

"What in the world about?" I wonder out loud. "Just because I wasn't Phi Beta Kappa?"

"Nein, Du blöder Junge"—"No, you silly boy"—my stepmother replies. *"Er ist so aufgeregt weil Du mit dieser verflugten Schickse schläfst."* "He is so upset because you are sleeping with that goddamned *shiksa*."

I'm off—planning to meet "that goddamned *shiksa*" later on in my travels—for the archetypal 1969 postgraduate hitchhiking trip around Europe, and, as always, I am certain my father is going to die while I am gone.

As always, too, my father's got one of his "secret" mailboxes—this one located in the *yekke* summer haven of Fleischmanns, New York—to which his "dear son" has been instructed to write if he has any, as my father puts it, "secrets between a son and his Dady, which no one else should know."

I *do* have a secret, in fact—or what I hope isn't really a secret—which is that I love him, and I want him to know it before he drops dead and the wicked witch of Jackson Heights has utterly convinced him that I'm a no-good ingrate who wants nothing more from life than to fuck shiksas and the inheritance of his paltry shares of AT&T. So, before leaving for Europe, I send the folllowing epistle to P.O. Box 483, Fleischmanns, NY 12430:

Dear Dad,

Before leaving for Europe, I just wanted to write to you and let you know that—despite everything Alice may try to tell you about me, and convince you of—I am a loving and devoted son, who is grateful for everything you have done for me.

You should, I hope, be able to realize this for yourself, but I know that Alice works on you night and day to convince you otherwise, and that she would like you to believe that I am a no-good, ungrateful person, who has no feeling for anything but girls and pleasure. But it is not so: I love you, and am devoted to you, as hard as it is sometimes for me to realize that you are married to someone who spends so much of her energy to turning you against me, and against everything I do.

So—since we can never know what the future will

bring—I wanted to say this to you—as you suggested, in secret—before leaving on my trip. I look forward to seeing you, in good health and spirits, when I return, and hope you will have a wonderful and restful summer in Fleischmanns.

> *Your loving son,*
> *Michael*

But my father's secret mailbox, it turns out, has a Freudian trapdoor of its own: The night he receives this letter, just as I'm winging my way over the Atlantic, he conveniently manages to leave it, open, on the kitchen table, where my stepmother is sure to—and does—find it. *"Solch ein undankbarer und neidischer Junge,"* she informs him upon reading it: "Such an ungrateful and envious boy."

Something within him, I'm convinced by now, must be sure she is right.

We're back from Europe (Daphne and I are now living together), and I'm teaching German—at the time a relatively painless way both of staying out of the draft and of having to decide on a "real" future—at a high school outside Binghamton. Late one night the phone rings.

It's my poor cousin Amos—my *brother*—his voice quivering with discomfort on the other end, who has been given the rather dubious assignment of saving me from the clutches of the golden *shiksa* with whom I am, for the most part happily, living.

"Hi, Mike, how ya doin'?" he—the only person on the planet whom I still allow to call me "Mike"—begins.

"I'm fine, Amos, and how are you?"

"Everything's fine here too. Listen, let me get right to it, okay? Ernst [my father was called by his middle name in the family] asked me to call you because he's worried about you and thought I might be able to help."

"*Worried? Help?*—What exactly do you mean, Amos?" I can feel my poor cousin's increasingly palpable discomfort on the other end.

"Listen, Mike, I really didn't want to call you, and I'm really uncomfortable about this, believe me, since it's really none of my business, but you *know* how Ernst is. I think he's just worried that you don't quite know what you're getting into, living with this girlfriend of yours, and he just asked me to call and talk to you."

Had I a bit more distance from all of this, it might now occur to me: My father—never all that "worried" while my stepmother was torturing me and ruining what was left of my childhood—is *now* worried about me, while I am happily living with and fucking my girlfriend, two hundred miles away in Binghamton, New York. What he is *really* "worried" about, I should realize, is that I am doing what *he* was never able to do: *I* am living with Claire Haas. *I* am fucking and eating and humping the golden *shiksa* he had to give up. I am saying: *To hell with Judaism and Hitler and the Nazis and religiously obsessed and persecuted fathers.* I am trying to live my life.

"Listen, Amos," I say, "I appreciate your calling, and I realize it wasn't your idea, but, really, I'm doing quite fine, and I wish my parents would just leave you—and me—alone."

"I understand, Mike," Amos commiserates from the other end. "I just promised Ernst I would call, so I felt that I at least had to do it."

"No problem," I say. "I understand." And then I hang up.

But I don't, of course, have such a liberating distance on all this. Something in my father's sick message, as always, strikes home: I turn back into what should be my own life, thinking I am the no-good, the vagrant, the wounding and ungrateful son.

Several weeks later, there's yet another late-night phone call. This time, on the other end (paid for at her own expense—an ominous sign) is the voice of that great harbinger of doom, my stepmother.

"There's been a terrible accident, and your father is in Flushing Hospital," she quickly informs me, no doubt hearing those long-distance seconds clicking away. "You must come home right away." My stepmother—I've, by now, become accustomed to this fact—only refers to her house as my "home" (after all, I don't even have the keys) when there's trouble and she needs me.

"I'll be there as soon as we can," I say, motioning Daphne out of bed, but the line is already dead on the other end. Some five hours later, or as quickly as unrenovated Route 17 and my 1964 Plymouth Valiant will take us, we are driving down the West Side Highway, just as a magnificent sunrise filters through the polluted skies of Manhattan. We stop at my friends Larry and Charlene's apartment on the Upper West Side, where I am both planning to unload "the goddamned *shiksa*" (I don't, after all, want to give him another heart attack to boot) and call the hospital to see about visiting hours.

"I'd like to inquire about my father, Julius Blumenthal's, condition, and when I might come see him," I tell the hospital operator. "He was admitted last night after a car accident, I believe."

"Mr. Blumenthal's condition is listed as critical," she informs me after a brief pause. "If you are his son, you can see him anytime."

By now the tears are already streaming down my cheeks, as I

run down the five flights of stairs from Larry's apartment and lurch, nearly hysterical, into my car. Like a bad imitation of a James Bond chase scene, careening madly around slow-moving traffic and double-parked cars, I make my way over the Triboro Bridge and race right through the toll booth without so much as blinking an eye—except, that is, to wipe away the tears. I have visions of entering the emergency room just as a white sheet is being pulled over my father's face, with some overly solicitous nurse turning to me and saying, "I'm so sorry, Mr. Blumenthal, you're just a few minutes too late. Your father was such a lovely man."

Pulling into the hospital parking lot to the accompaniment of screeching rubber, I leave the car, keys and all, in front of the entrance and run into the lobby, madly looking for someone to point me in the direction of my father's last breath. "He's on four East, in the Intensive Care Unit," the desk person on duty informs me, and I'm off, taking the stairs three at a time. As I turn, nearly vomiting from anxiety and exhaustion, into the ICU door, I'm met by what should, perhaps, have been a predictable sight: My father, his right leg suspended in some sort of traction, is holding a nurse's hand in his, just on the verge of planting a kiss thereupon, as I enter the room.

"*Ach,* my dear son!" he exclaims when he sees me. "God bless you, you are here. The nurses here, God love them, they are taking such good care of me."

"But wait a minute," I say, turning to the nurse in what must seem more like anger than relief. "They told me at the front desk and on the phone that my father was in *critical* condition. *This,*" I motion toward my rather comfortable-looking *père*, "doesn't look like critical condition to me."

"Oh, my," says the nurse. "I suppose someone should have told you: They place *every* patient who has a previous heart condition on the critical list, whenever he or she comes in as the result of an accident—just in case. But your father—and such a charming gentleman he is—is doing just *fine*, Mr. Blumenthal, you don't need to worry about a thing."

By some miraculous twist of having discovered literature too late and excelled at taking tests too early, I find myself—my father's wish that I become either a pharmacist or a veterinarian notwithstanding—in law school at Cornell, where I seem, at least during my first year, destined to be one of the class stars. I am naively determined, to both the delight and irritation of my professors, to follow Yeats's suggestion and "hold reality and justice in a single thought."

During the summer between my second and third years (I spend my first law school summer working as a stonemason's assistant on the Cornell Grounds Crew, where my boss calls me "Meathead"), I find myself, on the recommendation of a friend in the third-year class, working for a man named David Souter, then deputy attorney general (under future Sen. Warren Rudman) of the State of New Hampshire.

At my interview with Souter—during which we seem to disagree about virtually everything, aside from our mutual affection for Emerson and Thoreau—I find myself face to face, for the first time, with someone for whom the law is not merely a profession but both wife and mistress (Souter, a thirty-something bachelor, still lives with his mother in Ware, New Hampshire). A former Rhodes scholar and Harvard Law School graduate, he is as serene and polished as I am nervous and rough, but we seem, nonetheless, to like each other, and—*voila!*—before I know it, I'm the only summer intern in the Criminal Division of the Office of the Attorney General of the State of New Hampshire, working on cases for whose opposing side I feel a far greater natural sympathy than our own.

Souter, whose thoughts seem as hermetic and focused as mine seem decadent and wild, seems pleased with my work nonetheless, and I, indeed, try to take advantage of every possible opportunity to steer our conversations *away* from the law and in the direction of Thoreau and nearby Mount Monadnock.

It's that infamous "Watergate summer," the TV screens and papers filled to the brim with embarrassing revelations about our president and his men, and, on my last day of work—when Souter and Rudman take me to a *very* Republican-seeming Concord restaurant for lunch—they also present me with a letter commending my work in their office and telling me that "in this summer, when some in our profession have been shown to be so derelict in their duties and lax in their ethics, your work in this office and your association with us has once again confirmed our conviction that lawyers, indeed, can be the best of men."

After lunch, alone with Souter in his office, I inform him—although I have already interviewed, at his suggestion, for a clerkship with local Federal District Judge Hugh Bownes—that I am thinking of taking some time off after law school to write, a plan that meets with a somewhat less than enthusiastic response on my boss's part.

"I would be careful, if I were you," he counsels me, both affectionately and, no doubt, wisely. "The law," he adds, with the air of someone who knows, "is not a very forgiving mistress."

Judge Bownes, in fact, *does* offer me the clerkship, which I at first accept and then—in one of those self-destructive career moves many a better writer has taken before me—decline, only to accept instead the profoundly unpoetic sounding position (for which I don't even recall having interviewed) of staff attorney for the Bureau of Competition of the Federal Trade Commission in Washington, D.C. I've decided that—in terms of a choice of venue, at least—I am a bit more Henry Miller than Thoreau, safer in a city than in the New Hampshire woods.

Arriving in Washington in the fall of 1974, fresh from having passed the New York State Bar Exam, I am immediately assigned to an unbelievable-sounding case—a study of anticompetitive practices in the California raisin industry—the initial work on which involves my spending several hours each day interviewing Armenian raisin farmers in the area of Fresno, California.

Immersed as I am, day and night, in the world of raisins, this line of work also results in some of my first nonamorous poetic scribblings. The first line of one such poem, entitled (what else?) "Raisins," suggests that I am a young man more likely headed for Madison Avenue than for the Harvard English Department. The poem, which begins "A raisin is some sunshine you can eat," contains at least one memorable couplet I still—though I have done everything possible to forget it—recall: "A raisin is a little Black boy/Left in the bathtub too long."

Knowing even less about literature than I do about law, I immediately send this masterpiece—along with several other "poems," and a brief "biographical note"—to one of the few literary magazines of whose existence I am even aware, a periodical called *Field* published by the English Department of Oberlin College, in Ohio.

In roughly the amount of time it would take a plane to fly from Washington to Oberlin and back, my "poems"—along with their stamped, self-addressed envelope—are back in my mailbox, with the following miniepistle appended, in pencil, to my "biographical note":

Dear Michael Blumenthal,

Don't ever lay a trip like this on any decent magazine. . . .
It marks you.

The Editors

P.S. "Raisin = little Black boy" particularly offensive!

Thus go the sterling beginnings of my literary career. My legal career, alas, fares hardly any better. Unable to cope either with the FTC's utterly impersonal, prisonlike edifice at the corner of 6th Street and Pennsylvania Avenue, NW, or with any more interviews with Armenian raisin farmers or the executives of California agricultural cooperatives, I spend most of my afternoons, after slinking off to lunch, at the Washington Zoo on Connecticut Avenue, staring at the distended throat sacs of the gibbons, and hoping I will catch a glimpse of the two giant pandas in the act of mating.

I'd like to see, for a change, how *they* do it: Perhaps there's something there to be learned by the likes of me.

Finally, during my late twenties, while I'm working for Time-Life Books in Washington, D.C.—still vainly searching for my father's ever-withheld blessing—I think I may have finally gotten (in my parents' eyes, at least) this "woman thing" right:

Her name's Anne, and she's not only Jewish, but *German-* (or, rather, Austrian-) Jewish; from a well-off, somewhat more assimilated suburban family in Bethesda, Maryland. She has a father with a well-paying, secure government job, a design business of her own, a luxurious condominium in one of the better sections of DC—What more could my parents possibly want?

"She must be sick and not telling you about it," my stepmother whispers to me in the kitchen the day I bring Anne to my parents' house for *Shabbos* dinner.

"Sick? What in the world are you talking about?"

"Diese Frau ist doch so dünn—das ist doch nicht normal." "The woman's so thin—it's just not normal," my stepmother replies.

"Das Mädchen lügt Dich doch an," my father, ever the jealous suitor, comments later that evening. "That girl is lying to you."

"Lying to me? About what?"

"Her age, *Du Dummkopf!* She must be much older than she is telling you. *Sie weiss, diese Pollackin"*—She knows, this Polack—"what a good catch you are." My parents seem to believe that the son of Julius and Alice Blumenthal is such a rare catch that women will go to any length—even to the extent of lying about their age—in order to snare him. Having thus arrived at my parents' house enamored of a healthy-looking, relatively well-built twenty-eight-year-old woman, I now find myself—in the eyes of those whose approval I still stupidly and hopelessly crave— in love with an aging, sickly looking anorexic, not to mention a liar.

What kind of woman would possibly please them? I wonder. Who could possibly be Jewish enough, German enough, rich enough, pretty enough, young enough, fat enough? Naive as anyone looking for love in all the wrong places, I can't yet see— for the dark forest of my parents' combined animuses and neuroses—the clearly visible trees that stand directly before me: *No* woman in my life has ever been "good enough" for the son of *Julius Blumenthal, Fine Furs.* No woman ever will.

Sometimes the whole business—my swapped families, my dead mother, my evicted grandmother, my loveless stepmother, my psychologically crippled father—are simply too much for me, and even my *echt Yiddisch*, Borscht Belt–trained sense of humor can no longer come to the rescue.

On one such occasion—during a period in my mid-twenties when all of life is seeming particularly hopeless to me and no one among my increasing army of psychotherapists, Freudian and Jungian, seems capable of offering a solution—I find myself once again in the basement of my stepmother's house in Jackson Heights (the only part I'm allowed to inhabit), sitting at the typewriter. Maybe I'm writing a poem—who knows?—but what I *do* know is that, amid all the turned-off lights, opened mail, listened-in-on phone calls, and impermissible showers, I'm trying, like a turtle with its head tucked into its shell, to reclaim my battered boundaries under the rubric of something that might approach art.

My stepmother, for a welcome change, has taken a walk to the mailbox—the closest she ever comes to an urban adventure—and my father, who's been seated upstairs at his office desk and who, perhaps, detects that his son is in a near-catatonic depression, comes downstairs in an effort to resuscitate the depleted paternal air that exists between us.

"Is something the matter, dear son?" he says, trying, I realize, as best he can to create some intimacy within the linguistic, intellectual, and historical abyss that yawns between us. "A father and his son can have some secrets, no?" he continues, putting a new twist on a line that, in the past, has merely provided another convenient avenue to betrayal. "Come, tell your papa what is on your mind."

I am some twenty-six years old, with a law degree from Cornell, and I'm in no mood, really, to tell my "papa" what's on my mind, nor, even if I wanted to, could I find the words to do so. But something in me nonetheless breaks down on hearing the question; and, bursting into large, uncontrollable sobs, I place my head in my hands atop the typewriter and begin wailing—appropriately enough, in German—*"Ach, ich bin sooo unglücklich."* (Oh, I am sooo unhappy.)

My father, not knowing what else to do when confronted with such naked emotion, rushes right to the liquor cabinet, which contains the one alcoholic beverage—a bottle of Hennessey—my parents keep in the house for the relief of angina pectoris, and pours each of us a healthy shot.

"No, thanks, I don't want any." I sob, trying to control my own body's heavings. "Just please leave me alone."

My father, it will often occur to me later, is no doubt really trying, in his own way, to communicate. He really *wants,* I believe, to help. But there's been too much water under our collective bridge—too many betrayals, too many cursed girlfriends, too many wicked stepmothers. And, as I return my head to my arms atop the typewriter and continue sobbing, I hear my father's slow footsteps going up the basement stairs behind me.

Then, a few minutes later, I hear the sound of his own heartrending sobs coming from the bedroom upstairs.

I meet my first wife, Kendra, while sitting at a café in Washington, D.C., reading Italo Calvino's *Italian Folktales.* I'm now working as producer for West German Television Network ZDF, and it's one of the only times in my adult life I'm *not* actively looking for a woman.

The second she walks into the café and sits down beside me, though, I'm a goner. Green eyes, a wide, gap-toothed smile, dressed in L.L. Bean duck boots, blue jeans, and an embroidered white Mexican-style blouse that make her look like she's just been out horseback riding.

She has, in fact, done virtually all the things I've dreamed of and lacked the courage or aptitude for: five years of salmon fishing in Alaska, bicycling alone through Poland and Hungary, sailing with a Greek sea captain in the Mediterranean, organic farming in rural Ohio, the triathlon in Honolulu. She's the antithesis of the burdened, ever-thinking, inert self I so want to be rid of. And who knows but that I may be the same to her.

By midafternoon, we're in bed—or, at least, on the grass. And—over the next six months or so, until our wedding—we hardly ever emerge from some coital or precoital position or, when we do, only in order to assume a new posture *en plein air.* From the banks of the Tidal Basin to the hills of the Shenandoah Valley, I shoot my desperate seed into her, hoping to find in her beautiful, Polish-inspired, Midwestern face—like Proust in his grandmother's—the entrance to another soul, but unable to find anything beyond myself. And one afternoon on a friend's secluded deck in Sperryville, Virginia, from a position too intricate and lovely to name, I ask Kendra to be my wife.

My parents greet the news of their son's impending marriage—as part of which I assure them both of my great happiness *and* that any and all children will be brought up utterly, utterly Jewish—with a deafening silence, followed by a pair of reluctant grunts when I inform them that I intend to drive up to their summer cottage in Fleischmanns to introduce them to their future daughter-in-law.

My father's been suffering from a twenty-nine-stroke-per-minute heartbeat and a terrible case of shingles, but exhibits his characteristic charm ("Hello, Sindra," he says, butchering my fiancée's name in the traditional manner. "God loves you, and so do we") when we arrive. Within a few hours, however, the atmosphere, seemingly benign at first, takes what should have been a predictable turn for the worse. After supper and the Jewish "Blessing After Meals," my father, à la Jack Nicholson in *Carnal*

Knowledge, asks Kendra to please come into the bedroom with him for a few minutes. The two of them leave the table and close the bedroom door, leaving me in the company of Alice.

Ever the naive and hopeful one, as I sit there hunched over my stepmother's (delicious, I must confess) apple strudel, I assume my father is bestowing his blessings and sentimental homilies upon Kendra, informing her in the process how blessed she is to have garnered a catch like me and a father-in-law like himself.

When, however, the bedroom door opens several minutes later to reveal Kendra's ghostly white face and my father's despairing visage, I suddenly begin to suspect that what transpired inside wasn't exactly a colloquy of benedictions.

"What happened?" I whisper to Kendra as she emerges from her obvious ordeal and reenters the kitchen.

"I'll tell you later," she whispers. "Just be quiet."

But now it's apparently my turn for a private audience with the failed rabbi. "Sindra, maybe you would be so nice as to wait outside," my father suggests politely, settling back into his chair at the kitchen table as Kendra opens the screen door and exits into the night air.

"I told Sindra," my father begins in German, "that we both welcome her into our family and wish the two of you every *Massel* for your future, but"—and now I begin to have a terrible sense of foreboding—"your old papa who has only a few years left only asks that she become Jewish."

Still shocked, though I should hardly be, something within me immediately rushes to my girlfriend's defense.

"It's fine with me if Kendra wants to convert," I say, beginning to tremble with the not-so-subdued rage of someone who—thinking he's been invited in for supper, has merely been set up for an ambush—"but I'm absolutely *not* going to demand it of her." Then, resorting to a moment of logic I should have known could only backfire when faced with the contralogical mechanisms of my parents' psyches, I add: "After all, no one in *her* family has asked me to become a Catholic."

No sooner is the word "Catholic" out of my mouth than my father, his black *Shabbos* yarmulke still planted firmly atop his head—followed immediately by my stepmother assuming the same position—lowers his face into his uplifted palms as if into a washcloth and descends into a long sequence of sobs.

Realizing by now that my parents' more or less "civilized" behavior of the preceding hours has been merely a seductive setup for what was to come, I rise from the table to rescue my outnumbered future wife from the porch.

"Let's get out of here," I whisper. "No," she answers calmly. "Let's just sit here and wait."

Within a few minutes my father, dry eyed and no longer wearing his yarmulke, emerges from the screen door carrying a small silver tray on which is perched his perpetual cure for all ills: his bottle of Hennessey. *"Kommt doch, Kinder,"* he says, looking more like a Holocaust survivor than I've ever seen him before. And, utterly ignoring Kendra's non-command of German, *"Lass uns ein bisschen Schnapps trinken."*

Not knowing what else to do, I grab a small shot glass of cognac from my father's trembling tray and hand another to Kendra. I'm trembling by now myself, tears running down my cheeks. *"L'chayim,"* my father says, bringing the glass to his lips. "God love you."

"Es ist nothing but *sex!"* My father spits the word out like a cobra when we stop, at his request, at the counter of a small coffee shop on Fleischmanns' Main Street the next morning, after I have taken him to his biweekly doctor's appointment.

"Vergiss mich" (forget me), he then adds when I try to respond, slamming down his spoon and walking out onto the street. When I follow him, sobbing, onto the sidewalk, he turns to me once more, adding the classic survivor's curse: "And if anything happens to me, it's your fault."

Utterly shocked by the cruelty of what my father—this man who, throughout my childhood and early adulthood, perpetually referred to me as his "million"—has just done, I, shaking with sobs, sit down in a wooden lawn chair in a private backyard just to our right. Across the street several denizens of Fleischmann's *"Adenauer bench"* stop to observe the all-too-clichéd scene taking place before their eyes.

My father, a lethal combination of hatred and pain oozing from him, sits down on the chair beside me. *"Schämst Du dich nicht?"*—"Aren't you ashamed of yourself"—he asks, giving voice to the obvious first priority of his concerns. "In front of all these people?"

Though I'm still some fifteen years from writing them, the words I used to describe my father's ill-fated choice of Claire Haas some fifty years earlier in Nazi Germany might, at this moment, provide me with a useful bit of insight:

". . . he may merely have wanted to strike back at his father for marrying a woman *he* so hated. He may have wanted to wound the man who had wounded him."

The day before my marriage to Kendra, I find myself seated in Mt. Sinai Hospital's postsurgical "Family Only" waiting room. My father, ever the master of timing, has entered the hospital the day before to have a pacemaker implanted. I'm almost wishing his long ordeal of mock dyings would finally come to an end, when the surgical nurse, carrying a clipboard and her most professional look of controlled compassion, emerges from the elevator doors.

"Is there a Mr. Blumenthal here?" she calls as she marches into the room full of potential widows, widowers, and orphans. My heart leaps into my gullet. I make a beeline for the elevator.

"I'm Mr. Blumenthal."

"Could you wait over there in the corner, Mr. Blumenthal?" The grim-faced young woman motions to me. "I need to talk with you alone when I'm done here."

A sudden, all-consuming chill takes over my body as I head for a corner of the room while the nurse conveys her various pre- and postmortems to the assembled relatives. How appropriate, I think as I light a cigarette and collapse into a chair. *How perfectly fitting*: my wedding and my father's funeral on the same day.

Finally, after what seems like hours, the nurse—suddenly wearing a lighthearted expression—comes walking toward me.

"He's dead, isn't he?" I ask half hopefully.

"Why, no," the nurse answers to my amazement. "On the contrary—he's doing just fine. We don't usually allow relatives into the recovery room, but your father is just *sooo* charming. He begged me to let you in so he could talk to you. I just didn't want the other patients' relatives to hear."

I feel a sense of shocked disbelief. "Uh . . . yes . . . he's very charming, isn't he?"

"He sure is. So, if you'll just follow me, Mr. Blumenthal, I'll take you down to the recovery room. But you have to promise me you'll only stay a minute, all right?"

"I swear." I'm still trembling.

A few minutes later, the green doors marked RECOVERY ROOM. HOSPITAL STAFF ONLY swing open to reveal a large, disinfectant-soaked room filled with perhaps two dozen bodies attached to a vast network of intravenous devices and life-support systems.

From somewhere in the middle of the room, I hear an all-too-familiar voice singing an aria from *La Traviata*.

"Just follow me, Mr. Blumenthal," the nurse motions with an almost inaudible whisper. "He's right over there."

In a surreal daze, I follow the sound of that familiar voice to the center of the room. There, his head propped up on a set of pillows and a white surgical towel wrapped around his chest, my father is holding the hand of yet another nurse, whom—in a kind of groggy, postsurgical stupor—he is now serenading with Mario Lanza's "Golden Days."

"Here's your son, Julius," the nurse whispers. By now she's almost lost her own sense of recovery room decorum as her eyes meet her blushing coworker's gaze.

"*Ach,* my dear son." My father's head turns away from the nurse to look up at me. "My million."

"How are you, Dad?" I ask halfheartedly.

"Everything *ist wunderbar.* I am in *wundervoll* hands here." My father is grasping both by now nearly hysterical nurses by the hand as he speaks.

"He's a marvelous patient . . . so incredibly cheerful," the surgical nurse smiles. "He even tried to sell me a fur coat. You're lucky to have such a wonderful father."

"Will you call Mama for me and tell her everything is fine?" my father asks, referring to my stepmother.

"Sure," I reply. "But then, if you're really all right, I have to go back to Washington—I'm getting married tomorrow, you know, and we're leaving for Italy the next day."

"*Ja,* of course I know," the suddenly serious patient replies.

"Mr. Blumenthal, I'm afraid you'll really have to leave now." The nurse, still trying hard to contain her laughter, is tugging at my shirtsleeve.

"I'll call after the wedding to make sure you're all right—okay, Dad?" I place a hand tentatively on my father's shoulder.

"*Jawohl* . . . But don't vorry—your daddy vill be fine."

"Yeah, I'm sure you will be." I turn toward the recovery room door.

"*Und*, dear son . . . ," my father's head turns once more in my direction as I begin to disappear through the swinging doors.

"Yeah, Dad?" I stop in my tracks, awaiting my father's parting words.

"Have a vonderful trip."

Given his rage at every sexually satisfying, or potentially satisfying, relationship on which I embark, along with his all-too-revealing repertoire of proverbs and aphorisms, it should require no expert on the Freudian or Jungian psyche to conclude that—beneath all of Julius Blumenthal's hand-kissing and schtopping of traffic—lies a sexual misery not likely to make his only adopted son's future with women easy.

"I couldn't enter her," he says of his first wife, my dead mother, when I ask him, much later, why they never had children of their own. "I was never attracted to her," he says of my stepmother, an aesthetic and psychological predicament I can certainly commiserate with but that must—for a relatively robust and high-spirited man of fifty-five—have made for something less than conjugal bliss.

"*Warum eine Kuh kaufen wenn die Milch so billig ist?*"—"Why buy a cow when milk is so cheap?"—my father, who had purchased two less-than-entirely-satisfying cows himself, philosophizes on the subject of marriage. Clearly, as a dashing young traveling salesman with a chauffeur and an expense account of his own—a bit like the late Ricky Nelson's immortal "Traveling Man," my father, the decidedly unkosher young furrier, had often sated himself at the udders of cheap milk.

On the subject of visits to women's domiciles, the great traffic schtopper is hardly more sanguine. *"Wenn Du zum Weibe gehst,"* he prescribes, quoting that famous German feminist and Jew lover, Nietzsche, *"vergisse die Peitsche nicht."*—"When you go to see a woman, don't forget your whip." Restrained from spilling his seed more randomly by the existence of his two connubial cows—with the first of whom he was, apparently, impotent; with the second, merely unaroused—my father is hardly a man likely to look with great favor on his son's having a sex life.

My father's blessings and curses notwithstanding, however, Kendra and I are married the day after his pacemaker surgery, on the same deck in Virginia where I had, in heat, first proposed. Not a single member of my family is present, the rabbi and I being the only Jews among the congregated, the *huppah* held up at each corner by a lapsed Catholic. My Jungian analyst has made me promise to take the phone off the hook during the wedding, because—as he puts it—"I wouldn't put it past the son of a bitch to die just as you're saying 'I do.'"

But my father doesn't die, and I do say "I do," and I spend the next four months in complete and utter terror of Kendra's abandoning me, of her one day discovering what an empty accordion of longing has sent his litany of desire into the air around her.

Until, one morning, shortly after receiving a call from Harvard offering me the Briggs-Copeland Lectureship in Poetry, and now armed with the convenient excuse (for launching what I will come to suspect, later, was merely a preemptive strike) that I am now "too good" for my Midwestern *puella* of the lustful flesh, I turn in our bed and wake to find a mere human being—a human being onto whom I can now heap the anguish of my self-loathing and emptiness.

The truth is my wife has, from the outset, probably been too much of a lover—too much of a *man's* woman—and not enough of a mother for my mother-deprived psyche to tolerate. Hardly capable of leaving her alone for even an hour without fear that she will abandon me, I now find a more psychologically convenient—and more personally flattering—way out: I turn and, in my wife's shapely body, see once again my grandmother's sagging flesh, the disfigured, imagined body of my mother, the sad, divided language of cunts and wombs. I feel again that hunger no mere mortal can ever satisfy, the emptiness no other human being will ever cure. And, to the extent that I am present to begin with—and, no doubt, in some unconscious act of loyalty and obedience to my sexually enraged father—I slowly, during our first year in Cambridge, start to disappear . . . like a bird taking off for another continent, like a spent prick.

My wife, however—lucky her—is not someone designed for too much grieving. She's a girl destined to land on two good legs: She marries her divorce lawyer and moves to Jamaica Plain.

∾

8 | HALLOWED HALLS

Once there were twelve bodies

where we now sit. I know it,

because there are still husks

where those bodies once were,

empty carapaces

overtaken during the mind's coup,

begun as a benevolent dictatorship

but now gone wild

(as all power does)

with its sense of itself,

and so we are all seated here, captives

of bad wine and too much to eat,

and grow quietly to hate one another

for the pure tedium of what we have become—

repeating the word *tenure*

as if it were a mantra,

while the body,

that old anthropologist

(the one true scholar among us)

stirs restlessly

in its prison of pomp and conceptions,

as if to remind us

how brief its tenure is,

how transient its publications.

—"ACADEMIC SUPPERS," FROM *AGAINST ROMANCE* (1987)

SO HERE I AM, a first generation, German-raised American child, the student perpetually behind Warren Goldfarb (now, to my amazement—but not my surprise—chairman of Harvard's Philosophy Department), the conflicted son of furs and eggs, suddenly Briggs-Copeland Lecturer in Poetry at that citadel of immigrant dreams, Harvard University. How has someone like me—someone who can't even decide who his real parents are—come to deserve this?

"I feel like a fraud," another first-generation Jewish boy, a famous and widely respected scholar in my department, confesses to me in an unguarded moment at the Faculty Club during one of my first weeks in Cambridge. And if *he*—a deeply educated and internationally known scholar, a former professor at Columbia and Brandeis as well—feels illegitimate here, then what should *I*, the classic Jewish impostor, a trained lawyer who is now playing a kind of Jewish academic *Hauptmann von Köpenick* (a fictitious German worker who created a scandal by posing as a captain in the German army in the years before World War I) feel like?

I, too, feel like a fraud, of course—a fraud, for that matter, in spades. Sneaking off into dark corners and deserted bars, secreting myself in my office at night, I play a manic, fear-inspired game of catch-up: Hesiod, Horace, Dante, Petrarch, Ovid, Milton, Pope, Hazlitt, Lowell, Heaney (sitting, at that very moment, in the office next door)—a kind of who's who of *Everything Blumenthal Is Supposed to Know and Doesn't*. Not trusting that I have a legitimacy of my own to offer, I attempt, night and day, to mimic the legitimacy of those who have occupied these hallowed halls before me.

How, I wonder, can a man like myself—five feet ten inches of *echt* Ashkenazi blood—come to resemble Robert Lowell, at whose New England blueblood feet students once sat in my very office? What will my English Department colleagues—all those *éminences grises*—say if they realize that, right here in their midst, cruising around Harvard Yard with a membership to the Harvard Faculty Club in his pocket, is an impostor who has not only not read *Ulysses* but not even *A Portrait of the Artist as a Young Man*, a frustrated satyr who prefers the masturbations and ejaculations of Charles Bukowski to the cerebrations of William James, the various *Sexus*es and *Plexus*es of Henry Miller to Faulkner's *As I Lay Dying*?

"Friends?" a graduate teaching assistant in the English Department replies when I inquire about her social life. "People at Harvard don't have friends—they have appointments." *"Happy?"* another responds to a related question. "People at Harvard aren't *supposed* to be happy—they're supposed to be grateful."

But there *are*, of course, those, like my newly appointed colleague, the African-American scholar Henry Louis Gates, Jr., who are happy and comfortable at Harvard—some among them who even seem to have friends. Within them, it often seems to me, some inner voice has always been calling out: *Harvard, Harvard,* while, within me, the same voice has been whispering a more melancholy tune: *home, home.*

"Amid such plenty," my friend Twig asks one day over lunch at the Harvest in Harvard Square, "how can such ingratitude exist?" And it isn't, I have to admit, such a bad question: "Amid such plenty, how can such ingratitude exist?" Why is a man with a great teaching job at a wonderful institution, with fantastic students in a beautiful city, with marvelous friends and a history of sweet, generous, interesting lovers, so glum? Why am I so filled with disdain that I can't simply sit back and enjoy it? That I need, as a friend describes me, "to be always up on the diving board, and never relaxing on the lounge chair?" What's so wrong with the life the vast majority of people would gladly give the final sagging chromosome in their bored, uninspired bodies for even a small snippet of?

"Amid such plenty," Twig repeats, "how can such ingratitude exist?" And so I sit there, a Blumenthal né Gern, finally at Harvard—finally (perhaps) making my parents, whoever they are, proud. Making appointments, trying hard to be grateful.

Despite all this Harvard, somehow, feels eerily familiar: the parent for whom *no* achievement, *no* sacrifice, can ever be enough. Books, prizes, grants, awards—what good are they, when the person in the office beside you has just won the Nobel Prize?

During my first year in Cambridge, the Pulitzer Prize-winner in history, Alan Brinkley, is denied tenure by the university. A person wiser than myself in the ways of academia—like my nonfiction colleague with all of one, widely praised book, who departs for a chair at Oberlin after just two years—would absorb Brinkley's lesson and get wise as well: The thing to do at Harvard is to get in and then, just as quickly, to get out.

At Harvard, in fact, I quickly come to realize (but not appreciate) there are only two kinds of people: the kind, like my friend and colleague Seamus Heaney, whom Harvard needs, and the kind—like me—who need (or, at least, are perceived as somehow needing) Harvard.

It is the first rule of life at Harvard that the latter can never, short of a miracle, be transmogrified into the former, and one of the many ironies of my being there, it occurs to me, is that—just as only an institution with Harvard's clout and prestige could have afforded to take a chance on a relative "unknown" such as me—having come there (metaphorically) on bended knees, I will never, along with the rest of "my kind," be allowed—perhaps, I realize, because I am *incapable* thereof—to feel completely at home.

But, much as in the home of my parents—for whom, too, I will never make enough money; never marry a woman rich, or Jewish, enough; never pay sufficient "dividends" on their original investment—here, too, I, trapped by some feeling of relentless gratitude and unrequited love: I bleed, but I cannot commit the one act that has become my Hamletian bête noire: I cannot leave.

februar 26, '88

Dear Son,

Wir haben viel happiness mit your visit to us . . . wir danken you for all your LOVE STAY ONLY HEALTHY WITH US FOR MANNY YEARS TO COME. I hope that you had a good trip on Sunday—PLEASE TAKE CARE

OF YOU ON ALL YOUR WAYS—enclosed a POEM from our Rabbi's wife which she made to Viola (lady which I introduced to you in Temple on Friday evening . . . she was sitting on the table with us too. . . . Remember her?)

Mama und I found last week an unbeliefable Koincidence. . . . YOU WILL NOT BELIEVE IT, it is a mirakle. I was going through my old papers—death announcements from the AUFBAU from this time when our dear Mama Betzele passed away 9.25.59 may she rest in Sholem, und Mama and I discovered that the announcement of the dead of her dear husband #2 Fritz who died in the same week was on the <u>SAME PAGE</u> in the AUFBAU right next to our MAMA. . . . IS IT NOT A MIRAKLE??? Imagine, that these two people who had in the same week such a Schlemassel—such a bad luck und tragedie—would come to be married. . . . I think it is AMAZING.

Enclosed I have made for you a Kopie of the dead announcements. . . . I think it will be very interesting for you. KEEP IT PLEASE AS A MEMORIAL of our dear Betzele, und of this strange Koincidence. Mama she was <u>amazed</u> by this discovery . . . jawohl, the life is funny, is it not so dear son?

PLEASE REMEMBER: 3-7-88 Helen's 90th birthday. Please take <u>good care</u> of her wonderful <u>KIDDISH CUP</u>— hold it in honor, ein present it was for you from her . . . we owe to her many, many thanks—CUP has a great value, about $1,000—she was our dearest friend—<u>MAY SHE REST IN PIECE.</u>

SORRY—you forgot to take with you the whole big ENVELOPE filled with all LOVELY MEMORIES from Miss Eisenberg's time (you remember her??? she was your first girlfriend love. . . . O Jugend O Jugend was

warst Du so schön!!), and of many many other lovely
MEMORIES. ALL LOVE FROM MOM . . . she is too
busy with cleaning . . . you know how she is if she has a
cleaning women? <u>Meschugge</u> . . . let her work.

LOVE,
DADY

I unfold the Xerox contained in the envelope. On it is a tattered obituary page from the Friday, October 9, 1959 edition of
the *Aufbau*. Staring up at me, in large boldface letters, is the following black-bordered announcement:

**On October 1, 1959, following a brief, severe illness
shortly after the completion of his 60th year of life,
my dearly beloved husband, son-in-law, our dear
brother-in-law, uncle, nephew and cousin**

FRITZ KAHN
(formerly Mannheim)

passed from us. In deep mourning:

**ALICE KAHN verw. Guggenheim
geb. Bernheimer**

**25–22 82nd Street
Jackson Heights 70, L.I., N.Y.**

**I simultaneously wish to thank those who sent them
for their much-appreciated expressions of sympathy.**

Directly catty-corner from the above announcement, on the same page, is the following piece of additional good news:

Our dearly beloved wife and mami, our faithfully caring daughter and sister, sister-in-law, aunt and cousin

BETTY BLUMENTHAL
geb. Gern

was forever taken from us on September 25, 1959.
All who knew her will be capable of measuring our loss and pain.

In the name of the grieving survivors:

JULIUS BLUMENTHAL
801 West 181 Street
New York 33, N.Y.—Vineland, N.J.

I stare silently at the twin obituaries for some time before folding and replacing the Xerox in the envelope. By now there is little surprise left in my father's unearthing of various "unbeliev-able Koincidences" and "mirakles." There is, in fact, beginning to be a terrible logic to it all, a kind of order.

I open the bottom drawer of my desk and drop the letter onto the long-festering pile of letters and obituaries my father has sent me over the years. Then I do the only thing I can think of as I survey the long history of coincidences and miracles I seem to have inherited as the birthright of that earliest exchange of which I was a part. I put my head down on the desk and begin to laugh uncontrollably.

Then I start to cry.

My parents are coming to Cambridge to visit me for the first time since I left home for college almost twenty-five years ago.

"Why don't you come see *me* for a change?" I say to my father when he asks—in a tone suitable for addressing a twelve-year-old—"So, when are we going to see our dear son again . . . for your dady's birthday?"

For some reason I like the thought of having my parents on my own turf. "It's just another typical parental power fuck," my friend Twig intones. "If parents never come to visit you in *your* home, they never have to acknowledge the fact that you're a grown-up."

My parents' home, indeed, *has* always been the focal point of my stepmother's relentless neurotic power. Throughout my late adolescence and early adulthood, whenever I have come to visit, she covers all the furniture in plastic, then fastens a Christo-like wrapping of tattered white sheets to the wall (lending an even more funereal pallor to their already bleak and lifeless abode) because, as she puts it, "You get the walls dirty when you lean against them."

What's more, there's never quite enough hot water for a shower (*"Das heisse Wasser ist sooo* expensive"), she habitually follows me around the house turning off the lights ("Doesn't the glare bother you?"), and it's virtually impossible to have even a moment's uninterrupted peace to talk on the phone ("Mikey, it's time for dinner") or read a book ("Can you read the stock market listings to me? My eyes are so bad"). So having my parents finally come to a place where *I* at least have some control of the choreography seems not at all a bad idea.

Apart from their getting on the wrong flight and my being unable to find them when they arrive at Logan Airport, the three of us spend a relatively pleasant weekend, eating at restaurants, walking in the Boston Public Garden, and meeting some of my Cambridge friends.

"Such a pleasure to meet you, Miss——," my father greets every woman I introduce him to, kissing her hand as he speaks. "God loves you, and so do I."

"Your father," my colleague Gail whispers to me after being subjected to this treatment, "is the cutest thing that ever lived."

"I know. God loves you, and so does he."

By the time I take my parents back to Logan Airport for the return trip to La Guardia, I feel a relatively benign, if not downright successful, weekend drawing to a close. Given their by-now-legendary penchant for making the wrong turn, getting on the wrong plane, or attending the wrong funeral, when we arrive at the airport I decide to walk them directly onto the Eastern Airlines Shuttle. Escorting them to seats 10D and 10E near the front of the plane, I recognize several local acquaintances, including a psychiatrist friend from Cambridge Hospital, already seated on the plane. ("My parents," I whisper almost apologetically as we pass. "Just up for the weekend.")

"Well," I kiss them both on the cheek as they settle into their seats, "I better get going before the plane takes off. . . . Thanks so much for coming." I start toward the exit, feeling a bit like an adolescent boy who has just set off a firecracker and wants to split the scene before it explodes.

"Ein Moment!" I suddenly hear the familiar sound of my father's voice, and—to my amazement—turn to see him standing in the aisle and reaching into his jacket pocket. Before I can utter a syllable in protest, out comes the familiar, cologne-soaked white handkerchief and Hohner B-flat harmonica.

"Dad!" I try frantically to abort what is about to happen. *"Not here—please!"*

But there's no stopping my eighty-five-year-old father. To the delight and near-hysteria of the 200-odd passengers aboard the shuttle, he raises the white, cologne-soaked handkerchief in his right hand, places the harmonica against his mouth with the left, and—waving the handkerchief wildly at me as I flee toward the cabin door—begins playing *"Auf Wiedersehen."*

Flushed with embarrassment, I run out the airport door and race to my car. I, for one, don't want to be pronounced dead before my time has come. I don't want to be welcomed prematurely into the dark, like Lotte Baumgartner, while a light still burns within me. I realize that—though I, too, wouldn't mind one day being an eighty-five-year-old man who still plays the harmonica—I don't want the only song in my repertoire to be *"Auf Wiedersehen."*

I don't want every tune I sing to be another word for goodbye.

A friend has read an interesting article somewhere: Old people with dogs are less likely to be egocentric and self-involved.

"Why don't you get them a dog?" he suggests on the subject of my parents and their perpetual medical crises. "Maybe that will help get them off your back."

I remember, with a profoundly muted affection, my stepmother's beloved fox terrier, Ami, the one living creature whom she has, to my knowledge, ever shown any genuine tenderness, and whose death distracted her from her own medical and pecuniary woes. *Who knows?* What worked once, I allow myself to hope, might work again.

So, a Harvard English professor with lots of free time on his hands, I begin working the phones, making random calls to veterinarians and dog lovers around the country. What dog, I ask, would be most suited to two eighty-five-year-olds obsessed mostly with their own dwindling health and financial portfolios? There is relative unanimity, it seems, as to the answer: a Lhasa apso.

Now, the only remaining problem: Where, on an assistant professor's salary, will I find such a—hopefully already fully house-trained—beast? I begin calling around to various dog pounds and animal shelters in and around New England, until— *voilà!*—at the Humane Society of Providence, Rhode Island, located a scant hour and a half from my own Cambridge door, I locate a year-old fully fixed and house-trained Lhasa, available to me, with shots, for a bargain price of sixty-two dollars, straight cash, if I hurry right down.

Barely ninety minutes later I'm at the door of the Humane Society, and—following a relatively meager amount of paperwork in which I swear to administer regular medical treatment and never, *never* to abandon the poor animal—I am the proud and, I hope, very temporary owner of a filthy white Lhasa, whom I immediately dub, in honor of his beloved and deceased predecessor, Ami der Zweite.

Within another hour and a half, we're back in Cambridge, and Ami der Zweite is in my bathtub, soaped up with avocado shampoo. My parents are spending the summer at their rented cottage in Fleischmanns, New York, and tomorrow—Surprise! Surprise!— I will make the six-hour drive and show up with their new roommate, upon whom, rather than me, or so I fantasize, they will shower their abundant excess neuroses and negative karma.

When we arrive late the next afternoon and I unleash Ami the Second into my stepmother's not exactly welcoming arms, the reaction is pretty much the one I had expected—and hoped would rapidly abate. *"Ach!"* she exclaims, her features squinching up into the prunelike configuration I have long associated with a downturn in the Dow Jones. *"Ein Hund . . . was sollen wir denn machen mit einem Hund?"* "A dog . . . what do we need a dog for?"

My father, on the other hand, responds to the new arrival by whipping out his harmonica and playing a quick rendition of *"Du, Du, liegst mir im Herzen,"* and then chasing the poor animal—insofar as an eighty-five-year-old man with a pacemaker is capable of chasing anything—around the cottage, trying to administer a kiss. It is going, I realize, inhaling deeply, to be something of a getting-to-know-you phase. Ami der Zweite, for his part, looks confused and terrified.

I've budgeted my own maximum tolerance level for my parents—ten hours, not including sleep time—for this visit, and, besides, I have to teach a prosody class the next afternoon, so I just grit my teeth and tell myself things are guaranteed to get better . . . the dog, everyone has assured me, is the *perfect* companion for two old, ailing, neurotic German Jews.

But two days later, when I'm back in Cambridge already filled with pride at the rapidity and cleverness of my canine achievement, the phone rings, with my stepmother's voice on the other end.

"Du musst diesen Hund sofort wieder abholen," her nearly hysterical voice informs me. "You have to pick this dog up again right away." Apparently my father has been chasing the dog around the cottage for most of the two days—and then halfway into the village after his leash got untied from a lounge chair—until, now, the ever-ailing man is experiencing chest pains once again (my fault, of course), and (the inevitable threat): Who *knows* what might happen if I don't get the dog out of the house right away?

And so, some twenty-four hours later, after frenzied calls to local vets and dog shelters in the Fleischmanns area, I'm back at my parents' cottage, and, an hour later, Ami der Zweite—soon, no doubt, to be renamed Bobo—is a terrified inhabitant of the office of Dr. Mark Twillmann, D.V.M., of Margaretsville, New York.

I, meanwhile, have to get back to Cambridge to teach my Thursday class on the villanelle. Neither man nor animal nor saint nor God, I realize en route, can help me shoulder the burden of my parents: They are mine, I realize, for the rest of their lives.

~

9 | AGAIN THROUGH NEW EYES

Yes, this too shall come, at some difficult turn

and, when you emerge from it, it shall seem

as if the body of flesh were the metaphor of all light

on which the dark bird of love has come home to roost,

and the city of angels shall be the city of dust,

and the dreams of the young child who flew

and the man who fell from the uprootedness of air

shall be one, and nowhere will be somewhere

and the *else* a *you*.

—"SOMEWHERE ELSE," FROM *AGAINST ROMANCE* (1987)

DURING MY FORTIETH YEAR I return to my aunt and uncle's now overgrown and no longer egg-producing New Jersey farm and sleep in the same bed in which, twenty-three years earlier, my grandmother died.

She had died miserably—blind, lamed by a stroke, following her daughter into the grave by seven years in that terrible inversion of the life cycle in which a mother survives to bury her own child. The day she died, I—not realizing she was so close to the end—took my driver's test in Queens, rather than go to the place of the egg and watch an old woman die.

But now, a grown man, I am sleeping in her bed. I am sleeping in the room my father Julius built for her almost thirty years ago, after she was evicted from my parents' apartment by the advent of my stepmother. And I realize, as I lie there gazing up at the ceiling, inhaling the long-gone scent of my grandmother and of chickens and of eggs, that—for my grandmother, at least—the place of the egg was the place of death, and the place of the fur was the place of life.

I realize that it was the life of fur, not the life of the egg, that rescued her from Nazi Germany, that it was the life of fur that nourished and gave her a family and a home and a place of light until that fateful morning when her daughter's dead body was taken from that apartment.

I realize, as I lie there, that—for the old woman who died in that same bed twenty-three years earlier—the place of the egg was a place of darkness and loneliness, not a place of life. And now I am here—at the crest of my life's curve, the midway mark—lying on her deathbed, in the place where, until the time of my mother's death, the lives of my two star-crossed families intersected.

I am lying, in fact, on the cusp of life and death. So when I dream, that night, that the birds descend from the trees and are walking along the ground eating from my hand, I know that I am dreaming the dream of life and death, and that I, too, might survive that bed of death to rise once more into the light.

I remember the first time I ever mentioned my dreams of

becoming a bird. I was sitting in my Jungian analyst's office in Washington, describing how I had taken off from the ground and flown toward an owl-like creature sitting on a wire. I remember how good the dream felt, how light and transcendent.

"It seems to me it's a dream about not being grounded," my analyst responded, puncturing my bubble of contentment. But who, in his right mind, I thought at the time, *wants* to be grounded? After all, didn't people *fall* to the ground (as, I later realized, they *fell* in love)? Didn't things *grind* to a halt? Wasn't a thing that had run *aground* something broken, defective?

Yet, over the years, the bird-wishes of my dreams diminished. The animals all turned terrestrial, becoming foragers and ground dwellers. The world became populated by trees, where once only birds had lighted on telephone wires strung between poles. Just days before arriving in New Jersey again, I dreamed of walking with my wife in some African savanna, looking for a tree to name after myself—a tree named Michael Blumenthal. Maybe, I realize, it isn't a man's place to resemble a bird. Maybe it's a man's place to resemble a tree.

Sitting in my aunt and uncle's living room, on the same sofa where I once spent nights nestled between the bookends of my two families, I gaze around at the photographs on the walls and cabinets. There are my biological sister, her husband, and their two teenage daughters; then my biological brother and his wife and their two adopted children. Then there's a picture of my dead mother and my dead grandmother. As I look around, my actual mother—the woman from whose living, intact body I slid into the world—sits in the green upholstered chair beside me.

But I, Michael Charles Blumenthal né Charles Michael Gern am almost nowhere to be found. Not in my "parents'" house— with its ubiquitous photos of my stepmother's two dead husbands, my own dead mother, and a single photo of myself, aged about twelve (where, I realize, he would have liked to keep me forever) on the table of my father's study—and not here. I am the missing link, the one who's been given away, the one who—even now, at almost forty—continues to vacillate between the fur and the egg. There has, in fact, I suddenly realize, been only *one* venue where my own shining face has received star billing: on top of Helen's piano at 801 West 181st Street, apartment 29.

"I have always wanted another father," I once wrote in a poem. "You *have* another father," my psychoanalyst reminded me at the time. And sure enough I do—sitting right there, in the rocking chair in front of me, the sliver of bullet still embedded in his arm. The truth is, I have had two of everything—two mothers, two fathers, two siblings, two versions of manhood, two homes. And all I want is to have *one*—to have the womb and the cunt, the fur and the egg, living and dying, in a single place.

Shortly after returning from my visit to Vineland, I go for the first time to visit my mother's grave, located about an hour from New York in Beth El cemetery in Westwood, New Jersey.

I drive through the cemetery gate and, after asking directions to burial plot "F-11," park my car, and walk up the hill toward where the guard has directed me. Soon I am standing near her grave, the one I never visited as a child.

But now I am in a man's body. I look out over the low hills of New Jersey, over the vast valley of stone slabs . . . white as her empty bed was white, white as the pail into which she began to pour back her life. In all directions, names from my childhood— Heilbronn, Schoenbach, Hertz, Meyer, Hirsch, Guttman, Monat, Rosenthal—call out from their cold litany of stone, old *davener*s reunited once more in a synagogue of hedges, a vast democracy of marble and flowers.

Then, suddenly—just off to my left, on an aisle —I find her:

BETTY BLUMENTHAL

nee Gern

1907   1959

I find her, mother of no body, mother of affections but not of flesh, right beside my grandmother, who—in one of those wild reversals that has made a kind of myth of my family—followed her here:

JOHANNA GERN

nee Neumark

1876–1966

Suddenly I understand why I have become what I am: a man who needs to bear himself into the world each day by speaking his life. I see how the tidal surge of grief needs to come ashore, how the force that drove no water for so long needs to well up inside the tangible body of flesh until a new wave can rise behind it. I see how, for almost thirty years, I have dipped the wafer of my grief into my mother's dying and partaken of it; how, left in the world to save her, I cannot save even myself.

I place my black prayer book against her headstone. Something very much like speech rises from the water behind her. I recite the words I never had the chance to speak in her name: *Yisgadal v'yiskadash sh'may rabbow* . . .

I weep my mother dead. And she is dead.

∾

A few days later I am sleeping in the basement of my parents' house in Queens, in almost the exact spot where my stepmother's ninety-nine-year-old mother Lisette fell down the darkened stairway and died some twenty-five years earlier.

Suddenly I wake in the middle of the night, hearing a commotion in the bedroom above. I turn on the lamp on the night table and stare at the clock. It is 4:00 A.M.

Naked, I run upstairs toward the faint light in my parents' bedroom. A small old man in a blue bathrobe, my father, is standing beside the bed. He is cradling his wife's head—a toothless head, with caved-in cheeks and closed eyes, that hardly seems among the living—against his body with one arm. In the other hand he holds a thin blue pail. My stepmother is retching into the pail. *"Ach, mir ist's so schlecht,"* she moans, heaving in an eerily familiar manner over the pail. "Oh, I am so sick."

I stand for a moment, transfixed, staring at the two old people before me. For a few seconds, I can't move. "What's the matter?" I finally ask.

"Ach, mir ist's so schlecht," my stepmother repeats the words. A torrent of vomit spouts from her, missing the pail and landing on the bedsheet. *"Ach, mir ist's so schlecht."*

I walk over to the side of the bed beside my father and take my stepmother's head in my hands. It feels like a dead weight against my palms. As she continues vomiting into the pail, small rivulets of spittle flow down the side of her mouth and over the lip of blue plastic.

"Let me hold her—she's too heavy for you," I say to my father. The old man, trembling in his bathrobe, backs away. I pick my stepmother up in my arms and set her in a chair beside the bed so that she can sit upright. I notice as I carry her that her green nightgown has risen over the top of her legs, revealing mounds of sagging blue and red flesh, reminding me of my grandmother's body. The air around her has the faint odor of rotten apples. Though she lies impassive as a stone in my arms, she seems light to me now, as though not even the weight of the dead and the dying can overpower me any longer.

My father, meanwhile, has gone into the kitchen to make tea. When he returns, I kneel beside the limp old woman, feeding her the tea in spoonfuls. She inhales it, making loud slurping sounds. Still naked, I stand in the center of the room watching my two nearly ninety-year-old parents. I feel a sense of calm coupled with disbelief, a feeling of sadness bordering on detachment. I reach behind the closed door to find my father's other bathrobe. It's too small, and, when I try to put it on, the sleeves reach only two thirds of the way down my arms, just past the elbow.

Finally my stepmother stops vomiting and falls into a nearly comatose sleep. "Why don't you lie down—there's nothing more you can do now," I say to my father. He does as I tell him. I stand at the foot of the bed and gaze at the two helpless people sprawled before me. I suddenly think again of the dream I had several months before. "Poor Meyer," I spoke in the dream, putting my arm around a blind man walking toward me on the street. "Poor Meyer."

My stepmother is starting to snore in the chair. Her head has fallen entirely to one side. Beside her on the radiator sits the blue pail. The only other sound in the room is the faint humming of the fluorescent ceiling light. Slowly I walk over to the chair where she is sleeping. I place my left hand gently below her head, my right arm just below her thighs, and lift her almost lifeless body of flesh and bones back onto the bed. Then I prop the head of this woman who has never wanted to call me son against a pillow. I place the down comforter over her and turn out the reading light mounted on the headboard.

"Go back to sleep," I say to my father, who lies on the bed, nervously gazing at the weakened body of his second wife. "She'll be better in the morning."

"*Jawohl*," my father replies limply. "*Was ein* blessing that our son is here on this night . . . like the Messiah, our Savior. God loves you, and so do I."

"Yes," I repeat under my breath. "Like the Messiah, your Savior." I turn off the light and back out of the room toward the basement stairs. Slowly I close the door behind me and go downstairs to bed.

I gaze once more at the clock beside the bed. It is 5:20 A.M., March 1, 1989. I turn off the light on the night table beside me. I take in a deep, almost mournful breath that I don't release for a very long time. I feel a strange sense of relief, almost of calm, as I close my eyes.

Then I fall asleep.

∾

10 | REBIRTHS

Say you have finally invented a new story
of your life. It is not the story of your defeat
or of your impotence and powerlessness
before the large forces of wind and accident.
It is not the sad story of your mother's death
or of your abandoned childhood. It is not,
even, a story that will win you the deep
initial sympathies of the benevolent goddesses
or the care of the generous, but a story
that requires of you a large thrust
into the difficult life, a sense of plenitude
entirely your own . . .

—"THE NEW STORY OF YOUR LIFE,"

FROM *AGAINST ROMANCE* (1987)

IT IS HARDLY TWO MONTHS later when, while taking a much-needed "break" from my tour group during a brief trip to the Galápagos Islands, I meet Isabelle, the woman who is to become my second wife, at an outdoor café in Quito, Ecuador.

It's not, in fact, her I first notice, but the woman she is with—a dark-haired, dark-skinned woman I am sure is Ecuadorian. Starting a conversation with the two of them on the pretense of needing directions, I discover, to my surprise, that they are French, and about to take a trip to the nearby Indian village of Otavalo, which I had wanted to visit as well.

"Est-ce que tu veux venir avec nous?" Annick, the dark-haired one, asks in French. Her companion, a more-or-less gray-haired woman in a yellow sweatshirt and purplish pants, seems far more interested in reading her mail than in talking to me. Having no other plans for the day, and being not at all averse to a small side trip in the company of two rather attractive, single Frenchwomen, I quickly agree, and head off to my hotel to pack an overnight bag.

During the hour-long bus ride to Otavalo, I can feel my attention—in part, simply because she speaks better English than her companion—shifting from dark-haired Annick to her graying friend, Isabelle. There's something about her shy smile, her kindly eyes, her knowing gaze—even her consolingly gentle voice and endearing French accent—that I find more and more attractive as the bus crosses the equator toward Otavalo. By the time we finally register (in two separate rooms) at the small, inexpensive *pension* the women have located in their *Guide de Routard*, both Isabelle and I seem to have the same idea in mind: All it takes, later that night, is the excuse of needing—just as Annick happens to be leaving their room—to borrow a toothbrush.

～

About a month later—after I have returned from my brief trip to the Galápagos, and after Isabelle and I, a couple by now, have also returned from an "exploratory" trip to Boston—we are again lying in bed in a small village outside Quito. I am gazing into her eyes. With my right hand I trace a path around the tight little nests of wrinkles on the sides of her mouth. With the other hand I part the wisps of gray hair that fall flat against her forehead, wanting to see more of her face, to know her more deeply.

I realize she reminds me of no one in particular, yet of something very close, very personal, very familiar. She reminds me of life and of death. Of the mother into whose living face I once gazed, and the mother into whose near-dead, glassy eyes I stared hours before she was carried from my life forever. I feel, in this bed with her, very much at home. "Home," I remember a line of Robert Frost's, "is the place where, when you have to go there, they have to take you in."

It's not so much passion I feel with Isabelle as a kind of tenderness and sense of security. Some words I wrote earlier about my father's marriage to my mother might, in fact, have served me well here. "And what did it matter that he felt little of the passion he had felt for Claire Haas for this not exceptionally pretty Jewish girl who shyly reached her hand toward him, hardly daring to look up? It wasn't, after all, passion he was after any longer, but safety—not really a wife he had been looking for all these years of kissing women's hands, but a mother—a mother at whose living breasts he had never fed, into whose living eyes he had never had a chance to gaze."

But, on this particular night at least, I feel Isabelle shudder with pleasure as I rise, pressing myself more deeply inside her. *"Te amo,"* I whisper. *"Te amo mucho."* Never speak in heat, I hear my own advice reverberating again. But I now realize that heat may be the *only* place from which men and women speak of the true longing in their hearts—of wishes as deep and fundamental as the wish for cure, or the wish for a happy ending.

"*Te amo también,*" she answers. There is a long moment during which we gaze silently into each other's eyes. I move my right hand along the wide curves of her hips, feel my scent mingling with hers. Outside there is a rustling in the treetops, the summer breeze, and the scent of honeysuckle coalescing into the bright morning light. It sounds to me, from within that narcissistic haze new lovers are prone to, like applause, a beneficence of light and air that has gathered entirely for our benefit. "*Que bonita es la luz en los arboles,*" I whisper, circling Isabelle's mouth with my hand. "*Que felicidad.*"

"*Si,*" she agrees, puckering her lips against me, kissing my fingers. "*Que felicidad.*"

I look again into Isabelle's face. I feel a familiar tingling in my loins, a near-numbness at the tip of my penis. "I'm not sure it's safe," I hear her say halfheartedly as I close my eyes and give in to the feeling of pleasure and sadness that draws my entire body toward its center. I feel her, too, submit, giving in to some force larger than will or control or foresight or rationality, a force both transcending and including us.

Soon we are both moaning in our separate languages into the morning air. I feel a sudden loss of myself, of the tangible world in which there is so much struggle and pain and pleasure and mystery between our days of living and dying.

And then—both knowing and not knowing what I am about to do, led on by something larger than thought, more generous than reason, more dangerous than hope, more naive than experience—I shoot a wet, warm stream of my living seed high up into that dark womanly place (the place of the egg) where the yearning for light first meets its maker and begins to dance.

∾

"I don't think we should go through with it."

It's a Sunday afternoon in early October, and Isabelle and I are sitting in the café of Boston's Museum of Fine Arts, where we have finally decided to have *the* talk concerning what to do about our pregnancy. Some two months have now passed since that morning in Quito when, just before first leaving for Boston, we went to the clinic near the Old City, opened the tattered envelope with Isabelle's name on it, and read the words *"Positivo para embarazada"* scribbled on the scrap of paper inside.

I have been thinking, since our returning to Cambridge more than a month earlier, long and hard about what to do about this potential human being—my child—that is beginning to make its way toward life in Isabelle's belly. "I think," I continue, "that we'd be better off waiting until we know each other a bit better—until, you know, our relationship is on more solid ground and we're really able to *choose* whether or not to do something as dramatic and irrevocable as having a child." I notice that the very word *choose*—that fickle verb I have so long yearned to make my own— makes me nervous and uncertain, as though I am talking about something I don't really understand the meaning of.

"After all," I go on, trying to evade the look of sadness and disappointment I see crawling onto Isabelle's face, "we've hardly known each other four months. We must in fact," I continue, trying to make a bad joke, "have one of the shortest meeting-to-conception times in the history of romance."

"Yes," Isabelle, suddenly very much the provincial French Catholic girl, looks into my eyes as she speaks, slowly and thoughtfully. "But the fact is, Gringo, that this child already exists. There's no changing that or pretending it's not true."

I, already a veteran of three abortions, know she's at least partially right—there is no pretending that this child, or whatever it now is, doesn't exist—or that there will be no cost to me, or to life, in putting an end to its existence. Doesn't it seem, after all, that there is something in me that *wants* to be born, that *wants* to give life? And here, at this very moment, seated before me in the shape of a flesh-and-blood woman—it is.

"It's not," I continue stubbornly, in what I already suspect to be a half lie, "that I might not want to have a child with you when a better, more reasonable, time comes. It's just that we hardly know each other, to be perfectly honest—and we haven't exactly been having an easy time of it since we got back here from Ecuador." Isabelle and I, since returning to my "real" life in Cambridge, have had more than our share of misunderstandings, she—understandably enough—not finding the situation of being pregnant and in someone else's country particularly easy to adjust to; I, in turn, not finding her quiet nature and essentially nonverbal personality particularly compatible with the kind of life I live here.

"Yes," she agrees, "that's true. But the truth is also that there may never be a 'better' or a 'right' time—especially for someone with a past like yours."

"So what do *you* want to do?" I finally ask, fatigued by my own ruminations on the subject. There's a long silence as Isabelle continues gazing into my eyes, slowly stirring her yet-untouched cup of coffee.

"It's a child of passion," she finally offers up, slowly but firmly. "He was conceived in a moment of love."

"What does *that* have to do with anything?" I sense that I already know the answer. I am suddenly trembling.

"It's a good omen for someone's life." Isabelle, for the first time in our rather somber conversation, smiles slightly. "*You*, for example, would probably have had a happier life if you had been a child of passion." She pauses a long time before continuing, perhaps knowing that—in a conflict between an ambivalent person and an unambivalent one—it's always the unambivalent one who gets their way.

"So I'm ready to have it."

I am now, for the first time in my life, confronted with a woman who, despite my expressed wishes to the contrary, seems ready and willing to give birth to my child. For my own generation—the college-educated, pill-liberated children of Abbie Hoffman and Gloria Steinem—the prevention (or, at least, the termination) of even unilaterally unwanted pregnancies has been a staple, if not the centerpiece, of our self-actualizing creed. And though—given the fact of my conflicted paternity and feelings of being overwhelmed by my suffocating, geriatric parents—there dwells within me a substantial wish for a child of my own, this, somehow, seems not the time, or the way, I want it to happen.

My psychoanalyst, on the other hand—a kind and decent man whom I haven't seen in months and who, when I *was* seeing him, conveyed the belief that becoming a father would constitute a cure for all my earthly ills—has only a few words to say about my dilemma, when I rush to his office to discuss the situation.

"As I listen to your story," he says, pausing in his soft brown chair to scratch his rather Freudian beard, "I simply feel like asking, 'What are you waiting for?'"

My Harvard writer colleagues have two related reactions when I tell them I am going to have a child. "Aren't you," a woman novelist I work with, divorced and childless, asks, *"terrified?"* "I never thought," her male counterpart, a novelist from the Midwest who is about to have his second child, says to me in the hallway, "you were the type."

My analyst, a would-be novelist himself, seems to have another view of the matter: "You would," he has said to me on a number of occasions, "no doubt make a terrific father."

They are, of course, *all* right (the answer, I've found, as on multiple-choice exams, is usually "all of the above"): I *am* terrified, though I don't want to admit it, and I've clearly never *been*—whatever that may be—"the type." And I *would*, I'm often convinced, make a terrific father.

But all those subjunctives and conditionals are soon to be history, in any event: Though there may, in a minute, be time, as T. S. Eliot suggests, "for decisions and revisions which a minute will reverse," *this* decision has already been made—if not by me, then by life: Inside Isabelle's womb, already in the sixth month of his prenatal life, my son is busily making his way toward the light of this world.

Isabelle has become so heavy with the weight of what has been growing inside her that she can't get in or out of the bathtub without my help. I put my arms around the huge girth of her waist, feel her give herself over entirely to my arms.

"I think he already knows the sound of your voice," she says, suddenly smiling. "He can even hear you from the womb."

"How could he miss?" I joke, gazing at her distended belly. "I talk so damned much."

Falling asleep that night, I think to myself that it may very well be my last as a son who isn't also a father, the last time I can ask the question, Which father would you kill? Tomorrow, perhaps, there will be a child—*my* child—who won't, I hope, need to face the divided paternity of two fathers, who won't need to live his life in a chasm between blood and feeling. Tomorrow, perhaps, the sins of the fathers will no longer be so clearly visited upon the sons. But, at the same time—as I should, no doubt, have been that night nine months earlier when I had allowed my seed to spurt, unimpeded, into Isabelle's body—I am also terrified.

Nonetheless I allow myself to be eased into a deep sleep by the sound of Isabelle's breathing beside me. But it's only minutes later when I wake to a gasping sound from beside me on the bed, and a calm but firm hand on the back of my neck. I turn to see Isabelle heaving with a convulsive shudder that shakes the entire bed.

"It's happening," she stammers as her body quiets itself momentarily.

"Just relax," I say, jumping from the bed. A thrill—of both fright and anticipation—surges through my entire body, like the thrill of skiing fast downhill, or of making love to a new lover, of both control and abandonment. "I'm just going to take a shower and call the midwife."

As I disappear toward the bathroom, Isabelle grasps the wooden bed frame tightly with her hands and stares over at the digital clock on the night table. *Three minutes,* she times the space between the contractions that shake her entire body upward and almost off the bed. *Just three minutes.*

As I reenter the room, I hear a popping sound coming from beneath her abdomen. Water suddenly begins pouring out of her, soaking the bed in a bath of amniotic fluid.

"It won't be long now," she whispers shyly as I go to cover the plastic pad we had put on the bed with a new set of sheets. "No," I reply, feeling my breath get short. "It won't be long."

The words are hardly out of my mouth when what we both suddenly realize have been only mild contractions are transformed into all-consuming spasms. ("The most intense feeling of my life, Gringo, except maybe for death," Isabelle will say to me later. "It was like a shuddering of my entire being.") Seeing her face turn a near-crimson as she gasps for breath, I drop the sheets and run over to hold her.

"Let's go," I say. "I think I'd rather not have this be a home delivery."

By the time we get to the car and are heading toward the hospital in Malden, the contractions are coming almost every minute. I look at my watch for the first time. It's 3:45 A.M. Isabelle is squeezing my right hand so intensely I can't feel the blood circulating in my fingers.

The midwife is waiting for us when we arrive at the hospital, and leads us to a room on the first floor. "Just relax," she whispers. "It's no big deal. You're just going to have a baby."

The sun is just starting to rise. A wash of yellow light pours into the room as we enter. A nurse enters too, carrying a tray of apple juice and ice cubes.

"Don't push," the midwife keeps saying to Isabelle, who is now lying on her back on the bed, both knees in the air. "Don't push—you'll hurt the baby."

My hand just starting to be unnumbed from the force of her squeezing, I stand near the foot of the bed and gaze into the pulsating, near-mystical darkness of Isabelle's vagina, her cunt, and her womb. More blood than I ever imagined could be produced by a single living human is now pouring out of her. Not even the occasionally politically correct ideologist who lives somewhere inside me can deny it: It is hardly a pretty sight. In the midst of it all, I think I see a small, fleshy tuft of hair moving toward me.

"He's starting to crown," the midwife, remarkably calm through it all, says. "You need to start pushing now." The nurse, meanwhile, is holding a mirror over the side of the bed between Isabelle's legs so she can see the baby's emerging head. Her eyes seem to be leaping out of her skull like those of a fish gasping for oxygen. There is, she says, an unbelievable burning sensation between her legs.

"I can't do it! I can't do it! I can't push anymore!" she screams, as I stretch my right hand out to stroke her hair. But for the fact that I know who this woman is, I would scarcely recognize the seemingly possessed creature whose otherworldly moans now fill the room.

"Now's the time to think of our secret place," I say, whispering the name of the Ecuadorian volcano we climbed the previous summer. I haven't eaten for some twenty-four hours, but feel as if I am in a complete warp of time and space. In a kind of controlled stupefaction, I gaze at the emerging mass of pinkish skull and hair that is about to slide out of my wife's body. As my two hands reach, almost of their own volition, forward, I notice it is 1:00 P.M.—almost the exact time at which, more than forty years before, I myself had been born.

Suddenly, like a small, greased piglet, a tiny, breathless body—covered in blood, slime, mucus, and other effluvia so unmentionably grotesque that I will never find the words to describe them—slides into my waiting hands. Through the descending haze of my own tears and my own mute voice, in a motion so sweeping and natural, so organically whole as to seem planned and executed by the gods themselves, I—the man of the impotent father and sad, dying mother—arc the body of my blood-born son upward toward the waiting arms and intact breasts of his living mother, his life.

A few weeks after the birth of my son, I fly to New York to visit my parents, both of whom aren't doing well healthwise, to help with some personal details and shopping. My father has been diagnosed with cerebral arteriosclerosis, which seems to render his always scattered and repetitive mental functioning all the worse, and my stepmother, whose lifelong osteoporosis has, in recent years, made her spinal column resemble a camel's hump more than a human back, has broken yet another vertebra and is flat on her back.

My parents have greeted the birth of their only grandson with a funereal sobriety, so I am, as usual, prepared for the worst when I pass through my usual point of entry—the basement—into the customary darkness of my stepmother's house.

The first day of my visit includes a fruitless session with a social worker, through whom I am trying to secure some domestic help for my parents. I hope, ever cautiously, to flee the premises without any further mishaps the next afternoon when, to my shocked amazement, a small spill of water I cause while taking a shower throws first my stepmother, then my eighty-six-year-old father, into a tirade of abuse ("You bring nothing but unhappiness into our life—and then you marry another poor *goyische Schmatte*") so deranged and inexplicable that I resolve merely to use the "water off a duck's back" approach my psychiatrist has advocated and drive my father, as asked, to the wholesale kosher butcher's on the Lower West Side before I catch the two o'clock train.

We drive in silence across the Triboro Bridge and down the FDR Drive, I trying with all my human willpower to keep my eyes directly on the road and ignore the deranged verbal geyser seated on my right. When we finally arrive at Chambers Street, my father gets out of the car, where he is enthusiastically greeted by a small cluster of overweight men in bloodied smocks, with whom he shakes hands as though preparing to address a state troopers' convention.

"Shalom, Mr. Yarmolinsky. Shalom, Fred," my father serenades the two men, as he follows them into the warehouse. "God loves you, and so do I." He returns some fifteen minutes later, this time with two younger butchers in tow, carting four large bags of kosher steaks, lamb shanks, soup bones, brisket, and breasts of veal, which my parents will store in their basement freezer.

"God bless you, *Landsman*," my father says, kissing the larger of the two men on his bloodstained hand as he gets back into the car, "God loves you, and so do I."

A moment later we're driving silently up Eighth Avenue when my father suddenly turns to me. "Let's stop and have a coffee," he suggests, his voice exuding a thinly disguised rage. Our last such stop, in that small coffee shop in Fleischmanns, just before my first marriage, was an event I don't particularly want to repeat. "I don't have time," I reply coldly. "But I just want to warn you," I add, momentarily losing my grip on the "duck's back" approach, "not *ever* to talk about my wife that way again."

Whatever modicum of self-control my father is still capable of now goes right out the window. "Aren't you ashamed of yourself?" he rails, in a familiar refrain. "To talk to your sick old father that way?"

"And aren't *you* ashamed," I counter, straying even further from my limited Buddhist training, "of the way you behave toward me and my family?"

The words "my family" only set him off further.

"You are cursed by God," he says, taking his white handkerchief from his breast pocket and placing it over his face. "You will never find happiness.

"No one ever loved or wanted you." He begins sobbing. "Not even my sisters. I was the only one. . . . You were my million. I don't have anyone else but you. . . . I never loved Alice. I never loved anyone else. And sex . . . ," he adds, suddenly getting to the root of the problem, "sex, it never worked for me . . . not with our mama, not with Alice."

I am trying to keep my eyes on the road, to concentrate on the traffic, on not responding. Heaving with sobs, he puts his face in his handkerchief again. I realize that what this man so badly needs—what he's *always* needed—is to be loved, to be hugged, to be told that he no longer needs to kiss everyone's hand and bless them. But by now I've been too hurt and too wounded for too long, too often turned on and betrayed. All I can do is keep driving and try to remain silent.

"I was born to death"—he suddenly looks up again—"and now I am going back to death." I'm amazed at how quickly he seems able to move between weeping and railing.

"You should have waited until I was dead and rotted—until I was *verreckt*—to marry," he continues. "I would have bought you a house—we would have lived downstairs, and you could have lived upstairs."

At any other time the thought of sharing a house with my father and stepmother would have thrown me into convulsions of laughter. But now I merely struggle to maintain my silence, to work my way as quickly as possible back toward the Triboro Bridge.

"What did I do to deserve such a son?" he goes on. "I was always so good to you." He pauses, sobbing again. "And you were only interested in sex—sex and women."

I am thinking: This is not really happening; this is a dream. Just shut up and keep driving.

"You don't know what you are saying," I finally mumble. "You have suffered too much."

"It never worked for me, sex, never. I never loved her. You were my million. I sacrificed everything for you," he goes on. "You are damned, cursed. . . . *Der liebe Gott* will never let you find happiness."

He begins sobbing into his white handkerchief again. "Forgive me," he says, taking my right hand from the wheel and covering it with kisses. "Soon I will be dead. Let us go apart in peace."

I keep silent. We are almost over the bridge.

"Just be good to your stepmother when I am gone," he says. "She is all I have. Without her cooking I would have been dead years ago."

"Forgive me," he says again, kissing my hand. "I don't know what I am saying. Please don't say anything to Mama."

"Yes," I whisper quietly, as though to myself. "You don't know what you are saying."

I realize as I speak that—right there before my eyes—something has finally happened to my father that I have been waiting for all these years—something that will allow me, finally, to stop telling stories, something that will allow me to stop thinking about which father I would kill. For me, at that very moment, the man I am sitting beside as I make a sharp right onto the Triboro Bridge is already a dead man.

We arrive back at my parents' house in Jackson Heights. I carry in the meat from the car and begin packing my bags.

"You're not staying for lunch?" my stepmother asks.

"No," I reply, trying to keep the conversation to a minimum. "I've got to get back. I have a small son."

"I'll pack up some steaks and some challah for you and Isabelle," my father says, behaving as if the previous events had never taken place.

"Don't bother," I say politely. "We have plenty of food at home—and, as I've told you a thousand times," I add, exaggerating at least my own tendencies, "we don't eat red meat." I have only one desire—to get out of their house.

"Here," my father says, handing me a small foil-wrapped package with a note Scotch-taped to it and kissing me on the hand again. "At least take the challah . . . your mama made it fresh for *Shabbos*."

"Okay. Thanks."

Ten minutes later, still feeling as if I have been bludgeoned with an icepick, I'm on the Eighth Avenue subway, headed for the train station and the consoling arms of my wife. Feeling too defeated either to read or think, I peel the note from the foil package.

"For our dear daughter-in-law, Isabelle," it reads in my father's nearly illegible scrawl. "May you enjoy it in good health and with guten appetit. . . . God loves you, and so do we."

A few days later, in Boston's North End, I get a lesson in creative writing from a friend and colleague in Harvard's Expository Writing Program.

Still reeling from my father's words, I feel, somehow, the need to keep telling and retelling the story of our little journey down the FDR Drive to the kosher butcher's, as if by merely repeating the incident I can somehow purge my psyche and soul of its effects.

But if it's sympathy I'm after, my friend Doug the novelist's mouth—and, apparently, his heart—aren't the places I'm going to find it. "That's hilarious," he says, hardly able to contain a laugh as I relate the story of myself, Fred, Mr. Yarmolinsky, the kosher meat, the challah, and Blumenthal *père*'s various dark benedictions atop the Triboro Bridge. "That's one of the funniest stories I've ever heard."

And so, gazing into the mirror later that day, I, the Director of Creative Writing at Harvard University, see it again: Those who can't do, teach. My friend, bless his little novelist's heart, has just been trying to teach me something about aesthetic distance: In this to-me-so-tragic-and-dark little story of myself and my father, he sees something humorous and light—something, perhaps, I too should cast a Yeatsian "cold eye" upon, like death.

10 May 1992

Dear Berthold and Nelly,

I am writing to you today about a serious matter, which seems particularly appropriate since you are about to meet my son—who, as you know, is your own biological grandson—for the first time.

I have realized for many years—and even more so now that I have my own family—how painful it has been for me that neither (or both) of you, nor anyone in my "other" family, has ever fully explained to me the circumstances surrounding my birth and adoption. At the same time, I have had to live with this imperfect knowledge—and you have had to live with the pain of keeping the "secret" of it—and with all it has cost all of us psychologically and personally, for the past 43 years.

It seems to me that now—while we are all still alive—it is high time that someone told me the WHOLE truth . . . or at least what you know and can tell of it. I deserve to know. My son deserves to know. My wife deserves to know. And, I believe, *you* also deserve a chance to tell me, and to bare yourselves of what I know must be a painful and complicated burden.

While I have never spoken of what has been obvious to all of us, I have long known that—at least as a matter of blood—I am your son. And I would like, and deserve, to know more of what occurred during that strange time now almost half a century ago when I was born. No one should have to go through their entire life, as I have until now, with the story of their birth and adoption such a mystery. And I don't think either of you has any idea how much pain and suffering, and confusion, these "mysteries" have caused me . . . and may yet cause my son if they aren't clarified.

Why was I given away to Ernst and Betty? Whose idea was it? Why did they never have any children of their own? What was my mother's life like before she met Ernst? (Only Berthold, I think, can answer this.) My father's long-delayed and seemingly dishonest explanations of all this have never satisfied me, nor seemed entirely true. And you both know, of course, how painful and difficult his own birth and mother's death were, and how panicked and confused a man he is.

So—now, before it is too late—I am asking you to help me clear up some of these "mysteries." No one ought to be so much "in the dark" about his own origins, and I can assure you that—were the same thing or anything like it to ever happen to my own son—I would, as a father, make sure he knew the entire truth.

It would mean a great deal to me if you would finally tell me: How was this "arrangement" made? Whose idea was it? Why was I never spoken to or told about it? How sick was my mother when I was adopted? When did you first know that she had cancer? When was her second breast removed? It is unbelievable to me, and to those I know, that no one ever bothered to tell me the answers to these questions. And now—with your other grandson (also, I might remind you, adopted) about to be bar mitzvahed—I think it might be a good time to try and repair these wounds.

I know it will not be easy for you to speak about, or have to remember, these matters. No doubt, it was also a very painful and difficult time for you, having just arrived from Israel with two young children. But I, personally, would be very grateful to you for anything you can do to clarify these too-long-clouded questions. In the meantime, we all send you our love, and look forward to seeing you very soon.

Love,
Michael

Vineland, N.J.
5.16.92

Dear Michael,

We thank you very much for your sincere letter!—You wrote "it is high time"—but thank G'd, not too late, to answer all the questions you have to get, you deserved and no secrets!—Only the truth!—You can tell and trust me; <u>from our part no Secrets—never!</u>—Without complaining, I am not in good health anymore, but still around and asking myself, what was holding you up solang, to ask us many years earlier?—You had all the right to do so.—From our side, it was and still is my belief, that we would not "talk" behind "others"!—

And now answering your questions so good I can: My sister was always a great lady—loving, caring, faithful, true and dear to our family.—She never was sick, so lang I can remember at home.—Before I left my homeland, we met Ernst; 1936 our Father died and in the same year Omi and my sister Betty visited me in Palestine; Ernst and Betty were engaged and going later on to the USA, where Ernst had his family members.—1947, after all this years, we visited here. Once again, we were happy in the family!

Also 1947 Betty had her first Operation; she recuperated and she was later on again aktiv and happy.—1948 we settled on the farm and started a new beginning; new surrounding, language, hard working and trying to fulfill our Obligations; there it came, unexpected: Nelly was pregnant!—As a family, "all 5" (Omi included) we had not a "Idea" but in good intention that it was done, what we don't can change anymore, but we fulfilled my sister's longtime wish, to raise her child.—Which fault it was that they had not any children of their own, I can not answer.—Unfortunately it came different as we all were wishing for.—1958 the second Operation.

It is very hard for me to explain, maybe much harder for you, dear Michael, to understand, but this are the facts!—Hopefully, this letter will help not to mistrust us, but that <u>you never will change our belonging together in the future!</u>—If you need more Answers—we are ready every time!—We are looking forwards to see you on the 5.26, but that is not the right time to talk about this—this day belongs to Jonathan!—

Give our love, also to Isabelle and Noah!—

Love,
Berthold and Nelly

My uncle's letter, for the most part, tells me little I don't suspect or already know. They had "fulfilled my sister's longtime wish," and "which fault it was that they had not any children of their own" he didn't know. Nor did I, but for a brief, ambiguous admission by my father, during one of our few conversations about the subject, that he "couldn't enter" my mother. By now, at least, I have some idea of what "couldn't enter" might mean.

My aunt, the mother who had given up her eight-day-old son, was, as usual, mute on the subject—her usual unforthcoming self. Had it been depression on her part? Fear? A sense of economic panic? An act of the greatest unselfishness and familial generosity the world could know?

My uncle, in his own way, had tried to provide answers—not Freudian answers, but, as befitted who he was, simple ones. And now, with a lethal cancer growing on his breast and our next meeting "belonging to Jonathan," these were probably the best answers I was ever going to get.

"Now stand just a little closer to your aunt and uncle—there— That's it! Now—all together when I say three: *Cheeez!*"

I'm smiling for the photographer, my face wedged like a ball lodged in a metal fence between the aged, sickly-looking faces of my aunt and uncle—my mother and father.

"Okay, now. Let's have cousin Michael over here just a bit closer to the bar mitzvah boy's father, okay? Let's see you all hunker right in there. . . . *Thaaat's it!* A *big* smile now from everybody, okay? Nice and lovey-dovey now, let's all *squeeeze* right in there together and—when I count to three—say, *Cheeez.*"

My cheeks are starting to feel as if they're going to crack under the effort of all this smiling, but smile I do. It's my cousin's—my *brother's*—adopted son's bar mitzvah, and, as I stand behind these four people who are, in reality, my blood, I realize that I quite literally tower over the others. I am large, seeming, by comparison—as Walt Whitman once wrote of himself—to contain multitudes. Yet we all, I try to remind myself as my once-childish body towers over these four smaller, more fragile figures, are somehow embodiments of what E. L. Doctorow calls "the moral immensity of a single soul."

It has been only a month since my uncle Berthold—my *father*—had his cancerous left breast removed at the age of eighty-six. His face and expression already reveal a kind of ghostly air, as if he knows that his time here among the living is drawing to a close. His daughter, Judy—my sister—is also a creature in jeopardy: Fifteen years ago, in her early thirties, she too—in what is beginning to feel like a macabre family tradition—had a cancerous breast removed, and now, at nearly fifty, her hands are so racked by pain caused by nerve damage from the radiation that she can no longer work—can, in fact, no longer dress herself without help. And, as I look out onto her and her husband Curt, and onto her and my father, some lines of my own, from a poem entitled "The Cure," suddenly take on a certain ominous significance:

> Not just my family, dear God,
> but my times suffer from this,
> and soon it is as if the whole world
> were merely a single cell, dividing
> and dividing like mitochondria
> beneath a child's microscope

along with the poem's rather more hopeful ending:

>   . . . it is silly
> to think I am immune to this, and yet
> I do, and because I am trying to find
> a cure for cancer, because I want to save
> the breasts of all the beautiful women
> from the cold knife of the surgeon
> as it slices through my morning, through
> the stars and the river, because of
> this longing to stop things from dividing,
> I write this poem.

To Judy's left, her mother—*my* mother—sits in a wheelchair, her left knee so severely shattered in an auto accident more than thirty years ago, in which three of her best friends died, that she has progressively lost the ability to walk. And, beside her, just below my chin, stands her other son—my brother—whose own son, according to Jewish law, is about to become a man.

What, finally, is blood? I ask myself as I again force my cheeks apart at the photographer's request. Who are these people to me, and I to them? What force, what inexorable claims of destiny and blood, have brought us together once more—no doubt for the last time—in the gaze of this photographer's lens?

When the session is finally over, Amos puts his arm affectionately around me. "I'm really glad the three of you could make it," he whispers into my ear. "It's great to have you here." It's only been of late that I've taken either my cousin or his lifestyle—so different from my own—all that seriously, perhaps hiding my jealousy of his material comfort and cheerful good nature behind a smug sense of intellectual superiority—the kind of superiority, I now remind myself, that I hate. But today—indeed, the last several times I've seen him—he strikes me as an extraordinarily likable, good-natured, generous sort of guy.

Even his sister—*my* sister—whose life of financial struggle, sentimental homilies, bowling leagues, store-brand ketchup and frozen fish sticks I've often looked down on, seems to me this morning to embody a certain nobility, as I observe the grace and good cheer with which she refuses to draw attention to her many burdens, the obvious warmth and support that exist between her and her family.

We enter the synagogue, where, within minutes, in the first two rows are assembled—for the first, and no doubt last, time since my grandmother, Johanna's, funeral twenty-five years ago—all the living members of my two families, the confused and confusing cast of blood and affections and hatreds that has brought and raised me into this life. In the second row my small son, Noah, wearing a checked shirt, suspenders, and a black bow tie, is seated on my wife, Isabelle's, lap; she is just to my left; my father and stepmother noisily whisper to each other on my right. The rest of my family—the blood part, that is—are seated in front of us in the first row.

Suddenly, roused from my own reveries of amazement and mixed feelings, I hear the rabbi call out my uncle's and cousin's and nephew's names: "Will Berthold Gern, Amos Gern, and Jonathan Gern please rise and stand in front of the Ark." And then my own: "And would Mr. Michael Blumenthal please mount the podium as well."

"These Torah scrolls," the rabbi continues, opening the Ark and handing the first of the ornately embroidered scrolls to my uncle, "are herewith being passed along from generation to generation to signify the passing of our laws from generation to generation. We trust that you, Jonathan, who will now read from the Holy Torah that has been passed to you by your own father, and received by him from his, will take seriously the obligations and the rights which this coming of age as a man signify, and that you will enter into the Covenant which we are here today to celebrate with a sense of seriousness, purpose, honor, and reverence."

A few minutes later, Jonathan's *haftorah* and the accompanying blessings having been completed, the rabbi—with Amos's help—lifts the heavy scroll from the podium, carrying it to where I am seated, just to the left of the Ark. From where I am sitting, I can look down, now, at the aged figures of my parents and aunt and uncle, the somewhat amused faces of Judy's two daughters; the proud face of Amos's wife, Evelyn; at my own wife and son seated beside my parents in the second row. And, just as the rabbi places the embroidered satin cover and silver pointer over the scroll that I—the one odd piece in this jigsaw puzzle of fate and reunion—am holding, I stare out at my son and can swear I see his two-year-old face break into a wide, unambivalently joyful smile.

～

11 | SHE AND I

Don't have too many characters. The center of
gravity should be two: he and she.

—ANTON CHEKHOV TO A. P. CHEKHOV, MAY 10, 1886

We came out two others:

He-other and she-other together,

He-lover and she-lover together. And I said to myself,

Otherness is all. Otherness is love.

—YEHUDA AMICHAI, *OPEN CLOSED OPEN*

ISABELLE CLEARLY HAS HER work cut out for her, as do I. "Before you decide to marry a man," goes a piece of advice I've often heard offered to women, "make sure you have a chance to see him with his mother." But which mother, in my case, might that be? My biological mother, Nelly, who gave me away and then spent the rest of my childhood largely ignoring me? My adoptive mother, Betty, the sweet, kind, loving woman who spent the first ten years of my life navigating the bumpy road between my birth and her grave? My stepmother, Alice, the wicked witch of Dow Jones? Any way you cut it, it was hardly a pretty picture—or a very auspicious augury for a wife-to-be.

And there is, of course, the equally classically Freudian counsel to a prospective father: that the best thing a man can do for his son is to love his son's mother. But how, I wonder, can a man with a past like mine, married as the result of an accidental pregnancy, love *anyone*? In the schizoid world of my psychological needs, two sometimes opposed desires—the craving for passion and the need for security—dwell side by side. And if a divided heart, as Faulkner suggested in his Nobel Prize address, is the prerequisite for good writing, the inkwell of my heart must surely house an incipient James Joyce—or, at least, a Philip Roth—in the making.

Wanting, as the poet Randall Jarrell once so clear-sightedly put it, "the good whore who resembles my mother," I've married, first—in the person of my adventurous Jungian *puella*, Kendra— the good whore, and now—in the shape of more maternal (and, indeed, almost immediately a mother) Isabelle—someone much more like my mother. But, for me, after more than thirty years with my stepmother as my "mother," Isabelle has something I very much need: a generous, loving, and life-giving heart. And she knows something even—or, perhaps, especially—her Harvard professor husband doesn't seem to know: how to love.

So, in and around the person of my second wife, the repetition compulsion and the urge for rectification carry on a kind of holy war. Thickly foreign-accented, and, therefore, forcing me once again to utter my childhood prayers for a home ruled by perfect English; pregnant, and, therefore, depriving me of the role of "chooser" (rather than "chosen") I so covet, Isabelle simultaneously resurrects several of the most painful of my childhood ghosts, while, at the same time, feeding my craving for emotional security and unconditional love.

Yet what I want—perhaps even more than I want kindness and devotion—is to *choose*, to make love in impeccable, occasionally down-and-dirty, English. Instead, I find myself frequently feeling doomed, financially besieged, linguistically challenged. Yet perhaps I have "chosen" this as well . . . or, at least, chosen to place such interpretations on it. And within me, along with the knowledge that we are two essentially decent, kind, and well-intentioned people who want not to hurt each other, there still burns that eternal flame: *hope.* I hope to be healed, and I hope that, somehow, this marriage I have either stumbled into or—in a less than entirely straightforward manner—"chosen," will help me to heal.

Yet not all those who know both of us hold out the same hope. "I can't emphasize enough," a friend wrote to me years later from Paris, "that ever since I met you I have considered your marriage to Isa to be a monumental mismatch. I knew Isa earlier in her life, and I recognize in her many many virtues. But she was never your wife—in the sense of a romantic partner—and she was only the mother of your wonderful son by some kind of blessed but damned peculiar divine intervention. And what I felt for you, I would imagine a friend of hers would have felt equally for her.

"Maybe this is the real meaning of the story of Christ," his letter continues, "that Mary gave birth to Jesus without sleeping with Joseph, because symbolically only God should be held responsible for the miracle of our births. The imperfect unions of men and women cannot be held (should not be held) to be the cause of the magnificent miracle of life. In the image of God we create life, the fruit not of our accidental matings, but of the yearnings toward spirit which move through us like waves. So let us not, as parents, confuse the divinity of our offspring with the sometimes senseless biology of their origins."

~

She is quintessentially French. I am, in the loosest sense of the word, American. She always feels cold. I am always hot. In the winter, even if it isn't chilly, she does nothing but complain about how cold it is. Even in late spring there are large, fertile fields of goose bumps on her thin, beautiful arms, and I have known her, even in the Middle East in late June, to wear a woolen sweater around the house, to sleep in a lamb's wool camisole in August.

She speaks, since she doesn't speak much, only one language well, though she seems to understand so much more than I do, even in the languages she doesn't really speak. I, on the other hand, can make myself understood in several languages, yet have trouble focusing on the conversations of others.

She enjoys reading maps and navigating new places. I hate it, and quickly grow impatient and ornery. After a single afternoon in a foreign city, she will have mastered the public transportation system, be able to find her way to the centrum from the most desolate-seeming corners. I will get lost five meters from my own hotel or—worse yet—a new apartment. She hates asking for directions, preferring to gaze patiently at a seemingly indecipherable map for many moments. When we get lost, I am quick to blame her: She blames no one, but busies herself looking for secondhand shops and fruit and vegetable markets in whatever neighborhood we are lost in.

She loves old architecture, curved surfaces, rummaging among the trinkets and memorabilia of other people's lives at flea markets, the scent of flowers and herbs. I am always impatient to get where I'm going, missing virtually everything along the way. The only three things I've ever been able to love completely and unconditionally are my own disfigured face in the mirror and sitting at my desk making a kind of music exclusively with words—and, blessedly, my son.

She loves travel, unfamiliar places, a sense of the unexpected. I dream of living always in one place, burning my passport, etching an address in stone upon my doorpost, running for mayor in some town I will never again move from.

I love eating in restaurants—bad restaurants, good restaurants, even mediocre ones. She always wants to eat at home: fresh vegetables and better food, she claims, at a third the price. She hates the way I do the dishes and leave a mess after cooking. I like, on occasion, to do the dishes and cook, though I'm quite awful at the former, which I always do in too great a hurry, leaving all sorts of prints, smudges, and grease stains along the way.

She loves to watch a late movie—preferably a slow-moving, melancholic one of the French or Italian sort—and to have a glass of wine or two with dinner. I prefer rather superficial, fast-moving American films, fall asleep almost the second I enter the theater for anything later than the 7:30 showing, and can drink, at most, a glass of white zinfandel in the late afternoon.

She has little patience for, or interest in, pleasantries among strangers, preferring to restrict her circle of acquaintances to those she is truly intimate with. I enjoy talking to the garbage collector, the mailman, making small talk with the meter reader and taxi driver. The greetings "How are you?" and "Have a nice day" do not cause me to rail against the superficiality of America and Americans.

She is shy; I am not. Occasionally, however, her shyness rubs off on me, or, alternatively—as in the case of landlords who are trying to take advantage of us or rabbis who are too adamantly in favor of circumcision—she loses her shyness and grows quite eloquent, even in English, her vocabulary suddenly expanding to include words like *barbaric* and *philistine*.

She has no respect for established authority, and thinks nothing of running out on student loans, disconnecting the electric meter, or not paying taxes. I, on the other hand, though I have the face of an anarchist, am afraid of established authority and tend, against my own better instincts, to respect it. As soon as I spot a police car in the rearview mirror, I assume I have done something terribly wrong and begin to contemplate spending the rest of my life in jail. She, on the other hand, smiles shyly at the police officer, who quickly folds up his notebook and goes back to his car.

She likes goat's cheese, garlic, a good slice of pâté with a glass of red wine, tomatoes with fresh rosemary. I like sausages, raw meat, pizza, and gefilte fish with very sharp horseradish.

She claims I am a Neanderthal when it comes to food, a barbaric American animal who will die young of high cholesterol, rancid oils, and pesticides. She is refined and has a sensitive palate and a nose so accurate it can tell the difference between day-old and two-day-old butter. In Cambridge, Massachusetts, she spends many days in search of the perfect, vine-ripened tomato and just the right kind of basil for making pesto. She can't stand, for example, pine nuts that are rancid. *Rancid*, in fact, is one of the English words she uses most frequently.

At the cinema she hates to sit too close to the screen, and—if we're at home—refuses to watch movies on TV that are interrupted by commercials, claiming that it interferes with her "dream world." I like to sit near the front of the theater and tell jokes during the movie. I like almost any movie, as long as it is superficial enough not to disturb my world-view. She prefers dark, slow-moving, romantic tragedies, set to the music of Jacques Brel, which linger in her imagination for many days after, causing her to question, or reexamine, almost everything in her world. She remembers the names of films and actors, and prefers actresses who embody a kind of low-key sensuality and dark reserve. I adore those who are brazenly sexual and whore-like in their demeanor.

On those rare occasions when we've seen a film we both liked, she will, the next day—even the next month—remember every small detail of it: the weather in a particular scene, the shape of an awning, the way a blouse or a cloth napkin lay against the protagonist's arm or lap. I, on the other hand, will remember nothing, not even the plot, as if some premature and obliterating dementia had overtaken me during the night. Somewhat sheepfaced, I will ask her to remind me what the movie was about, who was in it—on occasion, even, what its name was—all of which she will generously do, never even pausing to comment upon my infirmity.

I either love or hate people, and find myself utterly incapable of having any interest in those I am indifferent to. She, though often equally indifferent to the same people, always seeks to find something interesting and unique about them, a pursuit I have neither the time nor the patience for. Something in even the most uninspiring of persons arouses, if not her conversation, then at least her curiosity, and—once she has been engaged with someone in any way—she retains a certain ongoing loyalty to them I can neither relate to nor comprehend. Though far less extroverted than I am, she will carry on a correspondence with any number of people, in all sorts of countries, and keeps a list in her address book of all the birthdays of everyone she has ever known and liked.

I consider every crisis a catastrophe, and will begin to fidget nervously and despondently whenever I am confronted with a late train, a rescheduled flight, or an incompetent waitperson. She considers each of these events a hidden opportunity, a portent from the gods, yet another manifestation of the world's independence and revivifying fickleness.

Though I have somehow been appointed the "breadwinner" of our family, I am extremely lazy: My favorite activity, as Freud said of poets, is daydreaming, my buttocks wedged firmly in a chair. She is never idle, raising domesticity to an art form, a Buddhistic perfection in every ironed crease.

Being a devotee of Bishop Berkeley's formulation to the effect that, if you can't see it, it isn't there, I prefer neatness to cleanliness: My idea of housecleaning is to sweep the large dust balls under the bed, stuff plastic and paper bags sloppily into a kitchen cabinet, cover the bed hurriedly with a creased down comforter, cram my underwear (freely mingling the soiled and the clean) into a dresser drawer. She is almost maniacally clean, sniffing each of my shirts and socks daily to make sure they don't need to be washed, vacuuming in corners, changing the pillowcases and sheets with the regularity of tides.

I like to buy cheap things, particularly clothes, frequently, wearing them once or twice until they fray in the washer or lose their shape, and then cart them from place to place without ever wearing them again. One of the things she seems to enjoy most is to go through my clothes closets, reminding me of all the cheap items I bought and never wore, or I have worn once, washed, and are now "totally out of shape." She buys clothes almost never, but always things of good quality, preferring to wear the same few things (always immaculately clean) time and time again.

I am the kind of person who can do many things at once, most of them rather imperfectly. She does only one thing at a time, but always with a sense of perfection.

I like to cook without recipes, freely mixing Marsala wine, mustard, artichoke hearts, candied ginger, maple syrup, and plums, hoping something capable of being digested will emerge. She always uses a recipe—except for things she has made before—but everything she makes is successful and delicious.

I would have been a rock star or a concert pianist—or perhaps, even, the proprietor of an illicit sex club—had I felt freer to follow my lyrical and immoral heart's calling. She would have been a sister in a Carmelite convent, or a gardener.

She is an enthusiastic and natural mother. I am a reluctant, though not unsuccessful, father.

She could have been many things, all of them having something to do with taking care of others or using her hands: a nurse, a dentist, a carpenter, a potter, a refinisher of furniture, a restorer of antiquarian books. I could, though I like to imagine otherwise, probably have done only the one thing I am doing now: putting words to paper.

I like to live part of my life in the if-but-only mode of wishful thinking and fantastical alternatives. She accepts the life that has been given her as her one possible destiny, without complaining.

She doesn't like to think about money—in fact, her refusal to think about it has, on occasion, gotten her (and me!) into heaps of trouble. I, while I don't like to think of it either, am usually left with the unpoetic task of having to worry about it. Since I have been with her, in fact, hardly a day has passed without thinking of it . . . almost constantly. She, on the other hand, worries about many other unpoetic tasks in our lives that have nothing at all to do with money.

I can imitate people from many countries, and with many different accents. She is too much herself to imitate anyone.

I like to have some kind of music playing whenever I am not reading or working. She usually prefers silence, or only to have music on when she is actually listening to it.

I will continue to eat even when I am no longer hungry, just for the pleasure of it. She eats only as much as satisfies her hunger on any occasion. I abhor all forms of table manners, eating with my fingers, chewing with my mouth open, taking food freely from others' plates, licking my fingers at the table, stuffing my mouth with large quantities, burping, and passing gas. She never eats before being seated at the table, waits for everyone else to do likewise, chews only small morsels at a time, and eats so slowly, and with such deliberate pleasure, that I have usually finished what is on my plate well before she is actually seated. Only twice in our eight years together have I heard her passing gas. Burping, never.

As soon as I make a decision, I immediately, and unfailingly, tilt toward wanting the other alternative. She immediately accepts and begins to implement any decision she has made. She often says that I am a neurotic and "special" kind of person; she feels that, living with me, this kind of behavior is the "statue quo." Occasionally, when I am in one of my periods of manic reconsideration, she smiles slightly in her slightly smiling French way, as if to say, "*Oy vey*, what a case I am married to."

I am often angry at others—friends, foes and family alike—and like to hold, and nurse, these angers for as long as is humanly possible, until I can almost feel them eating at my liver, like an earthquake with numerous aftershocks. She is incapable of sustained anger or hostility and would, I believe, forgive me (perhaps already *has* forgiven me) the most egregious deeds and betrayals, an attitude I have no desire to test to its limits. Even in her case, I like to remind her as often as possible of the ways she has disappointed and betrayed me. She, on the other hand, rarely mentions my betrayals and weaknesses.

I never cry, even when I am truly unhappy, yet I have a tendency to grow teary-eyed whenever an athlete experiences some major triumph, or after the last out of the World Series, when the players all rush to the mound and hug one another. She cries easily, even at sentimental movies whose pandering to sentimental feelings she despises.

I will take any kind of pill or medicine anyone recommends in order to relieve pain and discomfort. She prefers "natural" remedies. Although I am not terribly Jewish by religious conviction, I wanted to have our son circumcised when he was born. She felt it to be a pagan ritual tantamount to permanent disfigurement, and began assembling propaganda from various anti-circumcision organizations around the country depicting vast armadas of mutilated children with heavily bandaged penises. She won. She usually wins.

I think she is beautiful but too thin, and am constantly after her to try to gain weight. She thinks she is less beautiful than I do, but comments frequently about her "beautiful arms." When she was younger, in California, she wore her hair very short and looked like a kind of postmodern French punktress on her way to the wrong discotheque. Now I think she is much more beautiful and womanly, and, like me, a bit older.

When we met in Ecuador, she had rather gray hair and was wearing purple nylon pants and a yellow sweatshirt. She seemed, at first, more interested in reading her mail than in talking to me, a fact which I soon realized was due more to her shyness—and her passion for her mail—than to lack of interest in me. On the two-hour bus ride between Quito and Otavalo, across the equator, I slowly began to realize that she was quite beautiful, in an undemonstrative sort of way. The next morning I remember her companion bringing two glasses of fresh-squeezed orange juice to the room, along with coffee, and then our walking, hand in hand, above the town of Otavalo, where we finally sat in a small restaurant and her friend, Annick, took our picture. I look very happy in the photo, though not too handsome. She looks happy too, and very lovely.

We stayed in several romantic, small Ecuadorian hotels during those days, and I remember, not even a week after not having to borrow her toothpaste, looking down at her one night (or was it afternoon?) and saying, "I think I love you." "I think I love you too, Gringo," she replied. She used to call me "Gringo" in those days.

I remember talking to her an awful lot back then, and thinking to myself how attentively, and compassionately, she always listened. I myself am not such a good listener, except on occasion, so that—along with the sweet way she always said, "uh-huh, uh-huh . . ." and, "Yes . . . Yes," when I was telling her a story—it made a real impression on me. Back then, I don't remember her being nearly as sensitive to cold, or quite as thin—but, then again, we were in love and in Ecuador.

Sometimes, now, when I realize that we have been together for more than eleven years and have a ten-year-old son, I think that this is one of the major miracles of my life—and I'm sure she does also. I was so romantic then, that night in Otavalo, and so was she when, hardly a week later, she got on a plane from Quito to the United States and followed me to Boston. I remember her calling me, as we had planned, but I suddenly had a sense that the call wasn't quite long distance. When she told me she was standing at a pay telephone across the street at Porter Square, I ran down the stairs, not even bothering to button my shirt or pull up my zipper, and took her into my arms and carried her halfway up to my fourth-floor, rent-controlled apartment.

I was stronger in those days, and healthier, and so, maybe, was she. We were not so young, but very much in love, and there was a scent of laundry, somehow, wafting through my windows as we made love, on the mattress located on my study floor, for the first time in the United States of America.

Now, as I write this, I no longer live in that rent-controlled apartment, and that mattress, I am quite sure, is no longer on the floor. She is still beautiful, though—perhaps even more so— with her knowing eyes and beautiful smile and lovely French voice, and she is still, as a friend of mine once described her, *"une chouette"*: an owl.

Which is a wiser, more deliberate, creature than a fly.

~

12 | KAFKA'S FATHERS

Last night I dreamt my father dead,

That man whom life defeated 'ere I could.

I emerged, all bloodied, from the darkened wood

And placed an unheard blessing on his head.

Last night I dreamt I was a man

Who loved his wife, who overcame his fear

And kissed her, from her small toe to her ear,

As only sons of deadened fathers can.

Last night I dreamt, I dreamt I was a bear

And, as my own son whimpered in the night,

I gave voice to an age-old, stifled fright

And put my bear hair everywhere.

—"THE BEAR," FROM *THE WAGES OF GOODNESS* (1992)

IT'S JANUARY 1993 AND my uncle Berthold—in the weeks since my cousins Amos and Judy have moved him and my aunt Nelly to a retirement community closer to Amos's home—has been sinking rapidly. I'm in New York briefly from Budapest, where we are now living on a Fulbright fellowship, and Amos calls to let me know that his father has just been admitted to a hospital in Livingston.

I'm scheduled, the next afternoon, to take a train from Manhattan to Newark Airport to catch a plane back to Budapest. But something tells me there is another stop I need to make before leaving: I call my cousin to ask him to pick me up in Newark and take me to the hospital for a brief visit before I leave.

Entering his semiprivate room, I don't need more than a single look at my uncle, heroically trying to force himself upright in his hospital bed, to realize that this is the last time I will be seeing the man who is my natural father. Having all his life shared with his brother-in-law Julius the admirable quality of trying to be both brave and cheerful amid great physical suffering, he's still trying now. But it is obvious that he's fighting a losing battle.

I have only about half an hour to visit with him, a sadly emaciated figure, who, I now realize, has more and more come to resemble my grandmother Johanna, his mother. He trembles, trying to seem good-natured, as I hand-feed him a few of the cookies I've brought.

As I sit there beside him for what I know is the last time, it is those long-ago Monday nights in Washington Heights I am thinking of, those still-remembered quarters he tried to press into my ambivalent hands. I see again the bullet in his arm glistening in the New Jersey sunlight, his kibbutzniklike figure, decked in a Vineland Egg Auction sun visor and a white sleeveless undershirt, shlepping his buckets of eggs from the chicken coop to the egg grader, from the egg grader to the car.

It is *he,* I realize as I sit beside this dying man, who is, in some very basic and undeniable sense, the father of my life, a man who had loved me, under the circumstances, as best he could. He is my father who was not my father, my uncle who was not my uncle. A sweet and good-natured man, a hardworking chicken farmer, who did his best. And now, as he fades, slowly, toward the next life and I rise to enter, once again, what remains of my own, I bend over his weeping body and plant on his liver-spotted forehead, as tenderly as I can, a final blessing, and a kiss.

Two weeks later, at 3:00 in the morning, the phone in our apartment on the outskirts of Budapest's Fourteenth District rings. It's my cousin Amos on the other end, and I know as soon as I hear his voice what he has to tell me.

"Berthold died at home this afternoon at 2 o'clock." Amos's voice—usually possessed of a buoyantly let's-get-on-with-life quality—seems to be struggling to maintain its composure. "We were about to have him taken to a hospice, but, when the nurse came and examined him, she said it was just a matter of hours, so we decided to let him die at home. Judy and Curt and Nelly and I were with him when he died."

I—still the missing one, I can't help but observe—was not.

"When's the funeral?" I ask.

"Tomorrow. But there's no purpose in your coming all this way for that, Mike." My cousin's among the last remaining persons on this earth whom I still allow to refer to me by my childhood name. "It was good that you were here and had a chance to say good-bye to him."

"Yes." I suddenly hear my cousin—my brother—sobbing on the other end. "It was good. Thanks for calling, Amos.

"I'm so sorry," I add somewhat awkwardly, not quite certain

what, or whom, I was sorry for, but Amos has already hung up.

I, too, hang up and go back to bed beside the warm, half awakened body of my wife.

"What's up?" she mumbles from her near-sleep.

"Berthold died yesterday."

"It's a good thing you went to see him while you were in New York."

"Yes," I agree, "it's a good thing."

And then, as my wife falls once more into a deep sleep, another voice within me whispers, to no one in particular: *One down, one to go.*

I'm at work in my new studio along Budapest's Bajcsy-Zsilinszky út, the wooden shades drawn to screen out the hot summer sun, waiting for a friend to arrive. Suddenly, I hear the ominous screeching of brakes on the street below, followed, a second later, by a dull thud. I run to the window, pull up the shades, and look down from my fifth-floor balcony in the direction of Saint Stephen's Cathedral, where two cars, a white Lada and a yellow Trabant, are parked nose-to-nose, their drivers apparently arguing over who's to blame.

An immediate sense of relief floods over me: My original premonition of a terrible accident (I suddenly remember a man lying dead at the building's front door just days before) has materialized into nothing more than an ordinary fender-bender. But, just as I am about to turn back into my studio and resume work, I notice someone bending down behind one of the cars. Looking again, I can now see the source of the decidedly nonmetallic thud I've just heard: There, facedown just behind the second car, lying in a pool of blood and dressed in a green flannel shirt and suspenders, is a young boy, virtually the same age as my son.

"Dear V.," I hastily scrawl on the sheet of paper I tape to my studio door, "sorry—an emergency. Will explain later." Hardly fifteen minutes later, I burst through the door of Noah's kindergarten on Varosligeti fásor. It's naptime, a three-hour-long forced confinement in a group of small cots clustered (when it isn't too hot or too cold) on the school's outdoor patio, or else in the playroom, as they are today.

"Kis fiuk accidentós . . . nagyon rosz," I try explaining to the day-care workers, Vilma and Vali, in cracked Hungarian, and then creep tiptoe into the shade-drawn room, where, along with some half dozen Hungarian children between the ages of three and five, my son lies, faceup, asleep on a small cot. Propelled by a force entirely beyond cause or reason (and light years beyond desire), all I want to do is sit there and watch him sleep, to make absolutely certain it isn't—and will never be—him lying in that pool of blood at the corner of Bajcsy-Zsilinsky út.

"Papa," Noah whispers, opening his eyes some twenty minutes later. "What are you *doing* here? It's my naptime."

"I just came because I love you." I realize, unashamedly, that I have just uttered a line out of the worst kind of sentimental movie.

"Oh, Papa! Great! Let's go to the circus!" Noah jumps up from his cot.

"Anything you want," I say, taking my son's hand and walking him past Vilma's and Vali's slightly befuddled but somehow comprehending faces. "Anything you want."

The accident in front of my studio—along with my panic-stricken rush to my son's bedside—make me more acutely aware than ever that my life is at the mercy of forces I frequently neither care to acknowledge nor whose power over me I have sufficiently credited.

Married to a woman I may not have wholeheartedly chosen to marry, but now love and need, father to a son I hadn't really wholeheartedly wanted to bring into the world at the time, but now love, I can't help but begin to see my life as ruled by powers indifferent, and at times utterly antagonistic, to my own comfort and well-being. And why should my life be any different than most?

And here, once again, I see the mythic—and all too real—power of the abortion question: Before my son was born—when he was merely a somewhat abstractable "fetus" in my wife's womb—the very real, and very concrete, love I feel for him now had no location in space and time, no real existence in this world. Perhaps, of course, it was channeled (or sublimated, as the Freudians would maintain) into my work, or still being hoarded for some yet-unnamed future love, some as-yet-unconceived future child. But the moment my son was actually born, the moment at which he ceased to be an "issue," or a question and became a living, screaming, crying, laughing, needing human being, my love, too, was "born" with him—or at least transmogrified from some ulterior object or purpose.

Perhaps, indeed, I did not exactly want him to be born under the circumstances that brought him into the world. But once he was in it, my love became precise, located, absolute, unmodifiable. And then, of course, as my wife so astutely pointed out, there was yet another issue present for me in all this: In another time, or another place, in all likelihood, I myself—I who am writing this—would not have been brought into this world.

And, yet, this is not how I wanted it: I wanted to *choose*. I wanted to mount, against the world's campaign of obliviousness and indifference to a single man's fate, a campaign of my own, a campaign of freedom from my mother-deprived past, from all the reductive, psychiatric interpretations of my weakness and ineptitude. Having mastered the thrusts, counterthrusts, licks, and lappings of sex, why, I wonder, can I not now seem to master the seemingly equally straightforward thrusts and perambulations of the life that emanates from it?

But the answer, as usual, never lies far from the question itself: For, whereas sex is largely animal and intuitive, life—at least, human life—is convoluted and mysterious, ruled by forces more amenable to mystery than chemistry. Just as life in the now post-Communist countries is beginning to reveal the cracks and flaws in every simplistic ideology, so life in that postadolescent nation of the self reveals, daily, the simplistic fallacies inherent in any simple solution. Wish and counterwish, longing and counterlonging, freedom and security, desire and the end of desire, each with its vast armada of utterance and regret, insist themselves into my daily rounds, issuing forth into the ravenous air a confused, yet somehow not entirely dissonant, music of sighs and moans.

I love my son. I need, but perhaps do not quite know how to love, my wife. I long for my lover's singing and resonant flesh in the late afternoons. I want the securities of socialism but the consoling, though somehow often illusory, choices of capitalism as well. I want to be free to utter as many "fucks" and "cunts" into the uncensored air as I choose, yet I also relish the challenges of artifice and disguise—I need, for my art, both the marital sentry standing at the door and the lover waiting at my studio entrance.

"Everything I look upon is blessed," says Yeats. But at times everything I look upon seems cursed as well. A man falls asleep one night repairing socialist lampshades and wakes up the next day flipping meat at a newly opened McDonald's. If, after all, it is now possible to be a "free-market socialist," why isn't it also possible to be a faithful philanderer? A religious agnostic? A patriotic expatriate? Whitman, by his own boastfulness, was large, contained multitudes. Why is it, then, that I, a medium-size man trying to make himself at home in a world not entirely of his own choosing, can't manage at least to contain a small crowd?

And there may be another problem as well: One chooses, if one can, from some sort of stable center, from the self's locus of constancy amid all its external flux. But I, it sometimes seems to me (and to others) *have* no center: I am both a Gern and a Blumenthal, a chicken farmer and a furrier, an immigrant and an American, a son and a stepson. I am blood *and* water, divided and dismembered, a man trying to put all his eggs in a single basket.

We've been in Boston from Budapest for only a week, hesitating as always to make the inevitably painful, anxiety-filled visit to my parents. I am, at least, feeling consoled by the fact that it will be, as has become our habit since moving to Europe, somewhere "away" from my stepmother's house, someplace where the level of her ever-controlling neuroses can be checked by the presence of others.

That morning, preparing to leave Boston, we hesitate, weighing the option of delaying our visit yet one more day and going to a jazz concert. "Let's stay and go tomorrow instead," I suggest from the driver's seat of our already-loaded rental car. "It's such a beautiful day."

"No," Isabelle replies, without hesitation. "We planned to go today. Let's just go ahead and get it over with. We can take it slowly and stop for lunch somewhere."

So off we go, stopping for lunch at a diner on Route 23 near the Massachusetts/New York border and arriving at my parents' hotel, the South Wind in Woodbourne, New York, at around 4:00 P.M. I park the car, and Isabelle, Noah, and I begin wandering the grounds in search of my father and stepmother.

Suddenly, more than the usual uneasiness I experience on seeing my parents comes over me. Within minutes, as my eyes focus on a pair of blanketed figures lying in lounge chairs beneath a large maple, I understand for the first time the appropriateness of the term "white as death." The face I focus on as we walk toward the sleeping couple—my father's face—is clearly no longer among the living. He is lying on the deck chair, half asleep, his mouth open, hardly seeming to recognize us, and can't even summon the strength to rise from the chair to say hello.

"*Er ist schlecht beinander,*" my stepmother says—"He's not in good shape." This time the evidence speaks for itself.

"I don't think we're going to have to worry about visiting them next summer," I whisper to Isabelle. I'm completely shaken by the sight of a man who, even at ninety-one, seemed physically, if not mentally, robust the summer before.

"No, he looks pretty bad." Isabelle, usually the optimist in such matters, concurs.

"How is my dear nephew?" my father, apparently no longer susceptible to even a biological cover-up, manages weakly when we resurface from our room. "And my dear grandson?" By now, some knowing instinct in me—usually utterly phobic about using the video camera we bought at Noah's birth—is trying with all my might to capture my father's chalk-white image in the self-focusing lens. I am, something tells me, shooting the final scene of a long, painful script.

My father complies weakly, dangling his ever-present white handkerchief before the viewfinder and mumbling the obligatory words about God blessing us and being so thrilled to see his "nephew" and grandson.

"Lie down," I say after a few minutes, helping him back into his lounge chair. "You need to rest." Within seconds he's back asleep, his mouth wide open to reveal the gaping absence of the false teeth he misplaced somewhere before leaving New York.

"Er ist nicht gut beinander," my stepmother repeats.

"He just needs to rest," I force myself to utter a consoling lie. "He'll be better tomorrow."

Somehow, my father, ever the Old World gentleman, manages to get himself changed into a pair of beige slacks, his white dress shoes, and a seersucker summer sports coat in time for dinner. En route to the dining hall, he falls asleep, mouth hanging wide open, on each of the two chairs we stop to rest him in along the way. By the time we arrive at my parents' dining hall table, accompanied by their sweet, Parkinson's-disease-afflicted table-mate, an eighty-nine-year-old spinster named Edith, my father is asleep once more, roused only by my stepmother's periodic jab-bings and proddings, insisting that he eat.

"Ich habe doch kein Hunger"—"I'm not hungry"—he lamely protests, accompanied by my increasingly shrill implorings to my stepmother to "just leave him alone—he's tired," both to no avail.

Finally, all of us having, per usual, been collectively defeated by the sheer relentlessness of my stepmother's will, I offer to skin and cut my father's chicken leg for him. "God love you, dear nephew," he murmurs weakly, amid the slurping sounds of poor Edith hap-lessly trying to drink her soup with a straw, distributing far more of it in all directions across the table than between her lips.

Suddenly, feeling a pair of eyes upon me, I look up at my father once more across the table. As I do so, our eyes meet in a way I can't recall their having done in many, many years.

How can I describe the look I see there?—that strange commingling of fear and terror? But there is something else—something far more terrifying to me, something I had seen before in that coffee shop that long-ago morning in Fleischmanns and, more recently, as we drove across the Triboro Bridge from the kosher butcher's just after the birth of my son.

Having no better, or other, word for it, I must describe what I see in my father's eyes for what it unmistakably is: a stare of pure, naked, undisguised *hate*.

By 8:00 P.M., by which time we've put Noah to bed, it's obvious that my father is no longer fit for—or, to the extent he is still able to, desirous of—being up. I lead him, so weak that I'm virtually holding him up as we walk, back to my parents' room to put him to bed.

"Such a good nephew," he keeps repeating as I take off his pants and urine-stained underwear and help him on with his gold-colored pajamas. "God love you."

"Yes," I repeat in a whisper. "Such a good nephew."

My wife and I have brought my parents a bottle of Jägermeister—an alcohol-laced Austrian herbal curative—from Budapest, and I now pour my father a healthy shot of the dark brown liquid, thinking it may at least calm him and help him fall asleep.

"Such a good nephew," he keeps repeating. "Such a good nephew." As he lies down on the bed and I pull the blanket up to cover him, I keep thinking, for some reason, of the scene in the film version of D. H. Lawrence's *Women in Love* where Gerald lies down to die in the snow. There is something, now, resigned and defeated about my father as he lies there. With the usual ambivalence that accompanies touching him physically, I kiss him goodnight and go back outside to rejoin my stepmother and my wife.

About half an hour later, wanting to check on him again, I reenter the room to find my father, in a dazed and confused state, wandering toward the dresser. *"Ich möchte noch ein bisschen Schnapps,"* he says weakly. "I would like a little more *Schnapps*." Thinking there is nothing to lose by giving him a bit more in the way of a sedative, I pour him another hefty shot of Jägermeister and lead him, once again, back to bed.

"Such a good nephew," he repeats once more.

"Good night, Dad," I answer. "Try and get some sleep."

When we enter the room some twenty minutes later to take my stepmother to bed, my father is seated upright on the bed, holding a hand to his chest.

"Hör mal zu," he whispers, breathing with obvious difficulty as he speaks. *"Es röchelt hier drin."* "Listen—it's rattling in here."

Sure enough, a gurgling sound like that of a broken water pump is emanating from the middle of my father's ribcage.

"Take care of him for a minute." I motion to my wife. "I'm going to call an ambulance." Leaving her—the kindest, most forgiving, of the many *"verflugten Schikses"* my father has, for the past thirty years, cursed and damned—holding him tenderly by the hand and stroking his forehead, I run from the room.

I have, for thirty-six years, accompanied my father to so many doctors' offices, worried about him through so many illnesses, sat beside him in so many hospitals (their names—Harkness Pavilion, Columbia Presbyterian, Flushing, Doctor's, Elmhurst, Mt. Sinai—echo like a kind of liturgy through my mind as I drive), that it's hard to believe—as I follow the ambulance, red light flashing, through towns with familiar names like Woodbourne, South Fallsburg, Liberty, and Monticello—that this trip will be the last of its kind.

A strange calm fills me as I drive, somewhat akin to Emily Dickinson's "After great pain, a formal feeling comes." It's a clear, cool Catskill night, the ambulance and my car virtually the only vehicles on the road, and, as I drive, I'm aware of the fact that—perhaps for the first time in my adult life—my wish for my father and my wish for myself are one: that he won't survive the night. If there was ever a good time for him to die, I realize, it's now: He has "waited" for me and my family to arrive. He hasn't suffered a great deal. He has, his mind virtually gone, little to look forward to. His surviving my stepmother would be, from both a physical and psychological point of view, a disaster for everyone.

It's about 9:45 when we pull into the emergency room parking lot of Sullivan County Hospital. The rear door of the ambulance opens to reveal my father, still marginally conscious but quite heavily sedated to alleviate the congestive heart failure from which he is suffering.

"What a lovely man," the paramedic says to me as he rolls the stretcher through the automatic doors, and I picture my father, just moments before, in what will no doubt prove to be his last words, telling him: "God loves you, and so do I."

Several hours later, when the doctor on duty comes to get me in the waiting room, my father is already unconscious, his blood sugar up to an astronomically high 400, his kidney function virtually gone, his stomach distended, his forehead going cold. She asks me if "extraordinary measures" should be taken. "No," I reply, without a second's hesitation: "There've been," I add under my breath, "more than enough extraordinary measures already." Having spent the first twenty-five years of my life in constant fear of the fact that my father would abandon me and die, I am now seized by an opposing panic: He will live forever . . . Both of them, in fact, will live forever. An ironic little couplet I once wrote enters my mind as I stand there gazing at him:

> For years I struggled vainly to forgive them.
> Now I want merely to outlive them.

Seated beside my father as I wait for him to be taken upstairs to the cardiac unit, I stroke his head and speak to him softly in German, trying to let him know that someone—his nephew, his son, *does it really matter any longer which?*— is there. But he seems, at this point, already beyond all knowing, and I, in a certain sense, feel at a point beyond all feeling. My words, like Claudius's in *Hamlet*, rise up; my thoughts remain below. At just past 2:00 A.M., the nurses finally come to wheel my father upstairs. "You can stay here and try and get some sleep," the head nurse says, motioning me to a waiting room beside the elevator. "Someone will come and get you if anything happens."

At around three in the morning, wanting at least to see my father again, I slip into his room, where a solitary nurse is monitoring his life-support system. My father's head, now, is almost entirely cold. "He's on 100 percent oxygen," the nurse says. "And his vital signs are very low."

About a half hour later, as I lie on the sofa beside a soda machine trying to get some rest, I hear what sounds like an alarm bell ringing somewhere on the corridor, followed by the sound of running feet. I suddenly realize that, if my father is to die that night, I want to be there when it happens—not, as I have read was the custom in some ancient societies, in order to inhale his last breath, but, rather, simply to bear witness—simply to *be* there, this time.

I get up and hurry toward his room. But I'm already too late. A small cluster of paramedics, nurses, and physicians are gathered around my father's bed, vigorously trying to bring the dead man back to life by pumping his chest.

As I stand by the door and watch, an old fantasy—one I had thousands of times in thousands of different guises as a child—suddenly resurrects itself: I will protect him. I will not allow anyone else to hurt this man, whom life has hurt so much already. It is the same fantasy I had when I once contemplated my father being mugged by someone down in the fur market; the same fantasy I had about avenging myself on the man who, when my father once helped him up after a "fall" on a New York subway platform, reciprocated by stealing his wallet; the fantasy of beating the brains out of any young punk who would so much as dare take advantage of my aging, heart-conditioned, harmonica-playing father.

But my father, now, is beyond helping, and I, battered by so many years of betrayals and disappointments and curses and refusals, am beyond really wanting to help. "Wait in the other room," one of the nurses interrupts my reveries. "I'll come and get you." A few minutes later, she does.

"I'm very sorry," the nurse says, putting her arms around me and handing me my father's watch, ring, and wallet. It is 3:30 A.M., July 22, 1996. On this midsummer night in the Catskills, more than forty-seven years after he had come to New Jersey to "pick me up," my life with my father is finally at an end.

I should, I realize—if for no other reason than to support the moral ambiguities of my writerly vocation—stay in the room awhile with my father's body. Perhaps his ghost will have some message for me that his living self could never articulate? Perhaps—if I sit beside his cold, lifeless body, the yellowish ends of the oxygen tubes still inserted in his nostrils—some final insight, some poignant final farewell, awaits me . . . something I might have used, it now occurs to me, in this book.

But I don't want to linger, don't have anything more, at this point, to say to my father. He has been—since that long-ago time when I was forever accompanying him to Dr. Werther the cardiologist's—dying, and now, finally, he's actually gone and done it. Like the boy perpetually crying wolf, he's been crying death almost all my life. And now, indeed, he is dead. And I—the son who had been, up to the very last moments of his life, his "nephew;" the nephew who had never quite been his son—want to get out of that hospital, out of that room, away from my dead father's body.

Maybe, it occurs to me later, I *should* have done what I failed to do: Maybe I *should* have stayed in that room at Sullivan County Hospital, gazed, long and hard, at that dead body of his, and repeated, over and over, the words:

Now you are dead, you poor son of a bitch, and you can no longer speak your curse over every moment of potential happiness in my life. Now you can no longer curse my son and my wife and every other woman I have ever experienced pleasure with. You can no longer wish for me to repeat the sexual and marital misery of your own life. You can no longer inflict on me your dead mother and your wretched childhood and your sick religion and your miserable wife and your cruel Nazis and your sacrificed love. You can no longer fill my ears with your pious homilies, trying to convince me that it is better to be the victim of injustice than its perpetrator, that the way you call into the forest the forest will echo back, that whoever sleeps with dogs will wake with fleas.

You are dead, father who was not my father, pain that should not have been my pain. You are dead you are dead you are dead you are dead you are dead you are dead.

But that isn't, at that moment, what I want to do. What I want, right then, is just to get out of that room as fast as I can. What I want is to get back to my sleeping wife and son, back to something that is blood.

My stepmother, poor thing, is already a hysteric by nature; *this*—her third journey into widowhood, and the event she has dreaded now for some more than thirty-five years—will surely be too much for her to take. Isabelle and I decide it would be unwise to break the news to her without a doctor around to administer a sedative.

I go to her room, where she's already awake, having hardly slept, and tell her my father is resting comfortably in the hospital, and that we'll go visit him after breakfast. While she's eating, I go to the phone booth and call the doctor who treated my father when we arrived at the hospital, explaining the situation and asking if we might bring my stepmother to her office and break the news to her *there*, after which the doctor could, mercifully, administer a shot of some sort of tranquilizer.

The doctor, possessed of all the empathy of Attila the Hun, reluctantly agrees, and mumbles quick directions to her office, located on some country road in a rather remote Catskill village about half an hour from our hotel. I tell her we hope to be there by around ten.

After her usual breakfast repertoire of harassing the waitress for hotter coffee, softer boiled eggs, and a fresh grapefruit instead of juice, we pile my stepmother into our rental car and start down the road out of Woodbourne in search of the doctor's office. *"Ach, der Mann wird mir doch wieder gesund werden,"* my stepmother keeps repeating—"Oh, that man surely will get well again for my sake"—it, apparently, never having occurred to her that he might have wanted to get well for his own.

The doctor's office is a real killer to find, which we do only after getting lost several times and it being nearly eleven, by which time my stepmother is in a panic and, of course, wondering why I'm having such a tough time finding the hospital. I explain to her that I had told the doctor we'd stop by her office first, which seems to calm her a bit. Once we get into the doctor's waiting room, the doctor—whose Hippocratic oath obviously didn't include paying any special attention to ninety-year-old just-widowed women—keeps us waiting our turn, my repeated pleas notwithstanding, while she treats a variety of children with cuts and colds and a series of apparent allergy sufferers.

Finally, at almost noon, we're ushered into the tiny cubicle of a treatment room, where—while the doctor stands by granite faced and silent—I inform my stepmother that my father died during the night.

"*Ich dachte schon dass es dieser Mann nicht überlebt,*" she says—"I had a feeling that man wouldn't survive this," and then, after a brief series of "*Was mach ich jetzt, ohne den Mann?*"—"What will I do now, without that man?"—my stepmother's panic-stricken gaze around the room reveals, not so much the need for a tranquilizer, but the fact that she thinks she has misplaced her beloved pocketbook.

"I'm very sorry, Mrs. Blumenthal," the doctor, in an unguardedly sentimental moment, finally manages, before ushering us politely out of the room and welcoming the next allergy patient.

My stepmother's emergency care completed, we head straight back to the hotel, discussing the funeral and other arrangements along the way. To her unending credit, my stepmother manages to inquire at least once as to whether my father suffered before he died, which I assure her he didn't.

By the time we arrive back at the South Wind, it's lunchtime, and my now thrice-widowed stepmother is very much back in her usual mode of looking out for number one. To my wife's and my amazement, she exhibits an even-better-than-usual appetite: Appetizer, soup, a generous helping of the main course—pot roast—and a large piece of apple pie with ice cream for dessert.

"Ich muss doch richtig essen," she says. *"Venn nicht für mich selbst, denn wenigstens den guten Mann zu lieb. . . . Er hätte es doch so gewollt."*—"I have to eat well, if not for myself then at least for that good man's sake. . . . He would have wanted it that way."

Driving back to New York from Woodbourne for my father's funeral the next day, my stepmother decides she must first stop at the hairdresser's, even before arriving at her house in Jackson Heights. *"So kann ich doch nicht die Leute mich sehen lassen"*—"I can't let people see me this way"—she says, fondling her gray-white curls.

It's raining hard as we head down the New York Thruway into the Bronx, and my stepmother's beloved niece and nephew, Rosi and Alfred Oestrich—who will also inherit virtually everything she owns—are supposed to be waiting for us in front of her house, in what is now a drenching downpour.

"Don't you want to stop at the house first, and let Alfred and Rosi in?" I ask as we cross the Triboro Bridge.

"They can wait," says my stepmother of her two most cherished relatives, both close to eighty themselves, and not in the best of health. "I have to take care of my hair first."

"You're going to be in for an unpleasant surprise when you see your father's will," my cousin Edgar, the one truly decent member of my father's and stepmother's entire clan, informs me as we drive downtown from Alice's house in Jackson Heights to identify my father's body at the Riverside Memorial Chapel.

"Your father, as I always said, was a good man—but I'm afraid he was also a *Waschlappen*." *Waschlappen* is the German word for washcloth, or for someone who has no spine.

By now, of course, there's little that can surprise me. I'd be happy, merely, to not have my father come back from the world of the dead. I just want some peace.

"And as for Alice," Edgar continues, "*that's* still another story." My stepmother, it turns out, is the Homer of last wills and testaments. "Do you know," Edgar asks, "that I have no fewer than *nineteen* unsigned wills of hers in my briefcase, each of which she made out, and then was too cheap to pay her lawyer, Lissner, the hundred and fifty bucks to come out to the house and have it signed? Why, every time somebody brought her a box of chocolates or did her a favor of any kind, the woman went and changed her will."

This, too, comes as no surprise to me, having long ago realized that my stepmother was the living embodiment of one of my now-dead father's favorite half-Yiddish proverbs: *"Wer nicht gibt eret, gibt beret."* Something to the effect of: *Whoever doesn't give with warm hands gives with cold.*

Finally we find a parking space somewhere near the funeral home, where, after giving us the rundown of the funeral costs (a whopping $8,864), a very congenial African American woman escorts us into a private room, where my father's body, gazing expressionlessly skyward and draped in a simple white prayer shawl, lies propped up in a plain wooden casket

I don't—or, perhaps, can't—look for long, though I do look long enough to make sure it is, indeed, him, while Edgar, ever the good nephew in death as in life, places a hand softly to his lips and then onto my father's forehead.

A better man than I am, I think, but also a tad luckier: This man lying dead there in that wooden box was merely his uncle.

~

My father's funeral, not entirely unlike his life, is a study in irony: The Riverside Memorial Chapel's rental rabbi, a mellow-faced, convivial man by the name of Rabbi Jacob Goldberg, was, it turns out, also formerly the rabbi of the more-assimilated and less Orthodox Fort Tryon Jewish Center—the synagogue (both *too* assimilated and not sufficiently Orthodox for my frustrated cantor father) where all my friends, with the exception of Raymond Fleischhaker, were bar-mitzvahed.

As I hold my son Noah's two small hands in mine, we lift a shovelful of dirt onto the pine casket that contains his grandfather's earthly remains, and speak the words *"Yisgadal v'yiskadash sh'may rabbo, B'olmo deev'ro chirusay, v'yamleech malchusay. . . ."* But it is the words, once again, of the Irish bard Yeats that, somehow, reverberate in my heart and mind:

> Though grave-diggers' toil is long,
> Sharp their spades, their muscles strong,
> They but thrust their buried men
> Back in the human mind again.

Noah squeezes my hand, stares at the coffin disappearing beneath the dirt, and listens attentively to the rabbi's words. After the rabbi's tactful and entirely appropriate eulogy, it's now the ever-loyal prodigal son's turn to speak.

"My father," I begin, "was a man who lived his life, and died, by proverbs and aphorisms. *'Besser Unrecht ertragen als Unrecht tun'*—'Better the victim of injustice than its perpetrator'—he always said, and he was often—at the hands of fate, at the hands of his loveless stepmother, at the hands of the Nazis—the victim of injustice. *'Wie man in den Wald hinein ruft, so schallt es wieder her-*

aus'—'The way you shout into the forest, so it echoes back'—he said. *'Mit dem Hut in der Hand, geht man durch das ganze Land'*—'With your hat in your hand, you can pass through many lands.' Wherever he went, he had his hat in his hand, a flattering word on his lips.

" *'Es ist nicht nötig dass man lebt,'* he always maintained—It isn't necessary to live—*'aber dass man seine Pflicht tut'*—but to do one's duty. And he always, to his dying day, tried to do his duty. *'Möge er in Frieden ruhen'*—'May he rest in peace'—my father said at the death of many a friend and relative, and over many a grave. So let us say it now of him: May he rest in peace. Amen."

Following the service, Rabbi Goldberg comes over to shake my hand. "I hope we'll stay in touch," he says warmly, reminding me a bit of my father and the Officer Tumilinskys of the world as he places a business card in my hand. Looking down at the card, I see the following inscription:

MOURNERS' AFTER-CARE INSTITUTE

Rabbi Jacob Goldberg, *President*

"I'm afraid, Rabbi," I say, half laughing and half weeping, "you're about thirty-seven years too late."

I am seated in the office of my father's attorney—Michael D. Lissner, Esq., on West Fifty-seventh Street—a lawyer specializing in estate work for German-Jewish refugees. It is only thanks to my stepmother's generosity—a call to her regarding this matter having first been required—that I have even been allowed to *see* my father's will. Given my sense by now that every interaction with my father, living or dead, will lead to some sort of betrayal—

along with a warning from my father's nephew Edgar, who has already seen the will, that I am in for an unpleasant surprise—I'm prepared for the worst.

And the worst—a worst so ludicrous and incredible that it leaves me with little else to do but laugh at its tragi-comic dimensions—is exactly what my eyes are confronted with. The LAST WILL AND TESTAMENT OF JULIUS BLUMENTHAL consists of two parts, only the first of which—given the fact that my stepmother has outlived him—is relevant. In its operative section, after directing that my father's funeral expenses be paid, it consists of only one relevant sentence: "All the rest, residue and remainder of my real and personal property which I shall own at the time of my death or over which I may have a power of appointment, I give, devise and bequeath to my wife, ALICE BLUMENTHAL."

But the best, the most comically ludicrous, is yet to come—the section that *would* have gone into effect had my stepmother predeceased him:

If she does not survive me, then as follows:

1. TEN THOUSAND ($10,000.00) Dollars to Noah Blumenthal, presently residing at 40 Inman Street, Cambridge, Mass. 02139.

2. FIVE THOUSAND ($5,000.00) Dollars to *each* of the following:
   a. My niece, JUDITH WILLIS, presently residing at 1210 Kathy Lane, Newfield, N.J. 08344.
   b. CLAIRE HAAS, presently residing at 17 Bettenweg, Hainburg, Germany 64542."

And then, as if the shock and pathos of the above weren't enough, comes the posthumous clincher:

3. The balance of my estate as follows:
   a. FIFTY (50%) per cent thereof to the JACKSON HEIGHTS JEWISH COMMUNITY CENTER.
   b. FIFTY (50%) per cent thereof to CONGREGATION BETH HILLEL in Washington Heights, New York.

So there it is—in perfect English—the poignant final epistle of my father's life: Ten thousand dollars to his only grandchild; five thousand dollars to my biological sister, his niece; five thousand dollars to his *long-dead* former girlfriend (how, I think in a comic aside, were they possibly going to get it to her?), and *the rest of his estate*—this man who had a living son and a living grandson—to a moribund synagogue in Washington Heights that he hadn't attended in thirty years, and a local one in Jackson Heights to which he had hardly any historical connection.

Biology, I realize, gazing down at this incredible document, *must* be destiny: Nowhere on my father's last will and testament is there the slightest indication that he ever had a son.

I exit the A train at the 181st Street station, emerging into the late afternoon light just across the street from the apartment building where I spent the first sixteen years of my life, and begin walking toward Amsterdam Avenue, the same walk my father and I took on countless Jewish holidays and Sabbaths as we wove our way to Congregation Beth Hillel.

But now it is more than thirty years since I last took this walk, and I am very much alone as I stroll pensively through this once entirely German-Jewish-refugee neighborhood that has now become a Latin American *barrio*. What astonishes me, as the rhythmically musical sounds of Spanish, rather than German, fill my ears, is not that so few of the small shops and specialty stores I knew as a child have survived, but that *any* of them have: I marvel to discover that small, family-owned Joseph's Shoe Store still exists, as does Wertheimer's Department Store and Cushman's Bakery.

For the most part, however, it is a world transformed and unrecognizable: gone are the kosher butchers and the Daitch Dairy; gone is Hobby Land, where we used (discreetly) to shop for toys across the street from the synagogue; gone is the small fish market where I used to shop with my mother, marveling over the glistening, scaly rows of cod, halibut and flounder; gone is the foreign-language Heights theater where, on my first foray into the world of films, I saw *Der Hauptmann von Köpenick* in German with my father and Helen.

But now it is a different world as, less than two weeks after my father's death, I traverse the somehow smaller and decidedly shabbier confines of Congregation Beth Hillel and make my way to the third-row seat where my father's name plate was once (and should still be) affixed.

I search in vain for my father's name, but find, instead, only the weathered outline of its metal plate and a single lingering screw that once held it in place. I look down at the locked wooden box at my feet where my father always kept his tallis and prayer books, suddenly realizing that I have neither the key nor the slightest idea where among my father's remaining belongings it might be. I hurry to the back of the temple, taking a book and a prayer shawl from the piles for borrowing by the more intermittently devout.

I've come this night, having found myself in New York for other reasons, to say Kaddish for my father in this place where, on so many prior occasions, I—a young boy already lacking any real religious convictions—once stood beside him. Even tonight it is a writerly rather than a religious longing that has brought me—a longing for meaning, for the same kind of narrative coherence I strive for in my work, a wish to have my father's story end, at least in part, in the place where, for me at least, it began.

But, as I take my seat and futilely survey the minuscule gathering of no more than a dozen men in search of a familiar face, it suddenly dawns on me that it is not only my father who is gone: The faces I see in this temple he helped found (and to which he would have left fully half his estate), though mostly well past my own age, are no longer his generation's but those of the next. And *that* generation, I can see from the hunched backs and limping gaits, is dying out as well. Well over a decade ago, in fact, the congregation's current president informs me, the congregation was forced to merge with another, less Orthodox one nearby, merely in order to survive.

Gazing up at the stained-glass memorial windows, I see the commemorative plaques for my two childhood rabbis, Baerwald and Stransky—the rabbis, respectively, who didn't appreciate my jokes, and who wouldn't let me attend my mother's funeral—both long gone. Then, in the row just behind me, is the nameplate of the cantor with whom I studied for my bar mitzvah, Fred Kornfeld, also gone. Allowing my eyes, now, to wander along the decaying synagogue's walls, I realize that dozens upon dozens of new memorial lights have, in the decades since I last sat in this pew, been mounted on the walls; quite literally, the congregation of the dead now far outnumbers that of the living.

"*Yisgadal v'yiskadash sh'may rabbo, B'olmo deev'ro chirusay, v'yamleech malchusay . . . ,*" I again begin mouthing the words of the Jewish prayer for the dead in honor of my father. But, as I do so, I am well aware that it is not really his death I am mourning.

After the service I descend the flight of stairs leading to the reception room, where, almost thirty-five years ago, my bar mitzvah reception was held. A strong scent of rotted wood and urban dampness greets me as I enter the now poignantly empty and dilapidated room, filled with the cold, hazy light of bare bulbs and randomly strewn collapsible chairs. Not even an echo of celebration is palpable any longer, only a lost, unresurrectable world. I stop to urinate in the dank, rundown bathroom, make my way back up the creaking stairs, and turn out the lights.

On my way back to Fort Washington Avenue, I walk past the still-functioning pizzeria to which my friend Raymond and I impatiently ran each year after synagogue to break the Yom Kippur fast with a huge, fifteen-cent slice. I pass the old Woolworth's where once—now so many years ago it seemed almost a dream—I emerged, in a moment that now seems pregnant with meaning, holding what I thought was my father's hand, only to find myself mistakenly holding the hand of stranger. I pass the RKO Coliseum, now a multiplex, where, for seventy-five cents, I once saw a double feature of *The House on Haunted Hill* and *The Tingler*.

As I proceed down the lively streets, the sounds of a language I love but do not really speak fill my ears; the sight of young Latinos running and jumping, rather than old Jews limping, invades my eyes. Soon, my father's name, too, will be mounted beside yet another memorial light on Congregation Beth Hillel's crowded wall.

But neither he nor his world, I realize as I descend once more into the same subway station I so frequently entered as a child, exist any longer. The world of my father is gone. It is now the world of my son.

It's Thursday, September 6, 1996, four days before what would have been my father's ninety-second birthday. I've just gotten off an airplane from Tel Aviv, en route to what will be a month teaching in Boise, Idaho. But first my stepmother and I have some important business to attend to: Whatever, beyond the black borders of my father's will, may be left of my patrimony now awaits me.

Just after the 10:00 A.M. opening time, I pull my father's car up to a parking meter in front of the Chemical Bank's Jackson Heights Branch on Eighty-second Street and Roosevelt Avenue and open the passenger door to help my stepmother out. I deposit two quarters, giving us, as she reminds me, just an hour to accomplish our task, lest we have to deposit another quarter or—worse yet—risk a ten-dollar fine.

Entering the bank, my stepmother first carefully reaches into her pocketbook and removes the key. We inform the teller that we are here to get some things from my parents' safe deposit box. He directs us downstairs, where my stepmother, exercising every possible caution to make sure I don't see its number, hands the key to the attendant. After entering the vault itself to remove the long aluminum box, the attendant directs us to a small, private room off to one side where we can go about our business in complete privacy.

We take a seat, as I clear the flotsam and jetsam of various ashtrays and supplies from the table to make sure we will have enough room to accomplish the day's task. Then I lift open the lid of the safe deposit box, revealing two massive stacks of rubber-band-encircled stock certificates, along with a small zippered leather pouch, which my stepmother, in a rare outburst of seeming generosity, places in front of me on the table.

"Dass sin die Rings von Betty," she says. *"Sie gehören Dir."* "These are your mother's rings . . . They belong to you." Unzipping the pouch, I find three crumpled and rolled-up fragments of paper inside, parchmented with age, along with a Scotch-taped scrap of transparent plastic, in which sits a small diamondlike stone. Trembling, I open the first, from which a thin gold wedding band falls to the floor.

"*MY Wedding Ring*," I read my father's handwriting on the scrap of yellow legal pad. "*February 2.38 Freiburg Rabbi Dr. Sheuermann s.a.*" And then, in a different-colored pen, obviously written at a later date: "*TO MY SON MICHAEL.*"

Half wrapped around the small plastic sack there is a grease-stained dollop of paper, on which is written, once again in my father's hand, the words "*pleas WATCH the Brilliant stone which is lose in Papier.*" And then, on a separate smidgen of masking tape, which must once have surrounded the plastic, the words "*Belongs to son MICHAEL from Jettchen s.a.* [a distant cousin]"

Moving on through what seems to be all there is of my inheritance, as my stepmother nervously fingers her stock certificates beside me, I unroll yet another scrap of badly torn paper, this one white, from which a diamond-inlaid silver band with one stone missing and an oval-shaped gold ring bedecked with a white pearl tumble out. On both sides of the gold ring are mounted two small red stones surrounded at their four corners by tiny diamonds.

On the paper, in my father's inimitable calligraphy, is written:

DEAR SON! PLEASE WATCH the ONE LOOSE DIA-MOND STONE IN THE PLASTIC paper THE Ring with out STONES explanation: one stone is in this PLASTIC paper the other one Dear Michael you gave me to put on my SIEGEL RING/ which I wore till today *on happy occasions.*

Then, on the back, scrawled in the usual mélange of German and English, I discover the words: "*Von seinem Ring (silber) hat mir Michael einen Brillant STONE geschenkt um meinen Siegel Ring zu zieren.*" (Michael gave me one brilliant stone from his silver ring as a gift with which to decorate my signet ring.)

The event, as it still lives in my memory, had a slightly different resonance than the one described by my father: The original diamond-set silver ring had been given to me by my grandmother's cousin Jette in Denmark; my parents, without asking me, had simply *taken* one of the stones to fit into the black onyx setting given to my father as a seventieth birthday present by my stepmother.

Moving on to "package" three, a thick clump of yellowish paper surrounded by yet another rubber band, on which are scrawled the words *"Rings from Betzle selig TO Michael,"* I unravel it and allow an elongated-diamond-studded silver ring I immediately recognize as my mother's (the ring that was supposed, now on *two* occasions, to become my wife's, and never has) to thud onto the stock-covered table. On a second scrap of folded yellow paper, the top of which is decorated with my father's classic leaf-and-feather insignia and his equally characteristic combination of print and script, is written:

BETZELE SELIG RINGS TOOK FROM HER Hand on
the DEATH BED 9–25–59 8:45. We loved you so much
rest in SchoLAUM DEAR BETZLE! DR. Weismann took
the marriage Ring from her Hand.

Also inside the small packet containing my mother's ring is one of my father's old white business cards—"JULIUS BLUMENTHAL fine furs"—on the back of which is written, in a combination of red and blue inks (which extends, on one occasion, to a word and its umlaut), and of German and English: *"STERBE TAG From OUR Beloved Mami 9–25–58. DEAR LIESEL! Dieses gehört nur Michael zum Andenken an seine gute Mami Betty. Thank you!"*—"This belongs only to Michael, in memory of his good mother Betty."

My stepmother, by now, is in a near fit of impatience (the

meter, after all, is running), so, placing my bounty carefully in my jacket pocket, I unroll the rubber bands from the two massive rolls of stock certificates.

"We'll make three piles," she says, turning toward me. "One for the stocks which are only mine, one for those which were mine and your father's" (now hers as well), "and one for those which belong to you. Okay?"

"Okay," I say, nodding my head.

"Aber sei vorsichtig—But be careful," she adds. "Don't get them confused."

I assure her, with all my heart, that I won't, for there is, in fact, nothing to get confused *about. It is no longer a question of the handwriting on the wall,* I say to myself in a parenthetical moment of near-humor, *but of the typewriting on the stocks.*

And so our little game of financial triage begins as, slowly, from the Torah scroll of my stepmother's accumulated shares, the litany of her life and loves is slowly laid bare: 3,000 shares of Consolidated Edison: Alice Blumenthal; 5,000 shares of Exxon: Alice Blumenthal; 1,300 shares of Coca-Cola: Alice Blumenthal; 300 shares of IBM: Alice Blumenthal; 500 shares of Phillips Petroleum: Alice Blumenthal; 300 shares of Bell Atlantic: Julius and Alice Blumenthal; 500 shares of Pacific Telesis: Julius and Alice Blumenthal; 500 shares of Ohio Edison: Julius and Alice Blumenthal And on we go, for what seems to me, meter running and all, an eternity.

Every twenty-five certificates or so, a kind of financial hiccup enters into our proceedings as a stock certificate marked JULIUS BLUMENTHAL CUST FOR MICHAEL CHARLES BLUMENTHAL U-T [under the] NEW YORK UNIF GIFTS TO MINORS ACT, invariably bearing a purchase date from the early 1960s, emerges from the carnage. Whenever it does—before allowing me to place it on top of the strudel-dough-thin pile of what is now, irrevocably, mine—my stepmother brings the certificate virtually up against her face, lest there be some still-revocable error, and then, finally, with a tug that is the financial equivalent of a drowning person's letting go of a life raft, relinquishes it into my by-now-fatigued and trembling hand.

Within a half hour of this activity, with, my stepmother never fails to remind me, time running out on our meter, the three piles assembled before us—one a good twelve inches high, the second approximately half its size, the third in danger of being dispersed by the mere breeze from the ceiling fan—make glaringly obvious some things I have always, somewhere deep in my heart, suspected, if not known: The woman seated at the table beside me—this "mother" of mine whose sickbeds and traumas and emergencies and husband I have been attending to, now, for some forty years without having ever possessed even the key to her house—is an extremely wealthy woman; along with her own fortune, she has taken—with or without whatever "consent" he may still have been capable of—virtually all of my father's money. And there, spread out on the table before me in all its naked splendor, is the accumulated reward for my being—as my stepmother herself had always put it—*"zu gut, zu anständig, zu zart, zu weich"*—too good, too decent, too tender, too soft: I—the son who was never really a son, the boy who was always, actively or passively, discouraged from being a man—have been, for all practical purposes, disinherited.

"Wir müssen gehen—der Meter läuft ab," the three-times-widowed heiress says, gathering her beloved certificates in her arms the way a tired Chippewa woman might gather her infant.

Yes, I say, it's time to go. I have, after all, now been presented with the stark reality of what I came here to find out. At last—or so I hope—I am free.

∾

We return to my stepmother's house, where she wants me to begin reregistering my father's stock certificates in her name, and attending to various of her other numerous "financial" matters before leaving to teach for a month in Idaho the next morning.

"*Sei gut zu ihr*"—"Be good to her"—my brother's father-in-law, Abe Greenberg, had whispered to me as we left my father's funeral, intuiting, I'm sure, that there was money to be gained by my benevolence. But I realize by now—as I should have thirty-six years ago—that there's neither love nor money to be found at this venue, and I'm merely biding my time until the departure of Northwest Flight 861 for Minneapolis the next morning.

"How," I turn to my stepmother, hoping to get even a partial answer to some final questions, "could a man with a single son and a single living grandson possibly decide to leave *all* his money to two synagogues?"

She pauses momentarily, looking me—at least as nearly as she can come to so personal an act—in the eye. "Your father told me," she says, not a trace of apology in her voice, "that he didn't want the money he had worked so hard for all his life to go to a *goyische* family."

"And how about the car?" I—bordering now on pure desperation—ask, referring to my father's hardly-ever-driven 1992 Buick, parked in front of us in the driveway. "I'd like at least to buy it from you, since you can't drive it, and, when we come back to the States, we won't have a car."

"*Oh, es tut mir so leid*"—"I'm so sorry," my stepmother says. "*Ich habe es schon der Putzfrau versprochen*"—"I already promised it to the cleaning woman."

Growing increasingly numb, I remove a pair of folding chairs from the front foyer closet and my stepmother and I, in the noble tradition of her and my father, sit out on her concrete front porch talking—of course—about money. She's got the phone, courtesy of a long extension cord running from the kitchen, in hand, and—with a reluctance outweighed only by the prospect of the revenue it might ultimately secure—makes a "long distance" phone call to an acquaintance in remote, thirty-five-cents-a-minute Fort Lee, New Jersey. He is someone who, she has been told, may be able to help her reregister my father's German restitution *(Wiedergutmachung)* payments in her name.

Within seconds, ever the grieving widow, she's in tears, sobbingly imploring a certain ninety-one-year-old Mr. Weinbaum to *please, please* help her resolve this situation *immediately*—it is terribly urgent. There is, after all, some six hundred dollars a month involved, and she desperately needs the money. How else will she survive?

The phone call completed with only a tentative commitment by Mr. Weinbaum (who, no doubt, has been thoroughly exhausted by her hysteria) to come to Jackson Heights tomorrow and help sort out the crisis, my stepmother, after quickly putting down the receiver to assure there will be no further charge for the Grieving Widow Show, bursts into sobs—not out of grief at her husband's passing, but in a panic that she will be unable to survive financially without the added revenue of his reparations.

Notwithstanding some thirty-six years experience with this kind of behavior, I am momentarily stunned—indeed, almost moved to pity—by the sheer pathos of my stepmother's ravings. Here, seated beside me, is a ninety-year-old woman whose net assets, as I have just witnessed, must be in the *millions,* and she is here, literally weeping over a delay in getting yet another six hundred dollars a month!

There *is*, of course, something—were I someone less involved in, less wounded by, all this—heartrending and pitiable about it. What, I ask myself, in this woman's accumulated life experience, what pre- or post-Holocaust trauma, could have made of a potentially normal human being such a paltry wreck, such a bundle of impoverishments, that not all her accumulated millions can provide her—even now, at the age of ninety—with some consolation?

But, sadly, I feel myself to be beyond pity—I am trying with all my might, in fact, to avoid it in its most unappealing form: the one in which it is directed primarily toward the self. I turn away from the tear-struck figure beside me on the porch and contemplate the imminent departure of Northwest Flight 861, the flight that will transport me, forever more, far from her stocks, her prayer books, her saturated postage stamps, her pathetic and loveless life.

Back in New York a month later, I am walking along Riverside Drive with Melanie, a former student, with whom I'm discussing my father's death and—but for the piddling amount of stocks he was unable to divest me of—my virtual disinheritance. Melanie and I have, since her student days at Harvard, become friends, and one of the things I admire—and envy—about her, in addition to her literary talent, is that she's possessed of the kind of savvy, real-world smarts and lack of sentimentality which the offspring of Harvard professors and the like are usually more prone to than the children of Holocaust survivors. Indeed, when we meet at our appointed place, the Upper West Side Barnes & Noble, it's not *Rilke on Love and Other Difficulties* Melanie is reading, but *MONEY* magazine. My kind of girl, or so I wish.

As I begin recounting to Melanie the events leading up to my father's last hours, and the somewhat humorous though macabre ones following them, culminating in my visit to the Chemical Bank and my father's lawyer's office, I suddenly see a light go on in Melanie's eyes.

"How old were you when he put those stocks in trust for you?" she asks.

"Oh, about ten or twelve."

"And what happened to the *dividends* during all those years?"

"I don't know. I assume they spent them."

"They?"

"Yeah, my parents."

"But those dividends," Melanie says emphatically, turning toward me, "those dividends were *yours*. Who paid the taxes on them, by the way?"

"Well," I say, almost embarrassed by my lack of smarts as to fiscal matters. "For the last bunch of years, in fact, *I* did."

"Well, then," Melanie concludes with a prosecutor's assertiveness, "you really ought to *do* something about that."

Somewhere in the middle of her life's journey, Alice Bernheimer Kahn Guggenheim Blumenthal must have had a brilliant idea: Although the stocks that my father, early in their marriage, had set aside for me "under the New York Uniform Gift to Minors Act" were—to what must have been her acute disappointment—untouchable by either of my parents, the *dividends*, she must have realized, arrived quarterly, in checks made out to my father, and could be disposed of in any way my parents chose.

And dispose of them, indeed, is what they did: For the next forty-plus years, in fact, in an amount whose *net* worth I then calculate to be around $62,809.95, interest and appreciation not included.

But my stepmother's financial imagination hardly stopped there: Why not, she must have figured, send sweet little Mikeylein (and, later, his wife and son) the 1099 income tax forms and have *him* pay the taxes on the dividends *my parents* had already spent on themselves? Brilliant idea, eh?

And so I, dumb schmuck— not realizing, for some dozen

years, what it is they are doing, what it is, in fact, they have *already* done—proceed to *pay* the bloody taxes on money I have never actually laid eyes on. There are no limits, I will later realize, to a good son's blindness.

While still in New York, I also talk by phone from my hotel room in mid-Manhattan to my "aunt" Nelly—my *mother*—at her retirement community in Northern New Jersey.

In the now nearly forty-eight years of my life, she has never once mentioned the dark, badly contained secret that has dwelled, all these years, between us. But now, as we, rather obliquely, discuss my father's will and all my stepmother has done to facilitate my disinheritance—and I repeat once again the question I posed to my stepmother: "How could a man with a single son and a single living grandson possibly leave *all* his money to a couple of synagogues?"—a sudden uncomfortable silence momentarily enters into our conversation from her end.

And then—just as belated as Rabbi Goldberg's calling card from the Mourners' After-Care Institute—a long-withheld acknowledgment works its way through the telephone wires from South Orange, New Jersey, to my attentive ears in mid-Manhattan.

"If we had known that Betty was going to die," says the woman who, biology be damned, will forever remain my aunt—in words I realize it requires no small amount of courage, or pain, to utter—"we would never have given you away."

It's too little, and it's far too late, but I finally decide to do things the American way: I get a lawyer, a very sweet woman by the name of Ninette Bordoff, who's related to my cousin Amos by marriage and who—much to my son's delight—actually works for a firm with offices in the Empire State Building, the skyscraper of his dreams.

My stepmother—whose usual attorney, Michael Lissner, has probably had enough of her myriad unsigned wills and her unwillingness to shell out the measly $150 to have them signed—counters with a nice Italian gentleman named Paul Fusco, procured for her by her nephew (from her second marriage) and Man Friday, an insurance salesman by the name of Charles Selig. (Charles, ever the goodhearted fellow, will ultimately inherit $35,000 plus the house.)

The fact that she actually needs to *pay* this lawyer, I realize, must be breaking her little *echt*-German-Jewish heart, and I, for one, am not going to help her gather up the pieces. But I, too, who can much less afford it, have had to come up with a $5,000 retainer for dear Ninette and her colleague, a deeply congenial, bow-tie-sporting litigator named Gorman Reilly. Ninette and Gorman work for the kind of law firm that doesn't exactly do pro bono work for litigious nonlegatees.

When all else, finally, fails, Gorman and Paul decide to arrange a "summit meeting" at my stepmother's house, to be attended by what is hardly a Passover sederlike cast of characters: myself, my cousin Amos, my stepmother, her nephew Charles, and the attorneys for both sides. My father, if he is watching from some netherworld, must be finding even his "God loves you"s exhausted by this unlikely gathering.

"What we have here," Mr. Fusco, exercising the oratorical prerogatives of his profession, begins, "is the tragedy of a family that has lost its way."

"I beg your pardon," I interrupt, realizing that my stepmother's uglier-than-usual expression of ennui and disgust is no doubt exacerbated by the clicking away of her attorney's two-hundred-dollar-per-hour clock. "But what we have here, really, is a woman who perpetually *refused* to let me be part of this family. In fact, sir, what we have here is not a family at all."

It is, perhaps, futile of me to do so—unless, of course, the litany I am about to recite represents some personal purgation on my part, which it might—but I then go into a brief and radically edited recounting of the past thirty-five years *chez Alice und Ernst*, leaving out the water-soaked postage stamps, but providing the salient details of her progressive alienation of my father's affections, and the various slings and arrows of outrageous fortune that have befallen me at the hands of the not-so-merry widow.

Suddenly, coming from the other side of my stepmother's round kitchen table, I hear a rather unexpected sound. I look across, and there, holding his head in his hands, is my cousin—my *brother*—Amos, shaking with sobs.

"Go on," he says bravely. "I'm sorry."

What's to be sorry about? Lucky guy, I think. At least he can summon enough real emotion to cry. His blood brother, on the other hand, has the writer's disease: It's only on paper that he can weep.

∾

EPILOGUE I: HAIFA, ISRAEL

Full fathom five thy father lies;

Of his bones are coral made:

Those are pearls that were his eyes:

Nothing of him that doth fade,

But doth suffer a sea-change

Into something rich and strange.

—SHAKESPEARE, *THE TEMPEST*

THE HAND HOLDING the camera now is a more tranquil, more focused one: It is mine. As I rewind and review the film of my father I shot just hours before his death, I am seated in Haifa (where I am teaching for the year), just a few miles from my biological brother's and sister's birthplace in Afula, a short distance from the moshav where my biological parents met and lived.

It surprises me how little I feel as I gaze through the viewfinder at this man who, for forty-seven years, was the only father I knew; this man who, straining yet one last time to wave his white handkerchief into the air, already seems among the dead—seems, as I watch him now, to want only one thing from this life: to sleep.

When was it, I wonder half aloud to myself, that my father first began to seem so dead to me? When he first pressed my dead mother's nightgown against my lips instead of allowing me to say good-bye to her actual body? When he married the one woman I dreaded having as a stepmother, whom I knew from the start could never love or want me? When he first began to object to, to damn and to curse, every woman I ever loved or was even attracted to? When I first began to see that he was too weak, too confused, too betrayed a man ever to listen to his own heart—or even to hear what it was saying? When I first realized that I would never, no matter how deeply I craved it, have his blessing for the one act every son aches for his father to bless—his becoming a man? Or was it, perhaps, that day in his car crossing the Triboro Bridge between Queens and Manhattan, when he cursed and damned my wife, my son, my very life?

For so long, now, my father had been gone to me, for so long his deepest loyalties had been elsewhere. For so long—almost all his life, it now seemed to me—he himself had been like a broken record, mouthing the same "God bless yous" and "God loves yous" to everyone, everywhere, telling them all that they could "schtop the traffic."

When, I wondered, as I watched this nearly dead man in the pastel-colored sweater I once bought him as a birthday present valiantly try to seem alive for the camera, had I last—or *ever*—had anything actually resembling a conversation with him? Who was he—this man who couldn't father a child, who couldn't make love to his wives, who couldn't say what he meant, whose life had to be filled with secret mailboxes and secret addresses and secret bank accounts and, for all I knew, secret lovers—but, insofar as I could tell, no real friends?

Watching, again, the face that, hardly ten hours later, will be the face of a corpse, I try to summon up from memory's archives those moments that allowed me, for so many years and at so many bedsides, to be the dutiful son, the loyal son, the devoted son . . . the ever-hopeful son who, fifteen years earlier, in a poem entitled "Watching *La Bohème* with My Father," had written:

> But now, ourselves like two old tenors,
> we sit here, watching Mimi serenade
> Rodolfo, and I understand at last the tremors
> of our long singing, and its purpose. I don't degrade
> these long and lush librettos of dénouement anymore—
> I sit here, awed, as Mimi drags herself across the floor.
>
> And I reflect upon the long and painful arias
> of our duet, its strange and ancient repertoire,
> reverberant with rotten human bonds and barriers.
> Oh father, here we sit at last, in her boudoir,
> convinced the loveliness of song expels its sadness,
> that even tragedy, well sung, reveals a gladness
>
> In the unextinguished heart. And so at last
> we learn to love like this: the cindered past
> merely a prologue to our long cantata,
> the arias all sung, our dying's imprimata.
> For we have learned to sing together rather well—
> before the lights went out, before the curtains fell.

What, I wonder as the film unwinds back into gray from my father's last moments in the sun, if he had died back then, at that moment when, seated upstairs in my stepmother's house, I felt the momentary bond of two sad men watching a tragically beautiful opera together?

But my father *didn't* die then, and so I sit here now, wading through the intervening years of betrayal upon betrayal, disappointment upon disappointment, and try, even in death—out of some surely self-defeating feeling of loyalty to this man who, much like myself, was the child of a prematurely dead mother and a loveless stepmother—to remember the flawed and tragic figure who, all his flaws and darknesses notwithstanding, once tried to show me love.

Nights, now, as I lie in bed with my wife and a certain deep sadness comes over me about the various difficulties of our marriage, I realize that—for better or worse, like it or not—I am, in large measure, this man's son—if not by blood, then at least by fate. And that fate—which I experience not merely in my mind or heart or penis, or even in words, but in every fiber of my deepest, most involuntary being—tells me that, though we may exercise some small freedom in determining who we are and how we end up, the choice, in large measure, is not our own.

So now *I* have a son: Noah Gabriel Blumenthal—my biological father's only blood grandson, my adoptive father's only grandchild of any kind—named, first, for the last just man (the survivor of both God's wrath *and* his benevolence); second, for God's archangel who was the messenger of good news; and, lastly, both for my dead father and myself.

And what if that son, with his moppy brown hair and chestnut eyes, his ecstatic, pleasure-seeking nature and winning smile, his contagious laughter and love of LEGO, Smashmouth, and Mr. Bean had never been born? What if that soul had never been embodied into this world? What if I had, now, no child to call my own, no further blood that was mine, no place beyond this page in which to utter my sometimes-constricted love out into the world?

Gazing now, once again, at the film, I remember the man who, when I was a child, rose many a day singing, in mock Caruso, "Oh, what a beautiful morning. . . ." I remember the man whistling as he emerged from our fifth-floor elevator, bringing me a pound of my beloved Horn & Hardart's rice pudding, taking me downtown to sit on Santa's lap on Christmas Eve and buy a new car for my Lionel Trains. I remember the man on whose lap I sat in that Dollar-a-Record recording booth on Fifty-third Street singing "Golden Days." I remember the not-so-young widower with a blind mother-in-law and ten-year-old son who, on many mornings, got up to pack my lunchbox before going off to the fur district and who placed on our old Grundig Majestic a yellow 45 rpm record of Mickey Mouse and Donald Duck singing "School Days."

I remember, most of all, this man—my betrayed and betraying father, for better and worse—playing his harmonica, waving his white handkerchief, shlepping his furs from place to place, saying to all the world, whether he meant it or not, "God loves you, and so do I."

~

EPILOGUE II: JACKSON HEIGHTS, QUEENS

AS MY PLANE LANDS at La Guardia Airport, where my father uttered so many of his late-life *Auf Wiedersehen*s, the thought suddenly becomes entirely vivid to me: In just six days, I will be fifty years old. Just five years younger than my father when my mother died, two years younger than she was on her deathbed.

Some forty years later, it is my stepmother, at ninety-two, who is on her deathbed, and my aunt—my "real" mother—who is also in a hospital bed some fifty miles away in Livingston, New Jersey, having just taken several bad falls in the retirement community where she now lives, the last one resulting in a hairline fracture.

I haven't laid eyes on my stepmother since she fell down the two stone steps leading to her front porch some six months ago, breaking a hip and several ribs. After several days in critical condition in the Intensive Care Unit of Flushing Hospital, she was placed on a respirator—which she's been on ever since—when one of her broken ribs punctured a lung. After another month in the hospital, she was transferred to the Silver Crest Nursing Home in Flushing, from where she has now been released to around-the-clock care in her beloved house—in other words, sent home to die.

Now, perhaps, both these women—the woman who gave birth to me and the woman who, for forty years was (even now, I can hardly bear to say the word in reference to her) my "mother"—are dying. Two women who, cumulatively, never showed me a minute of anything that could conceivably pass for a mother's love, and, as I head toward my stepmother's house, these heartbreaking lines from my friend Stephen Dunn's beautiful poem, "The Routine Things Around the House" come to mind:

> Now, years later, someone tells me
> Cancers who've never had mother love
> Are doomed and I, a Cancer,
>
> feel blessed again. What luck
> to have had a mother
> who showed me her breasts . . .

But I, a Pisces, have *never*—with the blessed exception of those ten years with my dying mother and my blind grandmother—known "mother's love." And the love of women—the love of the two women who have loved me and become my wives, the love of many women who have tried—has never come easily to me. And I, a Pisces, don't want to be "doomed."

And yet, thanks, mainly, to this dying woman I am about to visit—this woman who came into the life of a grieving ten-year-old adopted boy who had just lost his mother, and who, instead of helping to repair his wounds, only deepened them—I find myself, at fifty years of age, *not* beyond redemption, but—perhaps, I am forced to acknowledge—beyond repair.

The father of a nearly ten-year-old myself, I am all too keenly aware of what he now possesses that I lacked, of what wounds at this very moment—because of wounds of my own which it may be too late (and that may be too deep) to heal—I am no doubt inflicting upon him as well: Wounds that hardly allow me to feel "part" of my own family, since these two women—my "mothers"—never let me feel part of theirs, never even let me have the keys to their house.

What do I wish for this woman whose certain deathbed I am about to visit? Part of me, I realize, wishes for there to be no end—no limit—to her suffering: My sense of justice—a sense that has always been mine, both with respect to the world at large and to myself—wishes for her, now, to suffer for all the suffering and lovelessness she inflicted on me. That part of me that, for so long and so long ago, wanted to kick her and beat her and punish her and make her suffer until she had paid for all my earthly pain, all the mothering she had deprived me of, now wants to be redeemed.

But, when I enter the house, the woman lying on that rented bed—a ninety-two-year-old thrice-widowed, gaunt, toothless, emaciated woman, a plastic tube inserted in her trachea and an intravenous feeding tube in her arm, her lungs powered by a machine, a large, infected, suppurating wound like Philoctetes' on her foot, and her care in the hands of two women whose only attachment to her is the check they receive at the end of each week—is a sight so pathetic, so heartrending, so—how else can I say it?—*sad*, that there is, in fact, little left to hate, little left to grieve for beyond a life lost in its devotion to smallness, selfishness, and the inability to love, a life so without *caritas* and *amour* that it diminished all who came in contact with it.

"She is," her nephew Charles says to me in the kitchen of what ought to be—though it feels like anything *but*—my home, "the last of a dying breed." By this he means, of course, the German-Jewish refugees from, and survivors of, the Holocaust.

For me, however, this is far too unspecific a group: For me she has been far too palpable—far too *individual*—an influence to be part of a "breed," howsoever shared their psychological wounds may be. For me, she was—at this very moment still *is*—one of a kind: the "mother" who could not be my mother, the woman who (along with the woman who bore me and gave me up) may have damaged forever my ability to love as I would choose—my ability, even, to love *myself* the way an intact human being should.

And in some sense, I realize, I am more like my uncle/father Berthold than even biology might have dictated: a man *not* with a bullet in his arm but with a wound in his heart—a wound he has no choice but to carry with him along the byways and sickbeds and chicken farms of this life. A man who—unlike the Greek warrior Philoctetes, rescued from his wounded exile on the island of Lemnos in time to aid in the conquest of Troy—*cannot* make use of his wound to help win a war, but must make use of it the only way a writer can: to help him write a book.

There is no self-pity in my saying this, merely truth. For self-pity, I know (being susceptible to *it* as well) requires nothing by way of courage. But truth does. And this—this pathetic, loveless woman lying on her deathbed, that somehow equally pathetic and loveless woman lying in a hospital bed in New Jersey—is a large part of my truth, as are the three good women (my dead mother, my grandmother, my living wife) who have helped me survive to speak that truth now, who have helped me to become the kind of father who will spare his son, as best I can, a similar fate.

It—this story—is just as much my truth as is my relatively

blessed station (all the preceding notwithstanding) among the world's huge emoluments of misery and suffering. "Griefs," wrote Frost, "not grievances," and it is our griefs, as well as our joys, that are ours to utter as best we can. Which, in fact, is all we *can* do.

My plane is about to leave once more. It is I, now, who must say *Auf Wiedersehen*:

I kiss my dying stepmother on the forehead. I walk out of the room.

$\sim$

| POSTSCRIPT

I, TOO, DEAR READER, would like for this story to end, believe you me. But there is, alas, a postscript, and—in literature, as in life—it was foreordained by all that preceded it.

Six weeks after I type the preceding chapter, while I am having breakfast with my family in Austin on a Saturday morning, the telephone rings. It's my stepmother's nephew by her second marriage, also her executor, Charles Selig, on the other end.

"I have bad news," he says. I know what he's about to tell me, but he's got it wrong: The bad news for me was that this woman was *born*.

"Alice passed away early this morning at Flushing Hospital." I take a deep breath. What am I supposed to feel? Relief? Joy? Sadness? Or am I merely to take inventory? I have, after all, still one mother left.

"You were the first one I called," Charles interrupts my reveries. "I wanted you to know before anyone else."

"Thanks very much, Charles," I say. "I'll call the rest of my family and let them know."

"I assume the funeral will be on Monday," Charles says. "But I'll let you know once it's arranged."

"Thanks," I say again, and hang up. Then I go back to the porch and finish having breakfast with my wife and son. My coffee, after all, is getting cold.

The funeral indeed *is* on Monday, and I look into flying to New York at astronomically high last-minute fares. On further reflection, however (I wasn't, after all, allowed to go to my mother's funeral, so why on earth should I go to hers?), it seems to me it would make more sense to invest the plane fare in my son's education. Given the likely contents of my stepmother's will, we'll be needing every penny.

My cousin Amos (should I, I wonder, now drop this ridiculous charade and simply call him my brother?)—in yet one final manifestation of our bizarre familial ecosytem of confused blood and convoluted fidelities—generously offers to go in my place. I have only one hesitation: If I am not there to actually *watch* her being lowered into the ground, will I *truly* be able to believe she is gone? But it's a risk I'm willing to take: Gratefully I tell him to go.

Four weeks later, a copy of the will indeed appears in my mailbox. In addition to leaving her house (plus $35,000) to Charles, it contains a bequest of $40,000 and all her Exxon stock to her nephew Walter (who, all the evidence suggests, had engineered a robbery of my parents' house several years earlier); $3,500 to her former plumber, Warren; $2,000 each to her various nurses and cleaning women; $15,000 to (where else?) two synagogues, $2,000 to my biological sister, Judy, and virtually the entire rest of her estate—worth millions—to her seventy-five-year-old niece and her retired doctor husband in Connecticut, who need the money about as much as Bill Gates.

I, however, am not—as I think I will be—entirely omitted

from my stepmother's generously dispensing posthumous spirit: "FOURTH: I give and bequeath the sum of One ($1.00) Dollar to my late husband's son, MICHAEL BLUMENTHAL."

So there it is, in death as in life. The Bettys die young, and the Alices dodder on into senescence, collecting their dividends. The bones of both Lucifer and Saint Francis rest beneath the same cold and tainted ground, contemplating justice. The world, after all, is a rather Darwinian place, in which the meek may inherit the earth, but the others—to paraphrase George Herbert Walker Bush—get the mineral rights and stock certificates. The rewards of virtue are often left to the typewriter, and those of cruelty and greed deposited in the bank, or left to rest between rubber bands in some basement vault in Jackson Heights.

A world in which the good are triumphant and the wicked punished, where virtue collects the dividends and evil pays the bills, is largely a poet's dream. In that real place we mostly inhabit, the power of evil, as the Russian poet Joseph Brodsky observed, all too often outweighs the power for good.

The one great equality in the end is that the air belongs to everyone, rich and poor alike—as does the grave. And though we may, as Yeats suggested, try "to hold reality and justice in a single thought," it is largely in the mind—and not in this savage, iniquitous world—that such thoughts can be unified. Yet it is, I believe, Romain Gary who should have the last word on justice: "And I have also learned," he writes in his beautiful memoir, *Promise at Dawn*, "that if, for me, there is no beauty without justice, yet life cares little for logic, and can be beautiful without being just."

"To Michael," my friend, the French-Canadian writer Nancy Huston inscribes her essay entitled "Dealing with What's Dealt," "who got a helluva hand." And she's right: I got a helluva hand, as have so many others on this earth. And it is the hand we are dealt, not the one we might have hoped for, that we must play. So I have tried—am still trying—in my own, no-doubt-bumbling way, to play it as best I can.

For those of us lucky, and blessed, enough in our misfortune—as was Philoctetes on Lemnos—to be endowed with art's capacity to transform our wounds into a bow, there exists at least the possibility of redemption, the hope that we can instruct others through the small heroics of our own struggles. But bows, too, are destined to inflict wounds—as art, by which the artist strives to heal himself, often wounds others along the way. And our wounds, our destiny, the unasked-for hands we are dealt, are—as this painfully-rendered poem of my own acknowledges— our oracles as well:

Oedipus II

The oracle said: *you will always be alone,*
But he kept falling in love, he kept
meeting lovers whenever the road forked
back into his own solitude.

The oracle said: *you will be childless,*
you will plant your seed only into the wind.
But he kept fathering children, kept squirting his seed
into the darkness of the wrong engenderings.

The oracle said: *you will be cruel,*
selfish, relentlessly disobedient.
But he kept mimicking kindness, altruism,
those small decencies he hated and resented.

The oracle said: *you must enter the darkness,*
you must learn to swim in it, live in it,

pass through it like a burrowing mole. But he
kept yearning for the light, kept flying into it
like a moth lured to its own extinguishment.

Finally, the oracle said: *you will spend your whole life
resisting this, you will pass all your days yearning
for love, children, the bright light of your own bettering.*

Now he was starting to grow tired. *Yes,* he said, *yes,*
looking up at the dimming light, his fleeing love,
his one child calling out to him from across the seas.

My son, born one month and forty-one years after I was, is
ten years old as I write these words. *Ten years old.* The same age I
was when my life fell apart. By the time *I* was ten years old, I had
one lost mother, one dead one, a perpetually dying father, a
heartsick grandmother, and was on the verge of acquiring the
loveless, penurious stepmother who would devastate my adolescence and early adulthood. And I am about to be fifty-two, the
exact age at which my mother died.

And here is my son: in a home with his biological mother,
his natural, albeit sometimes ambivalent, father: a child spoiled,
cherished, and—if not entirely planned—at least loved. And, in
this fall of my son's tenth year—the same fall during which my
own childhood went from a largely happy to an entirely
wretched one—a certain dark thought comes over me:

Do I envy my own son? Would I—in some dark, still somewhat
unconscious, repetition-seeking part of myself—like to inflict on
him, in this, the tenth year of his life, some of the same damage
that was inflicted on me? To, quite literally, dis-member his family
by fleeing from it? Am I, who is both burdened and blessed by a
consciousness infinitely more self-aware than my own tragic
father's, really to do no better than simply to repeat what was done

unto me? Could this possibly be the consummation of all the consciousness I have fought—and paid—so dearly to obtain?

But I do *not* want my son, my only God-given child, "calling out to [me] from across the seas." I do not *want* to inflict on him—however cruel my own—such pain and such a fate. Oedipus, it is true, may have had no choice but to kill his father and marry his mother: He may *not* have needed to extinguish his own gaze as well. Our oracles, like it or not, live *us*. But it is part of our task, and our struggle, to attempt—at least in some small but significant way—to alter *them*. Though our fates may be signed at birth, they are sealed and delivered only when we return to that dust from whence we came.

How, then, to reverse this cycle of misery, some of it my own? There is only one way, I suspect. To summon all the strength and will I have at my disposal, to look the dark oracle right in its very eye and when I come, like Oedipus, to the place of the three highways (where perhaps I am now), to take the one that doesn't simply lead back home? Yet no one should doubt the truth of this: "It is hard," as the writer Patricia Hampl so poignantly observes "to sever the cords that tie us to our slavery and leave intact those that bind us to ourselves."

Everyone, we must remember—even Alice Bernheimer Guggenheim Kahn Blumenthal—was once a child—once an innocent—no matter how much our black robes of judgment may wish to condemn them now. Though the wicked may triumph in the end, no one I know worth sharing a table with would say they ought to prevail. "The world," as the poet Edwin Arlington Robinson knew, "is a hell of a place, but the universe is a fine thing." A fine thing, Romain Gary would say, that "can be beautiful without being just." And it may be best, to take Richard Ford's advice and "just offer myself release and realize I am feeling anger all alone, and that there is no redress . . . and also know not to expect it."

The dead will not return to us—neither Julius nor Berthold nor Betty nor Alice nor Mother Teresa nor Princess Di—but we are on our way toward them, with our mixed litanies of curses and hallelujahs. And now, dear reader—though perhaps not as lucky as Jean-Paul Sartre, whose father went to the grave before he could crush him—I am done, at least, with two of them, and ready to move on . . . to somewhere whose destination I do not yet know.

And you who are reading this, you, too, can finally do the one thing all of us are truly able to do in the end: bow to the authority of life and say: *Amen.*

| ACKNOWLEDGMENTS

IN LITERATURE AS IN LOVE, one is always looking for the right person. In the former, at least, I looked a long time before finding my dear, intelligent, supportive and tough-minded agent, Lane Zachary, and my insightful, attentive HarperCollins editor, Robert Jones, who—with his able and good-natured assistant, Alison Callahan, and my meticulously alert copy editor, Sue Llewellyn—was everything a person could wish for to accompany him along that often rough and thorny road through literary life and his own mistakes. Any writer with such people in his life can do little else but praise the gods for his good fortune, and keep at it.

I am sadly forced to use the word "was" in the preceding sentence because, just after I completed the revisions of this manuscript, Robert Jones died of cancer at the age of forty seven. Though I was blessed—and cursed—to have met him in person only once, his kindness, decency, high-mindedness, and (in light of his grave illness) courage were immediately evident to me. It is also clear to me that, with his death, not only I, but the many writers and editors he worked with so caringly and generously, have lost a brilliant editor and a true friend. I would gladly sacrifice the life of this book to have that life returned to us once more. That being beyond human possibilities, however, I can only hope, and pray that its own existence will prove worthy of the confidence and care he showered upon it, and that its career will bring some further honor, however posthumous, to his.

Numerous friends have stuck with, and believed in, me and my work throughout the years, beyond the vicissitudes of luck and reputation. They know who they are, and are both too important, and too numerous, to be diminished by being named here. They have, however, my undying gratitude, and my love.

Sections of the chapter entitled "She and I," in a somewhat different form, originally appeared as a story by the same name in a fiction issue of *Ploughshares* 24, nos. 2 & 3, edited by Lorrie Moore, to whom I am deeply grateful for her confidence and support. Nor should I refrain from acknowledging that chapter's enormous debt to Natalia Ginzburg's marvelous essay "He and I," which in no small way inspired it.